THE WINDS
ERASE
YOUR
FOOTPRINTS

THE WINDS ERASE YOUR FOOTPRINTS

Shiyowin Miller

Library of Congress Cataloging-in-publication Data

Miller, Shiyowin, 1913-
  The winds erase your footprints/Shiyowin Miller.
  p. cm.
  ISBN 0-87961-263-0
  1. Platero, Luciano, 1909- 2. Platero, Juanita, 1905-
3. Navajo Indians—Biography. 4. Navajo Indians—Social life
and customs. 5. Interethnic marriage—Southwest, New. I.
Title.

E99.N3 P575 2002
979.004'972—dc21

Copyright © 2002 by Dolores Lynn Nyerges

Chester Kahn, Navajo Artist
Cover and Illustrations

Illustrations copyright © 2002 by Chester Kahn

Naturegraph Publishers has been publishing books on
natural history, Native Americans, and outdoor subjects
since 1946. Please write for our free catalog.

Naturegraph Publishers, Inc.
PO Box 1047 • 3543 Indian Creek Rd
Happy Camp, CA 96039
(530) 493-5353
www.naturegraph.com

Books for a better world

PREFACE

This account closely follows actual events that took place during the years 1930 through 1936. Juanita Standly and Luciano Platero met, married, and then moved to Luciano's home territory—the Cañoncito and Crown Point areas of the Eastern Agency of the Navajo Nation in New Mexico. Cañoncito was, and still is, a small, isolated community about thirty miles west of Albuquerque; Crown Point is located northwest of Cañoncito between Grants and Gallup, New Mexico.

This is the story of Juanita's and Luciano's life together. Juanita was born January 23, 1905, at Laclede, Missouri. When she was a toddler, Juanita's family moved to the Oklahoma Territory. She graduated from high school in Walters, Oklahoma, and her first job was at the First National Bank in Burkburnett, Texas. At age eighteen she moved to Los Angeles, California, and found employment at the Helman Bank in Huntington Park, California.

Juanita, who had a small amount of American Indian blood, had a life-long interest in Indian culture. Meeting Luther Standing Bear (Leksi), the last full-blood hereditary chief of the Oglalla Sioux, was like finding family. Standing Bear was a lecturer and author on American Indian life, history, and customs. As a part of his lectures, traditional Sioux dances were performed by a group of Leksi's students. Juanita became a member of this dance group.

Luciano Platero was born in the family hogan at Cañoncito, and was reared in the traditional lifestyle and customs of his people. Though his birthday is on record as October 22, 1909, this was most likely a "good guess" by the officials at Santa

5

Fe Indian School, in Santa Fe, New Mexico. The family later indicated that he was probably four to five years older. When Luciano left school, he joined a Chautauqua group that eventually disbanded in Los Angeles, California. Having learned the art of silversmithing from his father, he found employment as a silversmith in a prestigious Los Angeles shop. He also worked as an extra in the movies, having his screen name, Blue Cloud, listed in the cast of characters in *Spanish Acres,* staring Richard Arlen.

Mutual friends introduced Juanita and Luciano, and their friendship quickly blossomed into love. They were married November 23, 1930, and shortly thereafter moved to Cañoncito—Luciano's childhood home. To prepare his wife and offer a change of mind, Luciano had described every minute detail of the entirely different lifestyle Juanita would encounter, but she was still eager to meet this opportunity.

The story of their life together reflects the challenge of a "mixed marriage," making a home, and having a family within the Navajo community, and the events leading up to Luciano's tragic and early death. More importantly, it chronicles the intimate feelings of a young white woman who, in marrying a Navajo Indian, had to adjust to the customs and lifestyle of her husband's culture.

If the story suggests that Juanita did not suffer a great amount of "culture shock" in this transition, that is an accurate assumption. Juanita was a strong, independent, and quite adventurous young woman. Her love of the land and its simple freedoms were characteristic long before she met Luciano Platero; and through him she found many aspects of the Navajo lifestyle both admirable and valuable.

Luciano, too, was a special kind of man. Although he died when their two girls were very young, both daughters feel they know him very well through this story, the oral legacy preserved by Juanita, other family members, and the friends who shared personal experiences of their father. Luciano epitomized the best of two worlds—the American value system in which he functioned and the Navajo culture which defined his spirit and held his heart.

This is a bittersweet story of love, and of the reaching out of two cultures for understanding.

THE AUTHOR:

Shiyowin Miller was born Virginia Ann Potter in Kansas City, Missouri, on May 9, 1913. She began dancing at an early age and was teaching dance by the time she was a teenager. At age fifteen, after her father died, Virginia and her mother moved to Los Angeles, California. In California, she danced on the stage and in the movies, eventually becoming a choreographer.

Having Cherokee and Osage in her heritage, Virginia also cherished American Indian culture. She met Chief Standing Bear during her performing years; joined his dance troupe, was adopted as his niece, and received from him the Sioux name Shiyowin (Bird Woman). And in this setting, Shiyowin and Juanita became lifelong friends.

In the early 1930s Shiyowin married Lyle Miller.

Following Luciano's death, Shiyowin began, with continual assistance from Juanita, this story, *The Winds Erase Your Footprints*. In 1940–41, she and Lyle moved temporarily to New Mexico and lived in the little house that Juanita had built in Cañoncito. This is where Shiyowin worked on the first draft of her book. She and Lyle became part of the Cañoncito community, attended rodeos, feast days, all night "sings", and dances. Shiyowin and Juanita together authored some short stories, including the acclaimed *Chee's Daughter*.

After the outbreak of World War II, Shiyowin and Lyle returned to California, where she continued to work on the book. Shortly after returning to California, their first daughter, Anita, was born, and five years later, a second daughter, Dolores, was born.

Shiyowin's interest in Indian dance and culture continued through the years, and a new era began for her when she became involved in teaching dance at Pacific Ackworth Friends School in Temple City, California. She was a pioneer in the field of incorporating creative movement into children's education. Throughout her teaching years. Shiyowin worked continually to refine this story. During Shiyowin's last decade prior to her death in March, 1983 her daughter, Dolores, assisted with editing and final typing.

Juanita several times expressed amazement that Shiyowin had so accurately put into words her innermost thoughts and feelings as the writing of the story progressed. Juanita's daughters, Rosita and Tonita, consider Shiyowin's writing to be an accurate document of the times, with elements of Navajo lifestyle and mythology authentically rendered. More universally, it is an expression of hope, struggle, and individual courage. And personally, of course, it is the love story of a man and woman who together created a unique American experience.

THE ARTIST:

Chester Kahn, a full-blooded Navajo, was born February 24, 1936, on the Navajo Nation at Pine Springs, Arizona. Typical of the Navajo lifestyle of the time, his parents had no automobile and used horses and wagons for work and transportation. One of his childhood responsibilities was to herd sheep. Another of his responsibilities was to take care of the horses, which he rode to trading posts and traditional ceremonies. Already a budding artist, since there were no pencils and paper at the hogan, he drew with charcoal on the canyon walls when he took the sheep to water.

When Chester was sent to the Bureau of Indian Affairs (B.I.A.) Boarding School in Stewart, Nevada, he attended an art class conducted by the famous Navajo artist, Jimmy Toddy (Beatin Yazz), and from there his life-long painting career began. Through the years, he studied painting, jewelry design and pottery at various art institutes as well as private schools for portraiture, anatomy and sculpture. He has held many one-man shows and received rewards for his painting, murals and jewelry work. For twenty years Chester had his own painting, silver- and goldsmithing business, and has judged jewelry at the Intertribal Ceremonies at Gallup, New Mexico.

Chester Kahn comments that this story is a true and compelling recorded history about the Navajo way of life during the 1930s. Drawing from memories of his own childhood also in the 1930s, in a community not far from where the story takes place on the Navajo Reservation, he illustrated the story as he and his family had lived during those years. The author's daughter, Dolores, was amazed at how closely his illustrations resemble what she had envisioned for this book.

Table of Contents

ONE
Return to Cañoncito

It was the hour of half-light before the sun. The big passenger bus lurched along the New Mexico highway. Gallup was behind them, Albuquerque lay ahead. Long low hills, newly touched with snow, sloped back from the road and mounted into higher hills thickly grown with piñon and cedar. The mass of dark trees stood in sharp outline against the pale sky.

Juanita pressed her face to the cold pane. Wind had drifted the snow beside the highway, and long streaks of red earth showed through. *Red earth.* Her husband had spoken of it so often in the two months since they had been married—always with a strange yearning in his voice that revealed his love and reverence for this land.

The bus was gathering speed as visibility increased with the dawn. Clumps of trees close to the highway flashed by the window—startling shapes silhouetted against sloping hills of snow. Most of the passengers were still asleep. It was a relief to have no one staring at her or Luciano. Juanita reached down by her feet for her small overnight case, moving cautiously so as not to disturb her husband. This was a good time to comb her hair; there would be little opportunity before they reached Albuquerque.

She balanced the case on her knees and opened it, resting the lid against the seat in front of her. Her hand mirror propped against the lid, she began to remove the long pins from her hair. Her face looked pale in the mirror and her eyes were shadowed. Sleep had been difficult once they'd definitely come to a decision to move. She and Luciano had known all along that living in Hollywood, although exciting, was too superficial and impermanent for them, and that if they were ever to build a worthwhile life together, there was but one place to do so: among her husband's people.

Juanita began to brush her hair with long, even strokes. It fell soft and dark about her shoulders. She was a handsome woman. There was an intelligence and strength of character in her face that transcended prettiness. Her nose was straight, and her chin was strong and faintly notched. There was a long generous line to her lips and a straightforwardness to her hazel eyes, wide-set beneath dark brows. The outline of her face was elongated and oval, except for her wide prominent cheekbones, which were faintly touched with color. Holding one hand firmly at the back of her head she coiled her hair into a thick, loose knot low on her neck. Her fingers moved white and swift against the darkness of her hair as she placed the long pins securely in the coil. She freshened her neck and face with lotion, dusted powder lightly across her nose, and arched her eyebrows with her fingertips. While she was touching the bright lipstick to her mouth her husband stirred in the seat beside her. She closed the case and slid it to the floor. There was the beginning of a smile on her lips as she turned toward him. They looked at each other, saying nothing.

The bus slowed down to approach a graveled section of the road. It was full daylight, and the sun was an indistinct ball of pale yellow behind the clouds. More of the passengers were awake now, straightening their clothes, smoothing their hair, making small, furtive attempts to erase the sleep from their faces. Now and then the bus driver glanced into the mirror over his head and surveyed the passengers behind him.

As the road curved, Juanita saw a hoghan[1] ahead. Six-sided and built of logs with an earth-covered roof, it squatted in the center of a clearing. There was a brush corral off to one side of it, and a big-wheeled spring-wagon, its frame gray and weathered. At one end of the clearing was a pile of uncut wood and a rough, low platform that held a water barrel. Juanita had seen pictures of hoghans. This one seemed larger and more remote than she'd imagined them. After they passed it, she asked her husband, "The hoghan where your mother lives—is it like that one?"

Luciano stretched his legs before him and pressed his shoulders hard against the back rest. "I could go to sleep again," he said lazily, but his eyes belied his words. "Oh, that hoghan . . . yes, my mother's is like that, but different. In

---

1 The author has spelled "hogan" as "hoghan" an alternative to the Navajo *hooghan*, meaning home.

Cañoncito there are no forests except far up on the mesas, so the people there build with rock and adobe, mostly." He spoke quietly, as he always did, and the composure of his face did not alter—but there was an aliveness in his eyes and an undertone of excitement in his voice which were not lost upon her. Going home meant that much to him. The very inflection when he said "Cañoncito" revealed a little-boy eagerness behind the reserve and dignity of the man beside her. He leaned toward her to get a better view of the country ahead. "Not many hours more."

She was very aware of him. The smooth darkness of his skin, the flair of his nostrils, the sharply cut cheekbones, the jutting line of his chin, the large black eyes. And his mouth—stern and proud and uncompromising. When his face was intent like this, the pride of his race was strongly marked upon it. There was the imprint of an aloof, untamed people that contrasted with the dark blue suit, the low-cut shoes, the light shirt, and the conservative dark tie. Sometimes when she looked at him, dressed so correctly in white man's clothes, her mind remembered further back and she saw him again as she had first seen him—in a bright purple shirt, with a width of silver conches worn loosely about his waist. There were bracelets on his dark wrists, and white shell, deep blue turquoise, and much silver in his rings and necklaces. With a red silk scarf binding the black, black hair against his proud head, he was indeed the most imposing Navajo she had ever seen.

They rode along silently for the most part. He pointed out the Continental Divide. As they passed a small group of buildings he said, "That's Thoreau. There's a trader there, and up that narrow canyon is Crown Point—the Agency."

There was a thirty-minute stop for breakfast and then they were back on the bus for the last hours of their journey. The country flattened out from the highway. There were a few scrubby trees, but mostly great broken masses of rock upended on the plain. Legend said that the long, low hill of red rock—it seemed still molten, flowing—was the congealed blood of an evil Yei who had been killed long ago

Luciano was intent upon the unfolding countryside. They approached the little village of Acomita—pueblo houses of adobe, cornstalks piled high on top the covered corrals, and an orchard of bare-branched peach trees beside the road.

"Delilah Wolf's people live here," said Luciano. When they reached the villages of Laguna, the old one and the new, he continued: "My grandfather used to ride over here when he was a young man, on their feast days. I have heard him tell about the time he rode in the chicken pull and got the chicken. Were those Pueblos mad! A Navajo getting away with the chicken! They chased him almost all the way back to Cañoncito."

Juanita's eyes looked to the places he pointed out and she laughed softly sometimes when he spoke, but she could sense that the thinly-veiled, well-meaning curiosity of their fellow passengers was the same as the day before. It had renewed itself now that breakfast was over and a long, uneventful day stretched before them. She was conscious of each time the driver glanced in their direction. She tried to pull her thoughts back, to regain the privacy of earlier that morning, but it was of no use—the things about her intruded themselves. The bus seemed crowded, stuffy, and she was aware of the dirt and grime, the litter of orange peels and discarded cigarette and candy wrappers. It was a relief when the bus pulled up to a group of buildings beside the highway.

"Correo. Fifteen minutes."

Luciano was surprised. "I didn't know the bus stopped here. If there'd been a way to get a message to my family, someone could have met us here with the wagon."

Juanita and Luciano stepped down from the bus and walked away from the other passengers. The sun was midway across the sky, and a sharp wind blew. Juanita looked small and slender beside her husband, her wool skirt whipping about her knees and flattening against slim hips. But there was a strange similarity to them as they moved west along the gravel shoulder of the road and turned to face north—a similarity in the free rhythmic swing of their walking that spoke of an eagerness for living. They stopped and stood a long time looking into the distance. Luciano moved close, but did not touch her.

"Out there is Cañoncito."

The sun rays were level across the broken country ahead when they left Albuquerque in a rented Model T. After crossing the narrow bridge that spanned the winter-feeble Rio Grande, they turned off onto a dirt road which was nothing more than the well-worn tracks of wagon wheels. The road was not for speed, and the Ford was loaded down with their suitcases, a roll of blankets, the heavy kit of silversmith tools, and all the supplies they'd bought in Albuquerque. Laughing, they gave up trying to force the little car any faster and settled back to watch the country in the witchery of sunset.

"After all, we can't be late when they don't know we're coming," Luciano told her. Juanita knew from the studied calm of his voice that he thought walking would be faster. It had been at her insistence that they'd stayed longer in Albuquerque. They had rented a hotel room, bathed, and changed clothes. Juanita was tired and dirty from the bus trip, and it was natural that she would want to feel refreshed and at her best when she met her husband's family for the first time. Luciano suppressed his eagerness to be on the way and observed teasingly, "I guess one bath isn't too much to ask when it may be your last one for a long time."

They'd then gone to a hardware store and to a market. Luciano knew exactly the things to buy. As the supplies stacked higher and higher in the rented car, he explained gravely, "Sometimes food gets scarce out there. With two more to feed, my mother may need these things."

As they rode along, Juanita had the strange sensation of reliving something she had dreamed. Her husband had described the country so completely. Behind them stretched the Sandia Mountains, and farther to the south were the Manzanos. It was through a pass between these mountain ranges that the Navajos had come back from Bosque Redondo. To the north were the old volcano craters, three purple cone-shapes on the horizon. Some of the old people remembered a time when the smallest crater still belched smoke. Ahead were the high, white peaks "Walking Around Mountain." To either side of the narrow winding road rolling country stretched into the distance—country white with snow and dotted with yellow-tipped spikes of yucca, the convoluted arms of a dark, spiny cactus, and the dull green of low-bushing juniper. Out on the snow-covered plain, high-ledged mesas of many-colored rock rose stark and alone under the wide, empty sky. It was all as he had told her, only he hadn't said that it was wild and beautiful.

The road slanted now toward a brown, narrow stream of water between high, wide banks. Juanita could hear the slosh of muddy water about the wheels, lapping along the running boards, and then the car began to climb the sloping cut of the bank. Luciano looked upstream. "Not much water coming down this year." And then his voice assumed a tone of gentleness that he sometimes used between them. "The closer we get to Cañoncito, the more I wonder if I've really made you understand how difficult and strange it's going to be for you at first."

Juanita knew that he was thinking about the water. Before they left Hollywood he had tried earnestly to tell her of all the things to which she must become accustomed. "My people won't seem clean to you," he said. "Water, in Cañoncito, is more than a matter of turning a tap. But after a while you'll learn there's a difference between earth and dirt." The language would be strange, as would the customs. Sleeping on the floor, eating on the floor, eating strange food . . . Luciano did not want any of these things to be unexpected. And the bugs, they must not be unexpected either. Juanita laughed when her husband added that you didn't have to keep 'em when you got 'em, unless you wanted to.

Riding along like this, returning Lu's half-smiles when he looked sideways at her, it was impossible to believe that anything could be unbearable as long as they were together. "Of course," her husband was saying, "I'll have to get used to some things all over again myself. School softened me for that life even though I was home in summer."

Juanita laid her hand against his hand upon the steering wheel. "We didn't come here thinking that it would be easy to build the sort of life we want."

Luciano's face was impassive again, except for the excitement in his eyes, and he seemed to concentrate on driving. He looked more comfortable in the clothes he'd changed to: corduroys and Western boots and a heavy woolen jacket. When the road started winding downward he pointed to a mesa. "See below, those two hoghans? Some of my relatives live there."

Juanita looked, but in the failing light the shapes of the hoghans eluded her. "We're almost there, aren't we?" she asked. Then, pensively, "Lu, what will your mother think when you walk in with a wife?"

Luciano was slow in answering. "It may take time for some of my family to accept you, but my mother, I know, will welcome you."

A chain of hills stretched away from the road into the twilight. One big mesa, dark with distance, stood in broken outline ahead. Luciano slowed the car and nodded toward the expanse of land to his left. "That's my allotment—one hundred and sixty acres. It isn't even fenced yet."

It seemed a long time while they drove toward the big mesa. The light in the sky was almost gone, and the long, low hills guarded the canyon on each side. Then Luciano slowed the car and stopped. "Here we are." Juanita looked about her for the hoghan. Presently she became aware that the car had drawn up in front of what looked like a large mound of earth. The blanket was pulled aside from the hoghan doorway, and two full-skirted figures moved outside. Seeing a strange car, they backed up against the side of the hoghan and stood with their heads discreetly lowered. One woman was tall, full-figured, and young. She must be one of the sisters of whom Lu had spoken thought Juanita. The other, slender, older woman—that must be his mother.

Luciano got out of the car and walked over to them. He stopped beside his mother and put one hand gently on her shoulder. Juanita saw his mother lift her face to look at him, and then she leaned her head against him and began to cry. They stood a long time like that. No word was spoken.

Juanita sat waiting, smoothing her hand over the skirt of her jersey dress. She'd worn the black and gray jersey because it was warm and serviceable, not fussy looking, yet the flat red bow at the neck line was becoming. She wasn't nervous, but she knew that a mother must not think her new daughter-in-law unsuited to the life out here. She hoped his mother would like her. Three years was a long time for a son to be away. And then to have him come home not alone.

Luciano and his mother moved apart and he turned toward the car. Juanita got out and walked around the car to her husband. He spoke quietly to his mother and she looked up, her face composed behind the traces of her tears. Instinctively, Juanita held out her hand. The older woman took Juanita's hand in one of her own, and covered it with the other.

It was warm inside the hoghan. Juanita let her coat slip from her shoulders as she sat down on the sheep pelts that her husband's mother arranged for her. The floor was hard-packed earth, and the encircling wall was rock, plastered with adobe mud. There were heavy cedar logs laid on top of the wall, and a second row of logs slanted inward to form a dome. The dome was reinforced with smaller interlocking logs, with a smoke hole in the center. A small fire burned in the middle of the floor, its smoke rising upward. Hanging from a peg driven in between the ceiling logs was a kerosene lantern. A few sheep pelts were scattered on the floor, and blankets were rolled against the wall. Bits of harness and a bridle hung near the doorway.

Luciano came and stood beside her. He spoke to the two young women across the fire, who got up and came toward him, their eyes downcast, their movements restrained. "These are my sisters Il-tha-bah and Yee-ke-nes-bah."

One of the sisters touched the palm of her hand lightly to Juanita's, fingers scarcely clasping. The other sister touched hands with her in the same manner, shyly. As they returned to their places, Juanita noticed how their long skirts were wrinkled, earth-smudged, and their blouses worn, the bright colors faded. Their heavy black hair was combed, neat and shining into double loops tied with yarn. Seated once more across the fire from them, Juanita could see that they wore no jewelry, not even silver buttons. Their blouses were fastened with pins.

A young man in a blue workshirt and faded, dirty Levis came awkwardly to touch hands with her. That was Allen, and he looked like Luciano. The next brother in size was Khee. He smiled rather nervously, his front teeth seemed much too large for his slender, pointed face. The small boy was Wudy. "Wudy was a baby when my father died," Luciano told her. The other small children were Bijo, Il-tha-bah's daughter, and Phillip, Lorencito's son. "Lorencito is my oldest brother. My mother says that he has gone to Crown Point." The children stared at Juanita with round brown eyes. "You're probably the first white person the little ones have seen," said Luciano. "Do you think you have the family straight so far? There's still Lupe and Ha-nes-bah at school in Crown Point."

Juanita said "Yes," but that was not true at all. When he'd told her in California about his family it had been clear: she knew the names of those who lived at home and those who were away at school or married. Now the faces in the flickering light of the lantern seemed strange, and she couldn't fit any names to them.

Luciano started bringing the supplies in from the car, and Allen helped him. Their mother sat in a swirl of skirts by the fire, asking questions as Luciano went out, and being answered as he came back in. Occasionally she glanced up at Juanita, smiled at her, then busied herself with the fire, poking it vigorously and adding another stick of wood. Luciano's mother was small, and frail-looking, yet her movements spoke of capability and endurance. Her skin was weathered, and there were lines of humor about her eyes and mouth. Her features were delicate, but for all their delicacy they were marked by the strength of will, deep inner poise, and unwavering decisiveness of a matriarch. Yet equally as strong as the strength in her face was the gentleness—gentleness that came from crooning to babies in the firelight, from tending motherless lambs in the springtime. She turned back the frayed cuffs of her black velveteen blouse; her wrists were slender and agile as she took pans from the box cupboard behind her. She poked the fire once more and it blazed for a moment, highlighting her face, lighting her deep brown eyes, gleaming against the blackness of her hair, and glancing off in tiny points of light from the silver circlets in her ears.

Then she stopped, and exclaimed, "Eee-yah." Luciano was unwrapping the big iron Dutch oven, the large coffee pot, the tin plates and cups. Her eyes misted over, and she stroked the lid of the Dutch oven with work-gnarled fingers. She continued to make soft exclamations as her sons brought in sacks of flour and sugar, beans and coffee and baking powder, lard and salt. The children began to crowd around the doorway, and the older sisters fingered the supplies as they were brought in. They inspected the labels of the canned goods and lifted the sacks of onions and potatoes experimentally.

Juanita watched with interest as the preparation for the meal began. Everyone seemed to take part in it: the larger boys went out for more wood and a bucket of water, the older sisters peeled potatoes, slicing them into a blackened skillet set in the raked-out coals. One of them filled the new coffee pot with water, as Allen opened a can of coffee with his pocket knife. But their mother was the center of activity, kneading dough in a white enameled basin, her hands working swiftly and surely. All of the time she talked in soft-slurred syllables, and Luciano answered her. There was so much that she would want to know.

When the questions concerned Juanita, Luciano would turn and repeat parts of the conversation to her. So Juanita knew when his mother asked, "Where did you get her?" and Luciano answered, "California."

"What was she doing there?"

Luciano had trouble finding words that would explain her job as bookkeeper in a bank. His mother looked puzzled.

"How did you two come together?"

"Delilah Wolf, a girl that I knew at school in Albuquerque is married to a man in California. They knew Juanita."

"Her people, where are they?"

"Texas," answered Luciano, giving it the Spanish pronunciation.

His mother was working a piece of dough, stretching it into a large flat circle with her fingers. She held it up before her. "My daughter-in-law's hair is straight and black like ours and yet her skin is not dark."

Luciano smiled. "Many white people have dark hair, but with my wife it is thought that one of her people long ago was an Indian."

His mother seemed to ponder all that he had told her as she placed the dough into the skillet of hot grease.

Juanita stirred a little, restlessly. "Lu, I feel so useless. Do you think it would be all right for me to set out the cups and plates?" Luciano handed her the new tin dishes. His mother, watching, got out a folded flour sack, shook it and motioned for him to spread it before Juanita. "Tell my daughter-in-law that I am sorry we have no table."

The coffee boiled and the potatoes were fried and the round pieces of bread were done. Yee-ke-nes-bah set out a coffee can with sugar in it and a glass jar that held a few spoons. They began to eat. The potatoes tasted good to Juanita—hot and mealy and smoky. The coffee tasted bitter. She shared her spoon with her husband.

"My mother says they haven't had sugar in a long time," said Luciano.

The fried bread was strange to her—thick and crusty. Juanita watched and used it as the others did. Taking it in one hand, she bent it between her fingers and used it as a scoop for the potatoes.

Luciano's mother was watching Juanita's hands. Luciano caught her left hand and held it out so that his mother could see the rings. "I made them," he said proudly. His mother touched them, exclaiming softly over the deep blue, three-cornered turquoise and the narrow silver band with teardrops of silver around it. He was explaining to her how white people used rings in marriage and that his wife had wanted him to make the rings for her. "But, besides that marriage, we were married with the basket." His mother looked very pleased, and he went on to tell her of their Navajo friends in California who had held the ceremony for them.

Juanita remembered that from the first moment she had felt the beautiful implication of the ritual. She had dressed in an old, old squaw dress: dark blue weave with a border of red at the hemline, the upper part plain and fastened at the left shoulder. Her hair was loose. She sat on the floor to the right of Luciano, who wore a shirt of soft red velvet, slit leg trousers, and reddish brown Navajo moccasins. Juanita poured water over his hands while he washed them. He, in turn, poured water over hers. Then a round, woven wedding basket filled with cornmeal mush was placed in front of them. The mush was marked with lines of yellow pollen dividing it into four sections. Luciano dipped his fingers into the portion of mush to the east, and ate it. Juanita followed. They ate from the south, west, north, and middle sections. Their friends ate what was left, and then a feast of stewed mutton, squash, and coffee was laid before them. After the feast they were given advice by one of the old men about how to treat each other in marriage. The basket ceremony had satisfied something within Luciano. His telling of the ceremony seemed to satisfy his mother.

Luciano and his family talked on and on. The fire died down, and was built up again. Laughter, gestures, and a word here and there in English let her know that he was telling of their life in Hollywood. Juanita relaxed on the sheep pelts. She felt full and warm and drowsy as she watched her husband's face. Pride and sternness were suffused there with his joy at being home. Nothing that they had left behind in the city was worth this moment.

Luciano carried the lantern and guided her with his hand upon her arm as they walked from the hoghan to the square rock house that his father had built. Luciano explained that it was now used for a storeroom, but that at different times relatives had lived there. His mother would help clean it out in the morning. She had thought that the hoghan might seem too crowded for them, and that they would rather have this privacy. They opened the wooden door and stepped down into the house. In the yellow glow cast from the lantern, Juanita could make out a small window at one end of the room, a large trunk, several bags of wool, a pile of sheep pelts, and a funny little iron heating stove set up on thin, curved legs.

Luciano spread some sheep pelts on the ground and then went out to the car for their blankets and suitcases. Blankets spread over the pelts made a comfortable bed.

"Before we go to bed, I'm going outside for a while," Juanita told him.

"Wait." Lu went to the door and called over to the hoghan. Yee-ke-nes-bah came out, her hair loose and down her back. Lu spoke quickly to her in a tone Juanita seldom heard him use.

She smiled to herself. "I wonder if he's afraid I'll fall off a mesa in the darkness." But she walked away without protest with Yee-ke-nes-bah, silent, beside her.

The lamplight in the window guided her back to the rock house. Yee-ke-nes-bah left her at the door. Juanita said "Good night," and then realized that she wouldn't understand that.

Luciano was already in between the blankets. "I know I'm going to miss my pillow," he said in mock concern.

Juanita took down her hair and began braiding it. "I'm so sleepy that I doubt if I'd even miss a bed." She undressed and blew out the lantern. Lying there in the darkness, they talked over the evening, Luciano telling her the things his family had said that he hadn't had the opportunity to interpret for her.

"You know, I think you made a good impression."

Juanita sighed and lay quietly listening to his breathing, then, asked, "Lu, what is that fragrance in the air? I noticed it so strongly when I was outside."

"The smoke from the piñon wood my mother burns. That's one of the things you keep remembering when you're away from here."

TWO
The Chapter House

The door to the rock house hung open. Pale winter sunshine spilled into a long pool upon the adobe floor. Luciano squatted on his heels, leaned against the doorway, and watched Juanita as she moved between the suitcases and the cross pole that he had put up at the far end of the room. The jersey dress was covered by a red gingham apron, her hair was pinned up off her neck, and dark, damp tendrils curled at her temples. The rock house had been given a thorough cleaning this morning.

As she unpacked the clothes, shook them out, and hung them on the cross pole, she paused now and then in front of Luciano. But he continued to sit there, silent, preoccupied with something. She continued to unpack—he would tell her what it was in due time.

The rock house was pleasant with the sun shining in. Juanita had brushed the cobwebs from the small poles laid tightly together to support the adobe roof, then brushed down the walls and swept out the litter of loose earth, wool, and woodscraps. Luciano's mother had dampened down the floor with water sprinkled from a bunch of dried grass that she used for a broom. The thick ledge of the small, square window held a lantern and Juanita's sewing box. Their bed of sheep pelts was made up in the corner. The trunk was covered with a bright blanket and set in the middle of the room as a table. The books that they had brought along were spread upon it, and they had heaped red apples on a tin plate. The larger suitcases were stacked against the wall and covered with a scarf. This made an adequate dressing table to hold their toiletries. Luciano had split small lengths of wood for the stove; the wood, yellow-centered, was stacked inside the door for chilly mornings.

A room like this could be made quite livable, thought Juanita. And then, aloud, "It wouldn't take long to have our own home here . . . a room like this and a smaller one for a kitchen."

Luciano roused himself to answer. "Longer than you think. It will take time and work before we can live the way we want."

Luciano and Juanita had not come to New Mexico to live as his people did, nor to live as they had lived in the city. There was a life inbetween, which meant having the advantages of the Anglo-American civilization along with the freedom and beauty of this country, and the wisdom and culture of his people. What they sought was a middle path, and they knew gaining it would not be easy.

They had planned to remain in Hollywood until their stake was big enough for the right start in New Mexico. Work in motion pictures was good, and the Indian store where Luciano worked as a silversmith was prospering. He thought he could fight off the homesickness a while longer. But Juanita thought of the months that went by with no word of his family, only secondhand news when one of the men from his reservation came to work as an extra in pictures. She thought of his restlessness in the noisy, crowded city and said, "We have enough money for bus fare to New Mexico and enough to live on until you get a job. It should be as easy to save money there as it is here."

Luciano had argued against it, although going home meant so much to him. "We'd have to live with my family until I get work. That life would be too hard for you." But Juanita was not to be swayed. When she saw something worthwhile in the distance, rough going held no terrors for her.

Now the last dress was hung over the cross pole. Luciano still sat on his heels, his face serious and uncommunicative. Juanita sat down on the doorsill facing, out toward the compound. She drew her knees up, linked her fingers across them, and waited.

The compound sloped up around them like a shallow bowl, the large hoghan almost in the center, a beehive oven nearby. Their rock house was the smaller of two buildings that together formed an "L" shape. The long building with the pole roof and the fireplace was where Il-tha-bah and her family lived. Inside the south rim of the bowl was a brush corral and beyond that lay a wide strip of land beside the arroyo. It was pasture now, but Luciano had told her of a time when his father planted a garden there and grew corn and squash and pumpkins, beans and onions, carrots and chilies. Luciano's father had been almost wealthy. He had owned many horses. The income from their sheep and from his medicine work had amply supplied the family.

Beyond the pasture stretched low, flat land surrounded and broken in upon by mesas, and covered with straw-colored grass, yellow-topped bunch grass, and wind-gnarled cedars. There was no trace of yesterday's snow.

"There's a meeting today." Luciano stood up and stretched. "Would you like to go?"

"Wouldn't miss it." Surely he hadn't thought all this time about a meeting, thought Juanita.

"I was going to take the car back, but I thought my mother would like to ride in style to the meeting." He paused. "Besides, when I take the car back I'm going to make the rounds of the trading posts and see which one needs a good silversmith."

"I thought you were going to wait a few days and visit with some of your relatives."

"There'll be time for that when we come out weekends. My hands are itching to hold the silver tools." He flexed his long, powerful fingers.

Juanita smiled to herself, and thought, My husband is going the long way around to tell me what is on his mind.

"It would be all right to go to work sooner than I expected," said Luciano.

Juanita tilted her head back to look at him, and waited.

He began slowly. "It is worse with my family than I thought. My mother tells me that there is little left of what she and my father owned."

"How could it go so quickly?"

"A man's personal belongings are divided among his relatives. Most of my father's horses went to his brothers. There was that year's bill at the trader's. I don't know if the trader came after the payment, but my mother paid the bill out of her flock then, instead of waiting until spring and the increase. For two years now, wool and rugs have brought little in trade. Il-tha-bah's husband has gone to Crown Point to look for work. My mother has killed most of her sheep so that the family could eat."

"The other families here must be having a hard time, too."

"Most of them—except where there are men in the family who can get a job outside."

Juanita turned her face away from him. "And so?"

"I will get a job as soon as I can."

It was a short distance to the Chapter House. The squat stone and adobe building was just out of sight around one of the mesas that broke in upon the flat land, but they drove over anyway—Luciano, his mother and Juanita in front, Yee-ke-nes-bah in the rumble seat, clutching her blanket about her head. Luciano's mother and sister were wrapped in brightly striped Pendletons, their hair combed and tied carefully. A Chapter meeting was an occasion. Families came from all over Cañoncito.

There were spring wagons drawn up behind the Chapter House, paints and sorrels, blacks and buckskins tied to the hitching rack. When they drove up, the young men lounging about the door came over to the car, recognizing Luciano. As he got out, they said: "Yah-te-hay, my friend," "A-ha-la-ni, Luciano," "When did you get back here?" Most of them were his age or older. Some of them had cropped hair like school boys. They milled about him, shaking hands and asking questions. Her husband was not out of place among them, but it was noticeable that his cords and shirt were newer and cleaner, and his wide-brimmed hat was not as wide as theirs.

His mother and sister climbed out of the car and started toward the Chapter House. Juanita felt that she should follow them but she didn't. A taller man then joined the group. His hair was short and his clothes were a little better than those the others wore. There was strength in his face, and his features were sharp and clear cut. Luciano brought him to the car. "This is my cousin, George Abeyta. He is the

interpreter at Chapter meetings. George, this is my wife."
George shook hands with Juanita and stood beside the car
door as she got out. Then Luciano introduced the other young
men. Some of them were embarrassed, and stood staring
down at their feet, mumbling a greeting; others touched
hands with her and murmured "yah-te-hay" as their names
were spoken. It seemed every other name was Chavez or
Platero, yet their faces were strongly Navajo.

Inside the Chapter House it was the same. Luciano went first
to the older women and introduced them to Juanita, then he
went to the older men. All of their names were Spanish, and
their faces Navajo. Her husband had told her that members
of his family had worked for Spanish people and some were
called by Spanish names, as he was. But she was not
prepared for this avalanche of Chavezes and Plateros,
Sandovals, Abeytas, and Secateros.

The Chapter room was square, the walls rough rock inside,
the floor cement. In one corner was a woodstove, its potbelly
full of crackling piñon wood. Along one wall were sagging
wooden cupboards. Low benches were beneath the windows
and in rows at the west end of the room. The headman was
shaking hands with the old men and women around the
stove, then he stood waiting for the room to become quiet.

The talk began with the low price of wool. There was no
longer any profit in keeping sheep, and yet there was no
profit in selling them. From her place between Luciano and
his mother, Juanita had a good view of the assembled
Navajos. Most of the men wore Levi's and trading-store shoes.
Their black hair was bunched about their ears under a band,
or beneath a hat brim. Some of them wore jackets, but more
of them carried a blanket folded over the shoulder or wrapped
about them. The old men wore their hair long, tied in back,
and they sat with their feet drawn under them, only a bit of
their reddish brown moccasins showing. Women young and
old wore full wide skirts, bright blouses, and blankets draped
loosely from their shoulders. The double-loop hairdress
fascinated Juanita: one loop fan-shaped at the back of the
head, the other resting low on the neck. Both loops were held
firmly in the middle, wrapped round and round with strands
of white yarn.

Among the women sat a young man, too colorfully dressed,
with long hair hanging about his ears and held with an

elaborately beaded band. He was slender, his face delicately molded, his eyes soft brown and long-lashed. Juanita whispered to Luciano, "Who is he? Do you know him?"

"He belongs to that family but is never with the men. They say he speaks like a woman and spends all his time with beadwork."

The headman eventually arrived at the real reason the meeting had been called. A man of the community got up and said that two young men had stolen his horse and shot it. He pointed out two of the boys who had greeted Luciano at the car. They were not the least abashed. They grinned and admitted to the headman that it was true.

"Why did you shoot it?"

"For the meat."

While the headman and the judges were deciding what to do, the people talked among themselves. A baby wailed in the corner by the window and its mother lifted it, shielded in the folds of her Pendleton, to nurse.

The headman walked forward and seemed ready to announce the decision, when an old man appeared in the doorway, and walked haltingly across the room. He was a short, old man bent heavily over a gnarled stick, his face crisscrossed with wrinkles, his hair sticking out in wisps under the broad brim of his hat. He squinted his eyes as he neared the bench by the stove. There were many "yah-te-hays" spoken before he sat down. The headman waited until the old man was settled.

Luciano said, "That is my grandfather."

The headman told the young men they would be turned over to the Agency to be sent to jail for stealing. The community could not tolerate stealing, even for food. They could have asked at any hoghan for something to eat—they would not have been refused.

"What's this? What's this?" the old man asked rising.

The headman restated the case, explaining it to him.

"He is much respected, my grandfather," Luciano told her. "He was the headman here for a long time."

The business of the meeting over, the people gathered into small groups to exchange news, and to discuss the stolen horse. Round-eyed little boys and girls peered from behind their mothers at Juanita, just as the children in Luciano's family had done. The men and women directed friendly, curious glances in her direction—glances that rested long upon her in appraisal. She knew now why Luciano had asked her to wear the soft blue wool with the blue and gray checked jacket, and to wear her jewelry, even some of his. The silver bracelets jingled heavily as she moved. They must all see that he had done well in choosing a wife.

When the people around his grandfather began to move away, Luciano walked over and stood in front of him. The old man turned his head slowly toward Luciano, his eyes lighting. "My son," he whispered over and over.

"Grandfather, this is my wife."

"EEEyah!" breathed the old man in surprise.

Juanita gave him her hand. The old man looked a long time at her, and before he turned his eyes away, they were friendly. "Good," he murmured to his grandson, "good."

They sat down one on each side of him. "It was my grandfather who insisted I be educated. When he was a small boy he learned that the white people were many and strong." Luciano repeated this to his grandfather and the old man nodded his head gravely.

"I heard you had much work in that western place," said the old man.

"Yes, grandfather, but I lost that job."

"Yes?"

"I was working as a silversmith. A woman brought in a bracelet I had made for her a long time before. She wanted another one that same design."

"You couldn't make it."

"I said I couldn't. She said I must do it. The woman who owned the shop said that I must. But I couldn't."

"Ah."

"How could I explain to those women that designs are like growing? You can't go back to when you were shorter."

The old man nodded his head thoughtfully. "You were right, my son."

It was early morning. Luciano sat at the wheel of the Ford, his hat tilted forward against the slanting rays of the sun. Allen had saddled the bay and put a lead rope on Il-tha-bah's black mare. Juanita wasn't going. It would be late when Allen and Luciano started home and they would cut across country with the horses. That long, fast ride over unfamiliar country would be too much for her.

Juanita leaned against the car. "And both my hands will probably be paralyzed from sign talk when you get back."

"You'll get along better than you think," her husband told her.

Juanita watched the Ford as Luciano headed out across the flat land, Allen following with the horses, their hooves clop-clopping unevenly. She watched until Il-tha-bah's black mare was lost from sight behind the mesa. Then she turned toward the hoghan. Luciano's mother stood in the doorway.

Juanita had expected to feel at a loss without Luciano to interpret for her but her mother-in-law smiled and held the blanket aside as though nothing were unusual. Yee-ke-nes-bah had begun to wash the coffee cups from breakfast. Juanita looked about for something with which to dry them. Her mother-in-law handed her a folded flour sack and opened the cupboard door to show her where the cups belonged.

Khee finished his coffee and went out to herd the sheep. Juanita could hear the tinkle of a bell, the eager *baas* as the flock left the corral. Il-tha-bah sat back against the wall with Bijo on her lap. Bijo looked quaint and solemn-eyed in a skirt and blouse like her mother's; she dipped a piece of bread into the coffee and pushed it dripping into her mouth. Phillip and Wudy played on the floor near Il-tha-bah, pulling a block of wood along for a wagon, heaping scraps of kindling on it for a load. Now and then they spoke commands to the imaginary horses. When they got too near the center fire, Il-tha-bah made soft scolding noises in her throat and held out her hand to guide them away. Their overalls were caked with dirt from playing on the ground, and their noses ran until they stopped playing to sniffle or draw their sleeves across their faces. Wudy's face was streaked with tears shed the night before. Juanita noticed all this and more. The children were good-natured with each other—round-eyed, fat-cheeked, and quiet as they played.

Luciano's mother began taking the sheep pelts outside to air. Yee-ke-nes-bah gathered up some of the blankets, motioned, smiling, that she had left some for Juanita, and carried them outside to hang on the corral posts in the sun. While they worked, Yee-ke-nes-bah and her mother talked. Juanita could tell by the sound of their voices when they looked at her that she was included in the conversation if she only could understand. Together, they set things up off the floor. Il-tha-bah took the children outside, and then they swept out the hoghan and dampened down the floor. They were trying to include her in their housekeeping—to make her feel part of the family, not alone. They were kind and good people. No wonder Lu had been certain she'd be at ease with his family today. She wondered if her own people would have been as gracious in accepting Lu among them.

Juanita searched for a word to attract her mother-in-law's attention. This would be a good day to put her own bedding outside. What word did Lu use in addressing his mother? "Shi-mah." That was it. Juanita tried to give the word the same accent that her husband did. "Shimah," she said softly, not very sure of herself.

His mother turned, a surprised and pleased expression on her face. Juanita pointed to herself, and then toward the rock house; she made vigorous motions as if she were shaking out blankets. Shimah smiled and nodded that she understood. Luciano's sisters laughed aloud and nodded that Juanita had made them understand, too.

Juanita had just stripped the blankets from the bed when her mother-in-law came padding through the doorway. She put her hand to her mouth, laughing self-consciously, and then made gestures to Juanita that she would help.

When they returned to the hoghan, Yee-ke-nes-bah pulled the sewing machine from its place behind the trunk, and set it in the sunlight that poured in from the smoke hole, near the remains of the morning fire. She carried in a wooden bench and set it in front of the machine. As she came through the doorway she pulled the blanket up and hung it over a peg.

Shimah went to the trunk and pulled out the black satin that Luciano had brought her for a skirt, then she found thread and scissors and some scraps of bright purple fabric. Juanita guessed from the way they tore the material that there would be a wide ruffle at the bottom of the skirt. Shimah sat down at the machine and treadled vigorously, guiding the material deftly as she sewed the torn strips together. Il-tha-bah began to gather the top of the skirt by hand. Yee-ke-nes-bah brought the purple material and came to sit beside Juanita. She cut a few thin strips end to end, which would be used for the binding of the skirt. Juanita began to cut the purple material, too.

Lu had told her about his mother's sewing machine. His father had bought it and hired a man to come out and demonstrate how to run it. Shimah had been so proud; it was the first sewing machine in Cañoncito, and all her women relatives had come to use it.

About noon, Luciano's mother made a pot of coffee and set out a plate of fried bread from the night before. Juanita thought of the apples in the rock house. When she returned with them, Shimah was standing in the doorway waiting for her. As they sat on the floor eating, Luciano's mother and sisters talked, gesturing to give her an idea what the conversation was about. Sometimes they pointed to an object and spoke the Navajo name for it, then laughed merrily when Juanita stumbled in trying to repeat it after them. But under it all she sensed their friendliness—that they had accepted her.

In the afternoon the wind began to blow, at first in little gusts that eddied the sand across the compound, and then in larger gusts that caught the sand up in swirls and scattered some of it down the smoke hole. The wind whispered around the doorway, and whipped the blanket down from the peg with one long sigh. Skirt-making was abandoned while the women went out to bring in the blankets. Juanita thought she went alone to take in her bedding, but when she turned with the folded blankets in her arms, Yee-ke-nes-bah was beside her. Together they picked up the scattered sheep pelts.

All afternoon the wind blew. Fine sand came down the smoke hole, choking the fire. Several times, Shimah had to stop the sewing machine and clean sand from the bobbin slot and around the needle. Khee came in early with the sheep. When he brought in wood, the machine was pushed back and a fire built for the evening meal. Juanita took down the brush of long grass and swept the threads and scraps into the fire.

When the flames grew brighter and more distinct in the fading light, Juanita began to listen for the first sound of horses hooves. The mutton stew was almost done and Shimah had begun to make the fried bread when Juanita heard the horses. She went to the doorway. Allen came in first, his saddle slung over his shoulder. Juanita walked past him out into the darkness.

Her husband had led the mare into the corral and was sliding the bridle off her head. "Any luck, Lu?" Juanita asked.

"Lots of it. The man at the garage charged us for the mileage instead of by the day."

"I mean about a job." He knew perfectly well what she meant.

"Oh! Well, we went to a lot of places. Guess I looked the part all right, horse and everything."

He walked over to her. She could smell leather and horse sweat in the darkness. Juanita spoke softly while helping him. "But . . ."

"But no one needed a silversmith today." He sounded disappointed and tried not to show it.

"Lu, you wouldn't have gotten a job in Hollywood this soon."

"I know it. And I'm not discouraged. You seldom get a job the first time you ask. Maizel told me to come back and Bell said there might be something later. I'll go in again next week."

They had driven the horses to water at the spring below Des Jin, the big mesa north of Cañoncito. Luciano rode the black mare, and Juanita rode behind the saddle, holding onto his belt.

Lu would get a job soon. Their money would last until then. No reason to spoil the days with worry. Days like this one . . . magic days with the clouds piled high in the sky . . . cloud shadows across the mesas . . . shadows here and sunshine beyond . . . sunshine on Des Jin, bringing out the rose and purple of the rocky ledges . . . bringing out from the distance the dark green shrubs high on the crest.

They met two boys driving toward the spring with a water barrel in a wagon. The boys called a greeting. Luciano answered and rode on, laughing. "They said, 'Out here when a woman rides double with a man, she likes him'."

"You know very well that this is a matter of necessity, my husband; don't get any illusions."

"That's not the proper answer." Luciano turned in the saddle and smiled broadly at her. "You'll have to learn prettier speeches if I keep you."

Once they paused to watch a flock of bluebirds winging over the yellow grass, then they trotted homeward, driving the horses before them. As they approached the north rim of the compound they could smell the wood smoke, and saw it rising from his mother's hoghan. Once over the rim, they saw an almost-new spring-wagon and a well-filled-out pair of sorrels.

"My mother has visitors of some importance."

"Will you pardon me while I powder my nose?" Juanita slipped sideways to the ground and ran toward the rock house. She had time to take her hair down and recoil it, and was brushing horsehair from her black skirt when Luciano came after her.

"I took the saddle in. It's old Wounded Head and his wife and son who are visiting my mother."

"Wounded Head?"

"That's the only name I know. We've always called him that because of the scar across his forehead. He told people when he first came here that a bullet grazed him when he was fighting Mexicans."

The scar was the first thing Juanita noticed when she saw him sitting at the back of the hoghan. From where she stood in the doorway, the deep crease above his shaggy brows seemed to intensify the scowling expression around his narrow eyes. His forehead was high and narrow, his graying hair combed back severely into a double knot. The way he sat, with his long legs crossed and his slender fingers curled about the coffee cup, seemed to give him an air of complete detachment and indifference. When Juanita touched hands with him, his long face remained impassive, his thin lips silent, his eyes expressionless.

She was so engrossed in analyzing the sinister feeling this old man created, that his wife and son made only vague impressions upon her. His wife was middle-sized and middle-aged; she was chatting pleasantly with Luciano's mother. The son seemed a younger, thinner shadow of his father.

Juanita sat beside Luciano near the doorway. As she drank her coffee, she had the feeling of being watched, but when she looked up, Wounded Head's face was immobile, his eyes disinterested. She whispered to Luciano, "They have on a great deal of jewelry and their clothes are good; they must be wealthy."

"Yes, they own more sheep than anyone in Cañoncito. My mother said when he married into that family he was already wealthy himself in silver and horses."

Wounded Head set his coffee down before him and cleared his throat before he spoke. He addressed himself to Luciano's mother.

"He wants to know if we are married by that government paper," Luciano told Juanita.

"If he only knew what a time we had getting it."

Juanita smiled to herself as she remembered how the clerks in the license bureau had stared at them, and how one had slyly phoned the newspapers. Lu had been confused by some of the questions on the license. She had written: "Juanita Standley—twenty-four—white—single—female—birthplace, Missouri." Lu had written "Luciano Platero" and stopped. He didn't know how old he was, for one thing, and he also didn't know his mother's maiden name. They figured it out between them: Lu had been out of school three years, he had gone to school for fourteen years, and his age had been guessed as eight when he entered. Lu indicated his age as "over twenty-one." For his mother's maiden name, he wrote down her Navajo clan name, "Edge of the Water." For his father's name he wrote "Lorenzo Platero". He didn't know his father's real name—that would have to do. It seemed the only important thing was that they wanted to get married. The clerk had asked them to wait, and told them that there were photographers on the way. They hadn't waited.

Wounded Head was still questioning Luciano's mother: Did they plan to make their home on the reservation? Shimah nodded. The old man mouthed this bit of information. Was it distasteful to him? Perhaps he was one of the "longhairs" Lu had told her about, who did not approve of marriage outside the tribe. She must not resent his disapproval; after all, her own family had not exactly blessed this marriage.

Then Wounded Head and his family got up to leave. His wife paused before Juanita and spoke softly.

"She asks us to come visit them," Lu said.

The old man stood beside his wife, his slender fingers hooked into the heavy conches of his belt. He repeated his wife's words, but there was nothing in his voice or in his eyes that said Lu and Juanita would be welcome.

THREE
Pentz's Trading Post

It started very gaily, this hair-washing. Luciano built a small fire outside the hoghan. Although the snow from the night before was almost gone, Juanita and Shimah found enough in the shaded recesses of the arroyo to fill their lardpails. While Luciano set these around the fire, they went to dig the soaproot.

Juanita always enjoyed these times alone with Shimah. Differences in language were no barrier to conversation. Shimah talked softly and animatedly as they walked along, and more often than not a familiar word—linked with her gestures—transmitted her thoughts clearly. Each day the bond seemed to grow stronger between them.

Shimah carried a sharp stick with her. When they came to a good-sized clump of yucca, she dug around the narrow-spiked plants and uncovered a small root; Shimah packed the earth around it again carefully and dug around the next plant. This root was long and fat. She worked it loose from the plant and shook it to dislodge the clinging red soil. Shimah carried several of the large roots in her top skirt as they walked back across the pasture. Near the fire, she knocked the roots sharply against a stone and peeled off most of the tough brown outer layer. Pounding the pale yellow center softened and loosened the long fibers until the soaproot was ready for use.

Shimah lifted the lardpails from the fire, protecting her hands with her skirt. When she had the basin half-full of hot water, she tempered it with cold water and put the soaproot in, two hands full. As Juanita watched her douse the soaproot up and down, small broken fibers separated and floated on the water. She would never get that out of her hair, she thought. Never.

Luciano brought a sheep pelt over, and Juanita knelt beside the basin. Shimah was still ruffling the water with her right hand, working up a rich lather, while her other hand was held protectively above the splattering suds. A pungent, clean scent arose from the soaproot.

"You'll find this a little more involved than a beauty parlor," her husband teased her, "but our scalp scrubbing meets all competition."

Shimah washed Juanita's hair, working the lather through it, massaging her scalp gently. Then she added cold water to a half-filled lardpail from the fire, to use for rinsing.

"When we accumulate a few more lardpails we can have a bath, can't we?" Juanita asked Luciano.

"Who knows," he answered, placing the towel about her shoulders.

Juanita stood, head forward, her hair long and black in the sunlight; she shook her head, the drops of water flying. She ran her fingers through her hair, the pale, yellow shreds of fiber falling lightly to the ground. Luciano was washing his head now, in water that his mother had prepared. Juanita began to comb her hair carefully, the comb snagging and tangling in the still-wet strands. She stopped and disentangled the combings, rolling them into a little ball. The wind caught it and tumbled it over and over across the ground.

"Ah-yeeee!" Shimah exclaimed, and ran after the ball of combings. She brought it back and placed it carefully in the fire, watching as the flames consumed the hair, talking rapidly to her son. I am guilty of some small breach of custom, Juanita thought, and then was surprised at the gravity of her husbands' face. He sat back on his heels, his hair dripping, unheeded. "You must always burn your combings," he told her seriously. "My mother says never let any of your hair escape like that."

"I'm sorry, Lu," she began. "It was a bit untidy. But out here in the open I thought the wind would carry it away."

"That's just it: the wind might . . ." He stopped abruptly.

Juanita was puzzled. It was such a little thing for him to get upset about, and she had said she was sorry. "Is there some taboo connected with hair-combings?" she asked gently, trying to smooth the troubled look from his face. "If I knew of it I'd observe it—you know I would."

Shimah stood by, gauging the conversation by the tones of their voices.

Luciano was still disturbed. "It isn't exactly taboo, just don't be careless." It wasn't like her husband to speak so. He'd always been patient about explaining even minor things. She turned away to hide the hurt.

Shimah plucked at her sleeve, speaking gently and soothingly, as though to erase the hurt, the alarm. "Tell my daughter-in-law to give me her jewelry so that I can put it into the soaproot suds. That will be good for the silver and the turquoise."

Juanita resolved not to mention the hair-combing incident again, especially since Lu was moody, and preoccupied with looking for a job. The incident wasn't important, only puzzling, and it wasn't worth getting upset if she never found out its significance. There was so much she didn't know—it would take forever to explain in detail everything she asked.

And yet Lu did not mind telling her about the "ancients" who had lived on this land before the Navajos. Their pottery shards were scattered all over Cañoncito. Sometimes an especially large piece of an old thumb-nail design or a paint-decorated piece was found, and occasionally an unbroken cooking pot was exposed by the wind. These "ancients" might have been the ancestors of the nearby Pueblos. The small turquoise beads that were sometimes brought up from underground by the ants might be from their burial places.

It was fun searching the anthills for small pieces of blue among the tiny bits of hard, dark rock that the ants brought up. Some days Luciano rode alone to different hoghans, to talk with the men who had been to Albuquerque, Gallup or even farther, hoping to hear that some trader needed a silversmith. On those days Juanita rode out with Yee-ke-nes-bah. Her conversation with her sister-in-law was the same as with Shimah: gestures, one or two newly mastered phrases, and much laughter over small things. But they understood each other when one wanted to race the horses across the flat land, or when one thought she saw something among the dark rock bits around an anthill.

It was on a day like this, while out riding, that Juanita became ill—so ill that she could barely hold herself upon her horse until they got back to the hoghan. Yee-ke-nes-bah was sympathetic; she helped Juanita from the saddle, and walked with her toward the hoghan. Juanita shook her head. She was going to be sick—each moment made her more certain. She gestured for her sister-in-law to remain there, and started off for a clump of juniper near the arroyo. But Yee-ke-nes-bah did not understand, or else chose not to. She came running along beside her.

When Luciano came home that evening, Juanita was lying face down on the blankets in the rock house. Shimah had built a fire in the little stove and sat quietly by the doorway.

Luciano became alarmed. Where had Juanita been? Had she and Yee-ke-nes-bah met anyone while riding?

Juanita shook her head. The nausea was leaving her and now she felt empty and weak. She had no idea what was the matter. The illness had come suddenly—sharp pains in her stomach and intermittent vomiting all afternoon. Juanita thought of how Shimah had followed her each time she left the rock house, padding along beside her, scuffing out a place in the dirt with her moccasin, and then padding back to sit by the door patiently until the nausea overcame her daughter-in-law again. Perhaps Shimah had thought Juanita was frightened by this sudden illness, that her presence would be comforting. Instead it had embarrassed Juanita, made her feel doubly miserable. All afternoon she'd thought: If Shimah would only go away and let me be sick alone.

But Shimah hadn't. She'd loosened her daughter-in-law's hair and bathed her face, and tended the fire in the woodstove. Now she was talking to Luciano, quieting his alarm.

"Shimah says it is nothing to worry about. You have been eating fresh-killed meat and parched corn. Your stomach isn't used to it."

Shimah was probably right. Juanita had been eating more than she was accustomed to: fresh mutton roasted over the open fire, stewed backbone and chili, hot fried-bread. Juanita groaned faintly. Why did she think of those things just now, when she felt as though she never wanted to eat again?

Luciano was still concerned about her, days afterward, when they were getting ready to ride to Correo for supplies. "You're certain you feel well enough to ride that far?"

"Of course I am."

"Wear something heavy—the wind has a bite."

Juanita got out her boots and Levis, a corduroy shirt to wear beneath her leather jacket, a light wool neckerchief to tie about her head, and gauntlets. Luciano borrowed her yellow scarf to knot around his throat and tuck down inside his woolen jacket. He stuffed the bottoms of his Levis into his boots and pulled his Stetson down firmly on his head. "Ready?"

Allen's bay horse was saddled for Juanita. The black mare was still in the corral. "Lu, whose buckskin horse is that?" she asked.

"Mine. Allen just came back with him."

Juanita tilted her head to one side. "How did you do it?"

"Traded my red velvet shirt to George Abeyta."

"Oh, Lu!"

By this time they had ridden out across the pasture and were following the line of the mesas that guarded the canyon on the west.

"I had a feeling about that velvet shirt, too. But it's more important, the feeling a man has about a horse." Luciano was trying to explain something which was difficult to put into words. Juanita rode closer to him.

"I could always borrow a horse from my family, but it wouldn't be like having my own. I knew it wouldn't be wise to spend any of our money when there's so little left, but then I remembered the shirt. George would trade most anything for a real velvet shirt."

"I understand, Lu." Had she forgotten? This was one of the reasons they had come here: The feeling they both had for horses. They shared this feeling, as well as something within them that longed for free and open sky and earth. There was a certain power that went with riding a horse—a power that was the rhythm and strength of the animal, its swiftness. A power that was the keenness of the wind against your face, and seeing everything around you more clearly. And the power was stronger when the horse was your own. Of course she understood.

The buckskin hadn't been ridden much; he was spirited, but not unmanageable. He set a good fast pace and Allen's horse would not be out-distanced. Juanita had to keep a firm hand on the reins. As they rode they talked a little. There should be letters waiting for them from California. They would ask the trader what day he went into town for supplies; perhaps they could ride in with him sometimes.

The broken country opened onto flat land that sloped slightly upward to Correo. Juanita and Luciano let the horses out, bending low over their necks to escape the cut of the wind. Juanita could feel the sorrel stretch out beneath her as Luciano's horse nosed ahead. They arrived at Correo laughing and breathless. When Luciano got off his horse, and looped the reins about the hitching rack, there was almost a swagger to his movements which implied: Isn't that buckskin a beauty?

Pentz's Trading Post was a mushroom growth of buildings beside the highway. There were gasoline pumps, a garage, and a row of tourist cabins. Inside the largest building were the grocery store, lunch counter, and post office.

Juanita and Luciano stood next to the woodstove in the center of the store. The whole place was neatly arranged and clean. Along one wall were shelves of canned goods, sacks of flour, sugar, beans, and a long counter with a candy case at one end.

"Almost all the Cañoncito people come here to trade," Luciano told her. "Shall we see if there's any mail?"

Mrs. Pentz came through a door at the back of the store. "I thought I heard someone," she said.

"Our name is Platero. Is there any mail for us here?" Luciano asked.

Mrs. Pentz stepped behind the post office window. She was a small, wiry-looking woman. Her arms and face were deeply tanned, and her short brown hair was marcelled and pinned back neatly. "I remember you now," she said pleasantly. "You got off the bus here a few weeks ago. I couldn't help noticing you, walking down the road together." She colored faintly, then began to sort out letters from a small bundle of mail.

There were several letters from California. Two were from Nadine—Juanita recognized the handwriting—and one was from Waano-Gano, addressed to both of them in large black print. There was also a letter from her parents; she tucked this one inside her jacket.

"Where is Mr. Pentz?" Luciano asked.

"Outside, at the garage probably."

As her husband went out the door, Juanita said conversationally, to Mrs. Pentz: "It must keep you busy here."

"Yes, it does. Fortunately, everyone doesn't come at once, although in the summertime they seem to."

Juanita walked to the candy case. The children would like some of those striped sticks, she thought, and I might as well start ordering the supplies. She consulted the list from her pocket.

"If you have the order written out, just let me fill it," said Mrs. Pentz. "I know you're anxious to read some of your mail."

Juanita stood with her back to the woodstove as she read Nadine's letters. They were gay, cheerful—like Nadine. It seemed that people were still spluttering because she'd gone to the reservation with Lu. And Nadine missed her so much that she might have to marry Michel to drown her loneliness. Juanita smiled. As if she weren't going to marry Michel anyway.

Luciano came in behind her and stood reading over her shoulder for a moment. "Mr. Pentz said he drives to Albuquerque twice a week, and he'd be glad to take us along."

"Fine."

"We'd better get our supplies now and start home. It looks like snow."

As they rode along the line of mesas, the sky seemed to lower itself about them—a dome of pale gray. The ground and ledges of rock stretched before them in monotone.

They were almost home when the first large, soft flakes fell slanting across their shoulders. Snowflakes melted against the shaggy hides of the horses, and melted on the ground. The snow fell thicker, faster, closing about them like a curtain. Juanita looked up to watch the unbelievably large flakes floating down. Some fell softly against her face, clinging.

"I'll ride a little ahead", said Luciano. "You follow." And soon all that Juanita could see was the horse and man ahead.

This might be the arroyo at the end of the pastureland they were crossing, thought Juanita. It was. They stopped in front of the hoghan and untied the bundles behind the saddles. Juanita went with Luciano to turn the horses into the corral, and help carry the saddles.

Shimah had coffee on for them. They stood about the fire soaking up the warmth. Juanita opened the bag of peppermint sticks; Wudy was the first to investigate, then Phillip. Little Bijo scrambled from her mother's lap.

Luciano and his mother were talking. He began to laugh. "I can just see you weighted down in Navajo skirts," he said to Juanita.

"Lu, what on earth are you talking about?"

"Shimah objects to your pants."

"My Levis? Why?" Juanita looked questioningly at her mother-in-law.

Shimah smiled a little, pointed to the offending Levis and shook her head, then made motions of spreading out a long, wide skirt and nodded approvingly.

"Shimah used to ride a great deal. She says a full skirt is comfortable." Luciano was still laughing.

"But Lu, I like to ride in Levis. Tell her that I'm as accustomed to them as she is to a skirt."

Shimah was persistent: Women didn't dress like men out here.

Could she explain to Shimah that she was herself, not one of the women out here? That Lu had married her because he liked her as a person, not because she was white or Navajo. That she had married Lu, not because he was a white man or an Indian. It was clear in her own mind, but could she put it into words? Better not try. She was fond of Shimah, and the older woman seemed to return that affection, but she didn't want to hurt her mother-in-law, or appear headstrong. Yet this must be settled so that she could remain herself, not someone trying to "go native." Settling this, not just smoothing it over, would make it easier when other problems came up later on.

Everyone was so still around the cookfire, waiting. Juanita took time to think of exactly the right answer. "Ask Shimah if it is considered 'bad' to wear men's pants out here."

"She says, not 'bad,' the women just don't do it." Luciano was still amused, and looked expectantly at his wife to see how she would handle this.

"Tell her that when something is taboo, or an important matter of custom, I will try to respect her wishes. But in other things I must do as I have always done; to change would be like trying to make me another person."

Shimah considered her words for a long time.

"I hope she doesn't think I'm just being obstinate about a pair of pants," Juanita said quietly to her husband.

He started to answer and then stopped. His mother was speaking, the silver circles in her ears catching the firelight as she nodded her head slowly.

"My daughter-in-law and I understand each other," she said
gently.

FOUR
Luciano's Grandfather

Past dull red sandstone mesas, aged and lined by countless years of wind and rain—mesas rising tall out of the widening piles of dull red talus growing with slim-spiked yucca, long, thick-bladed bear grass, and slender young cedars—that was the way to the old grandfather's. Juanita and Luciano were walking. The ground beneath their feet was as red as the sandstone mesas, scarred by wagon tracks, and cut deep by sheep trails. Against the ageless rock and the rugged beauty, their worries seemed small and inconsequential. What if Luciano went to Albuquerque again and again, returning without hope of work? What if there were only a few dollars left of their savings? They could still walk out like this and fill themselves with all that was peaceful and beautiful until work and money slipped over the rim of conscious thinking.

The hoghan of the old grandfather was walled halfway up with red sandstone and the dome covered with the equally red soil. There was a brush shelter of thick, green juniper boughs beside it, the green of the juniper sharp in contrast to the red soil. The grandfather was glad to see them. He murmured a greeting over and over as he made up a seat of sheep pelts at the back of the hoghan. "I will get my wife. She is somewhere near here with the sheep."

Luciano pointed out the moccasins that the old man was making. "It's difficult to get deerhide any longer, so they use cowhide or horsehide. And the reddish brown color, the men make that dye themselves. They say if a woman touches it, it isn't any good."

"Why is that?"

"I don't know the reason. But that is what they say."

The old grandfather came puffing through the doorway, his face alight. This was an occasion. He added the last wood to the fire and started outside for more.

"Here, Grandfather, let me help you." Luciano arose and followed him.

Juanita could hear the tinkle of sheep bells, the soft, drawn out *ba-a-as*. This hoghan was smaller than Shimah's, and from the worn blanket at the door and the small number of supplies in the open cupboard, it was evident the occupants were feeling the pinch of bad times too. She shifted her weight, resting her legs. Would she ever get accustomed to sitting properly upon the floor with her legs curled beneath her?

Luciano and his grandfather returned with the wood, the grandmother came in behind them, wiping her hands on her skirt, talking rapidly to her husband; she was obviously excited. When she saw Juanita she was suddenly quiet, shy. Her smile was friendly as they touched hands.

"They have killed a sheep for us and we are going to be feasted," Luciano told Juanita.

The carcass was brought in and hung near the doorway. Juanita watched as the frail old woman wielded the knife expertly and severed the ribs from the backbone. She was so slender; her movements quick and birdlike; and her sharp old face was like a bird's, topped with the double knot of thin gray hair. She was plainly enjoying the preparation for this feast in honor of her returned grandson and his wife.

Luciano and his grandfather were already talking earnestly. There was so much the old man wanted to know about that western place. Sometimes the grandfather laughed until there were tears in his eyes. Then he would put out his hand, protesting: "Stop, my son, now you are only teasing an old man." Juanita watched the two of them together. There was a vital handsomeness about her husband's face; laughter in his large, dark eyes, on his long, slow-smiling lips. There was youth and strength in the way he sat: one knee up, one arm resting across it, the free arm gesturing smoothly with his words. That same aliveness was behind the wrinkled, weathered features of the other man, but dimmed like the faded red silk handkerchief bound about his head. Yet now and then the aliveness flamed as his grandson talked—flamed like dying coals briefly fanned.

The grandmother set out cups for them and poured the coffee. The meal was ready. She went outside and returned with the head of the butchered sheep. The gray wool was bloody. There was blood and mucus about the mouth and nose. The half-closed eyes were glazed. She set the head at the edge of the fire.

"Yah t'eh! Yah t'eh!" the old man commended.

"We should feel honored," Luciano told her, "that they have killed a sheep for us."

Juanita tried to swallow.

"I can see you aren't appreciating it," he added, grinning.

"I'm not honored when I'm deprived of my appetite." Juanita tried to avoid looking at the sheep's head.

"After we are gone they'll cover that in the hot ashes and leave it to bake slowly. The meat of the head is a great delicacy. My mother likes those strips of white meat around the eyes."

"Oh, Lu, as if looking at it isn't bad enough!"

He laughed softly at her discomfort and, now and then, cast sidelong glances to see if she was eating her mutton ribs with relish.

Juanita tried to control her quaking stomach. She might as well accustom herself to this now. There would be other sheep's heads around other cook-fires. She looked straight at the head. Ugly things, sheep . . . but the lambs were cute. Destructive too . . . the way they ate grass roots. They ought to be killed. After all a sheep's ribs were no less a part of a sheep than its head . . . and she was eating ribs; the head just seemed more personal . . . but she'd have to get over that. She looked into the glazed eyes, this time unwaveringly. Oddly enough the gagging sensation was leaving her.

She looked over at Luciano and smiled. "These ribs are good, aren't they?"

As Luciano pushed his cup forward for more coffee he addressed his grandfather. "It's been a long time since I've heard the story of the long walk. Will you tell it?"

The old man was pleased. He liked to tell that story. He settled himself more comfortably, sipped long from his coffee cup, and began. Luciano turned a little toward Juanita and when the old man paused to remember more clearly or stopped to sip his coffee, he interpreted the story.

As he spoke, Juanita could see the old grandfather as a round-eyed, fat-cheeked boy only a little larger than Phillip or Wudy. Grandfather told how his mother left the other children with a friendly Laguna family; they would be safer there. The soldiers were not after the Lagunas; it was the Navajos they wanted. Hiding far back among the mesas, crouching in caves, was not good for such a little boy, and yet he was too young to be separated from his mother.

But the Navajos could not hide forever. Their sheep and horses were rounded up by the soldiers. Few men dared to venture out and plant a cornfield. The people lived on roots and seeds and what wild game they could kill. And then other Navajo men arrived among the back mesas—men in good shirts, riding good horses. "If you come in now there will be food and blankets for all. 'The Roper' has said so. If you stay, the soldiers will hunt you out and destroy you."

And so most of them went to meet the soldiers and a few stayed in hiding. The round-eyed, fat-cheeked boy went with his family. His people were going where there would be food for all. He rode most of the way in a wagon with other children and the old people. His family walked along behind the wagon, and when at last it was too full of the old and sick, he was lifted out to walk with them. It was such a long walk, and he was bewildered and frightened by the white soldiers who rode along the line to keep the people moving.

At last they came to the fort, and the people began to build shelters along the river. Families who were related camped together. Before the camp was settled he became separated from his mother. He was afraid to call out, afraid even to cry, so he wandered around in the dark looking for her, trying to hold back his tears until it seemed he would burst. A stranger, a Navajo man, found him and took him by the hand. They went to all the camps until they met his mother who was searching for him. How good it was to be lifted into her arms, even though he was too big for that.

They camped at the fort a long time, and it was a long time of death and horror. Their old enemies, the Apaches, raided them. Sickness swept the camps until there were fewer and fewer people. There was never enough wood to keep warm, or to cook with. Some of the food the soldiers gave them was not good.

The people were losing their spirit. Then one day the soldiers said they were to be taken even farther away, to a place called Indian Territory. The women cried out against this, and the men too. They crowded about the tent to talk to the Chief Soldier who had come to sign the paper which would send them away. Finally, it was decided the Navajos could go back to their own country.

The little boy helped his mother pack their few possessions. As they were leaving, one of the soldiers, of whom he had been so afraid, unfastened his sword and gave it to the little boy who was trying so hard to be big. The long walk home was easier; going home was different from leaving it. When the family of Lu's grandfather saw the mesa Des Jin in the distance, they turned toward it, they and all their relatives. "We're going this way. This is our home."

The main body of Navajos continued to travel westward to the land which the government had assigned to them as a reservation, while the little boy and his relatives turned into the broken country which had been their home, and their fathers' home before them, and their fathers' fathers' home before that.

"I still have that sword," Lu's grandfather said. He lifted it from the trunk and unwrapped it carefully. The scabbard was black and curved. When the grandfather drew the sword, the blade gleamed in the firelight. Juanita sat quietly. The sword was a symbol of how the Navajos had been made homeless and subdued. She had read of Bosque Redondo—the long walk of the Navajos—but it had seemed like something which had happened long ago to a strange people. It hadn't been long ago. It had been in this old man's lifetime. And it had happened to children like Wudy and Phillip and Bijo, to mothers like Il-tha-bah and Lu's own mother, to frail old women like the grandmother.

"Didn't these people seem like human beings to the government?" she asked her husband.

"Probably not. We were a tribe of savages who barred the way of trade and new settlements. We fought with and stole from the Pueblos and Mexicans. It didn't matter to the government that the Pueblos and Mexicans stole women and children from our camps and killed our men. It didn't matter that some of the new settlements were on land we'd held for centuries. Then when the wise old Headmen counseled peace and the keeping of the treaties, the young men would not listen and kept on raiding and killing."

"But here in Cañoncito, was that true?"

Luciano questioned his grandfather. "No, the Navajos here had been at peace with the Lagunas to the west and with the Spanish at Ojo to the north for a long time. But they were rounded up. They were Navajos."

Juanita watched as her husband turned the sword in his hands, and, she thought, it is scarcely one man's lifetime since my people held Lu's people captive.

The next day they rode north to Ojo. Luciano carried a battered coffee pot tied to his saddle and a small bundle of fried bread and cold meat. As they traveled north, the country seemed even wilder; there were fewer hoghans. The rock colors were more brilliant; the rock masses twisted in a tortuous maze suggested the violence of their formation.

"It's almost as though the history of these people through the centuries has left its mark upon the country."

"Or that this country left its mark upon the people," Luciano replied.

They had ridden a long way. The vivid-hued eruptions of rock were behind them. Snow-capped "Walking Around Mountain" gleamed in the distance. The country around them was grassy with rolling stretches of good pasture land. Sprawled in the center of the grassland was Ojo: adobe buildings clustered on either side of a stream. "This was a land grant from the Spanish King to the Herreras, and some of them still live here," Luciano told her. "But it isn't as it used to be. From what my grandfather tells, it was like a little town."

Juanita and Luciano urged their horses across the stream and rode around the settlement. There was the old schoolhouse; the Herreras had hired a teacher who came to live with the family and direct the education of the children. There were long rows of stables and a carriage house and a high-roofed barn. To one side of the barn were heavy posts where beef carcasses were strung up. The Herreras had been self-sustaining, living off cattle and sheep and the produce of their gardens and orchards.

On a higher slope stood an adobe church with a wooden cross. A smaller building had been the priest's home. The priest, too, had been a permanent part of the settlement. He had performed baptisms, and had always helped at the Herrera's settlement, where men herded sheep and rounded up horses, and women helped at lambing time and with shearing. The Herreras gave them Spanish names to keep account of their earnings.

"I herded sheep for them one summer when I was home from school."

"The place seems deserted now," Juanita observed.

"Yes, most of them have moved to the Spanish settlement around Albuquerque."

On the way home they stopped among the high rock ledges where there was a spring. The rocks were honey-combed with caves. "This is one of the places where our people used to hide when the Apaches raided through here. They rolled rocks in front of the caves, and from their safe hiding places, they could shoot the raiders off their horses."

"Life must never have been dull in those days."

"Of course," Luciano paused, "we raided the Apaches too."

They gathered dry wood and built a fire in a recess among the rocks. Luciano filled the coffee pot at the spring.

"It was only during the last twenty years that traders would come among us." Luciano's even teeth showed white between his wide smile. "The first man to get brave built a rock house near one of the springs where our people came for water. I don't remember him much, except that he had a peg leg, and our mothers used to frighten us when we were bad, saying they would leave us with him."

"Then my uncle, Joe Platero, built a big place of rock and adobe. The walls were that thick," Luciano held his hands wide apart. "The ruin is still standing. All the people went there to trade with him. He had a huge fireplace in the store and kept a big fire going in the wintertime. That Joe Platero was progressive. He hooked up with Wright's Trading Post in Albuquerque and got his supplies through them, even brought out the mail. It was mostly from children away at school. Joe had to read it to their folks and then answer for them. But when Joe died no one kept the store going. Correo is the nearest place to buy and trade now, and sometimes a family will drive into Albuquerque in their wagon."

Juanita rolled her fried bread around the meat. "It doesn't seem possible. These people here are so close to Albuquerque—to the Lagunas—to Spanish people; their children go away to school and come home, and yet they live as they have always lived. Outside contacts don't seem to change them."

"The country hasn't changed," Luciano said simply. "Sometimes I think my people are like the rocks." He pointed his hand toward the towering ledges. "Wind and rain leave their marks, but that doesn't change them. Bosque Redondo taught the Navajos that they must learn to live with white people, but it didn't change them deep inside."

Luciano moved the coffee pot from the fire so that it would cool and they could drink from it. The sun had begun to descend in the heavens. Juanita could see their horses cropping grass on the flat below them.

"But going to school has changed some of them—like you."

Luciano's face became impassive across the fire. "You are changed while you are away, but you can't stay away, and when you come back, the other life slips off easily."

Juanita looked puzzled. "But, Lu, you wouldn't want to go back to herding sheep, to living in a hoghan and never having anything else?"

"No. I still want some of the things that living in a city taught me to appreciate. But sometimes I am a little mixed up. I feel as though the person who lived in California wasn't really me." He raised the coffee pot and drank deeply, then arose and carried it around the fire to Juanita. He half reclined beside her, touching his fingers to her hair as she drank. She set the coffee to one side and regarded him seriously. His eyes were dark—fathomless. "But I have only to look at you to know I was that one." He reached one hand to her shoulder and drew her down beside him, brushing her cheek with his own for a moment. Then slowly, firmly he brought his mouth against hers.

That Luciano was sometimes mixed up and doubted ever having been away surprised Juanita. And yet she could imagine how it could be. There were times, as they walked between the towering, red sandstone mesas, that she herself doubted the existence of any other place.

They had taken the horses to water and on the way back turned them loose to graze. "Would you like to see the canyon where I was born? It isn't far. Shimah goes there often for a certain plant to make dye." They circled to the west until they were on the other side of a low mesa. Before them stretched a narrow, deserted canyon.

"How do people keep land for their own when they no longer live upon it?"

"The families remember. There's seldom any quarrel over grazing rights. Sometimes a cornfield will be fenced but that's all. It was after I went away to school that surveyors came out here, and the government allotted one hundred and sixty acres to each Cañoncito Navajo. That was to give them a title to their land since this wasn't a part of the main reservation. Most of the allotments are where the families have always lived; the children's allotments are adjoining, although some of the allotments are at another place where the family may have camped before—like mine. Large families own whole canyons, but the people come and go over the land as they've always done, and the springs still belong to everyone."

The little canyon where Luciano was born showed no sign of recent habitation. An arroyo coursed its way through it. Scrub cedars grew among the rocks.

"Here's a pile of rock from our old hoghan wall."

"Is this where you lived when the truck came to take you away to school?"

Luciano had told Juanita about that day and she'd never forgotten it. How he was out with the sheep and his mother came after him. The truck was waiting, half-filled with other boys and girls going away to school. The driver said that Lu should take something to eat on the way since it would be a long time before they reached Albuquerque. For once, there was no fried bread left from the night before, and no meat. There was no time to cook anything. A pail of cactus apples was all his mother had. He took those. The other children teased him because that was all his family had given him to eat. Juanita could imagine him choking back the tears, eating his cactus apples in silence, hardly tasting them.

Luciano was kicking over the rocks which had encircled the floor. He let out his breath in a long whistle and stooped to pick up something, a ram's horn pierced with three holes. "I remember this. My father used to straighten his arrows with it."

Juanita turned the flat, curved horn in her hand. "Lu, tell me about your father. You've never said much; only that your family was well-off while he was alive, and that he was a good medicine man."

"There isn't much to tell." He turned and looked down the canyon.

Juanita felt as though a curtain was being drawn and that she was being allowed to see only what was in front of it. Strangely she linked this with Lu's reluctance to talk about the hair-combing. But what possible connection could there be between Lu's father and the hair-combing?

"My father was respected as a medicine man. He seldom failed to rid a patient of the evil that disturbed him. One of the special things he knew was a cure for rattlesnake bite. My brother, Lorencito, learned my father's songs, and the snake bite cure passed to him." Luciano started walking down the canyon slowly. "See that place ahead?" He pointed to a crumbling adobe house on top of the mesa. "My grandfather lived there until he got too old. All of those peach trees below are his. He planted them when he was a young man. They still blossom in springtime.

Juanita looked at the dark, gnarled branches against the sandstone mesa and wondered at the perverseness that caused her to ask, not about the peach trees, but again about Lu's father.

"Was it here in this canyon that your father died?" The words rang sharply against the stillness.

Luciano was slow in answering. "No, it was when my family was on the mesas, far west from here, piñon picking." That was all he said; his lips closed sternly and the muscles of his face tightened. Juanita walked beside him silently, asking nothing more.

FIVE
Wild Duck Dinner

There was one sack of flour, one can of coffee, and a half-pail of lard left; no sugar. That might last until the next trip to Correo. But buying supplies this time would take the remainder of their money.

"The food would last if you and I ate out," Luciano speculated.

"But we have no invitations to dinner," Juanita reminded him.

"That doesn't matter. Haven't I told you about the good old Navajo custom of feeding guests, especially if they are relatives?"

Shimah sat watching them. She could tell by the tones of their voices and the hints of laughter in their eyes that her son and daughter-in-law were teasing one another.

"How are things with George Abeyta's mother—good?" her son asked.

"Good, from what I hear."

"We will pay my aunt a visit. It's about mealtime."

When they arrived at the Abeyta hoghan, they hardly looked like guests who had come just for the meal. Both wore clean Levis: Juanita a dark blue corduroy shirt, Luciano a black wool one with a yellow kerchief knotted jauntily about his throat. He creased the high crown of his Stetson and set it on at a rakish angle.

As they walked to the door George met them and spoke a cautious greeting. They could see past him into the hoghan where someone lay huddled in a blanket, feet toward the fire.

Luciano asked, "Is someone ill here?"

"My mother."

"Is it anything serious?" Juanita asked.

"No, she's caught a cold and now aches all over."

Luciano began backing away. "We might disturb her. Just riding by," he said easily, "and thought we'd stop and see how things are with you."

George followed them to the horses. "How is the buckskin behaving?"

"Good. He's going to be a fast one. Have you worn the red shirt?"

"One time." George grinned at Luciano. "Now all the girls are chasing me."

"I should have told you. That's how I got my wife."

Juanita smiled at their foolishness and began to untie the sorrel's reins.

When they had ridden away from the hoghan, she laughed softly. "That was a nice try, my husband."

"Wasn't it?" He slouched dolefully in the saddle. "And what makes it twice as bad, my aunt is a good cook."

They rode along silently. "Race you!" Luciano challenged suddenly. He seemed barely to touch the buckskin with his knees, and they were pounding along the sandy floor of the canyon. Allen's horse could just hold the pace. Luciano slowed up at the head of the canyon. The buckskin was straining to go again. "Can't do much of that. Works up an appetite."

They took the wagon trail up out of the canyon and started at a more leisurely pace across the mesa. A large hoghan, flanked on one side by a long, brush shelter, stood at the far edge. The corral was circular and well-built of interlaced cedar branches. A new, green spring-wagon with bright orange wheels stood beside it.

"That wagon looks familiar," Juanita said.

"This is where Wounded Head lives." He drew rein on the buckskin, whistling softly.

"Lu, I don't like that calculating look on your face."

"Why not? There's smoke coming from the hoghan. Wounded Head's wife has asked us to visit them."

"I suppose a meal is a meal." Juanita began to smile.

"And custom is custom. They are sure to feed us. I've heard that Wounded Head buys quite a lot of canned peaches at Correo." Luciano smacked his lips softly and drew the back of his hand across his mouth.

"Lu, it hasn't been that long since we've had peaches."

They hitched their horses to a corral post and walked to the hoghan. Luciano drew the blanket aside. Wounded Head's wife greeted them from beside the cook-fire. She was dropping balls of cornmeal into a bubbling pot of stew. Juanita found that it was all she could do to keep her nose from twitching over this tantalizing aroma.

Wounded Head greeted them with warm words, but his face remained impassive—cold. His son extended his hand for a limp handclasp. Juanita and Luciano were given a comfortable place to sit at the back of the hoghan, but Juanita wasn't comfortable. She was conscious of her hair being disheveled from the race up the canyon; she tried to smooth it, putting one hand to her head unobtrusively. She wished that she had worn a skirt instead of Levis. Somehow she could feel Wounded Head's disapproval without seeing his face.

Luciano was talking to the two men. No, he hadn't yet gone to seek work in Albuquerque.

Wounded Head placed his fingertips together with elaborate care. Was it true that in that Western place, where Luciano had been, there was great opportunity for ambitious, young Navajo men?

Luciano misunderstood. Was his son planning to go there?

A thin, ghostlike smile passed over Wounded Head's face and was gone. He shook his head.

The stew was ladled into bowls and passed to them. Juanita cooled one of the pieces of meat on her spoon. That didn't look like mutton. She bit into it. Beef! Wounded Head and his family *did* eat well. Her husband had placed his hat on the bedroll behind him, and now his dark head was bent over the bowl of stew attentively. He looked up long enough to direct a sidelong glance at her when their host got up, took a can of peaches from the cupboard, and opened it with his knife.

The meal finished, they sat back looking into the fire, the men talking leisurely of unimportant things. Wounded Head's wife asked a few questions of Juanita, through Luciano: did she like it here . . . did she miss her own people?

It was a foolish thing. Her imagination was overactive, Juanita told herself, but she wanted to get away. The fire was bright, warming. Wounded Head's wife was pleasant. Wounded Head himself seemed almost friendly as he drew Lu into conversation, but it was a strong feeling that Juanita had—as strong as a cold wind—as dark as a deep shadow. She was relieved when Luciano finally arose to go. He thanked them for the good meal, and then the blanket over the doorway dropped behind them. She was first into the saddle and started toward the edge of the mesa.

"Not that way," Luciano called. "There's no trail, only rocks."

Juanita turned and followed Luciano as he picked his way down the other side of the mesa. Halfway down the narrow trail, Luciano took off his hat. Holding it at arm's length, he shook it carefully. Puffs of yellow dust scattered on the wind.

"I'll be more careful where I lay my good Stetson after this," he said, as he recreased the crown and thumped the brim with his middle finger.

Luciano and Juanita were standing before the window of the White Eagle Trading Post. They had come into Albuquerque with Mr. Pentz, and the whole afternoon was before them, since he would not be leaving until evening. Maizel's hadn't been so encouraging this time. Bell's was still postponing the new trading post. It was a hopeless round from curio shop to trading post to souvenir store. No wonder Lu is moody when he comes home from a trip to town, Juanita thought. It seems more discouraging in here. Out there, one day it's windy, the day after, it rains or snows, and then next morning, the sun is bright again. Makes you feel that just the coming of another day will bring better things.

Juanita went into the White Eagle with Luciano, instead of window shopping outside as she had done at the other places. Mr. Palm, the owner, was always cheerful and glad to see them, even though he had no need for silversmiths. He came from the back of his shop greeting them like an old friends: "Well, kids, you're looking good. Got a job yet?"

Mr. Palm was a tall, heavy-set man in his late fifties, and he looked rather pompous until he spoke in that deep but unmistakably jovial voice. His dark hair was thinning a little on top, his dark eyes twinkled pleasantly behind rimmed glasses, and his was the one friendly face they knew in Albuquerque.

"Just fixing myself a pot of coffee back here on the grill." He went on, not waiting for them to answer, "Won't you have a cup?"

There was cleared space at the back of the store: an old-fashioned roll-top desk against the wall, Navajo rugs and saddle blankets piled halfway to the ceiling, gaudily-painted tom-toms stacked one on top of the other, and pottery bowls wrapped in newspaper and piled together.

"This is the stockroom, too," Mr. Palm explained. He gestured about him, smiling ruefully. "You can see that I overstocked this season."

Juanita and Luciano pulled a couple of saddle blankets to the floor and sat down.

"That's all right for you kids," said Mr. Palm, drawing a chair out from the desk, "but I'll just sit here and be comfortable." He poured coffee for them and set out a box of stuffed dates. "Haven't seen a season like this since I came here from Sioux country. Why, I haven't had a customer all day."

Luciano smiled. "You traders all know the same story."

"Don't believe me? Well, it would pay me to close this shop for the rest of the season." He chuckled. "Can't do it though; I'm attached to the place. Of course, until times get better, I've always got a little to go on." He chuckled again and patted his middle.

"Is it this way everywhere?" Juanita asked. "People seemed to have money when we were in Hollywood."

"I guess the depression just hit us quicker here . . . and harder. Most people come here for their health or to see the Indians." He nodded to Luciano. "And our business is with the people who come to see the Indians. So, if people don't have jobs, they don't get vacations; no vacations, they don't get out here to buy a little bracelet to take back to Aunt Emma." Mr. Palm spread his fingers over his knees. "And that's about the size of it."

Luciano reached for another stuffed date. "In other words, an unemployed silversmith doesn't have a chance."

"I don't want to sound discouraging, but if I were you and handy at anything else, I'd do my job hunting along some other line."

"I used to be a fair mechanic," Luciano mused.

As they left the White Eagle, Luciano dug his hands deep into his pockets. "Mr. Palm is right. I've been slow in seeing this for myself. Kept trying because I'd rather work at silversmithing, I guess."

They walked along Central Avenue aimlessly. "Lu, I wish you'd let me try to get a job."

"It isn't that bad." He pulled back his cuff from the heavy bracelets. "There are still things to pawn."

They turned off Central. "Are you tired? Would you rather go to a movie while I try some of the garages?"

Juanita shook her head.

By late afternoon, they had almost circled downtown Albuquerque, and Luciano had left his application for work at every garage and filling station within that circle. They were walking slowly now, dejectedly.

"Surely one mechanic out of all those garages will break an arm cranking a jalopy," Juanita said hopefully.

"We should meet Mr. Pentz in an hour. Shall we quit?"

"Yes, and, Lu, I'm awfully hungry."

The Liberty Cafe was near the White Eagle. Juanita and Luciano sat down at the counter, opened a menu between them, and began to peruse the list of sandwiches.

"Do you see this?" Juanita pointed to the large printing:

Special Today * * Wild Duck Dinner $1.50

Luciano read it softly to himself, naming over the various side dishes that went with the dinner. "Are you as tired of fried bread and weak coffee as I am?"

"Not only that, but at the moment it seems absolutely necessary to my wellbeing that I have wild duck. How much money have we left, Lu?"

"A little over three dollars."

They looked at each other, smiling slowly.

They were finishing their soup when Mr. Palm came in. "Well, well, you kids still in town?"

Luciano indicated the empty stool beside him.

"No. Thanks just the same. Got a couple of cronies waiting in the last booth for me. Have any luck today?"

"Spent the afternoon going to most of the garages. No luck."

Mr. Palm was looking at the soup bowls. "Say now," his voice lowered sympathetically, "I hope you kids get a job right soon."

The waiter slid their plates on the counter, set a relish dish, piled high with green onions, radishes, and large, ripe olives between them, then lifted the heavy, silver covers. The roast duck was a golden brown; long-headed wild rice was covered with thick, rich gravy. Two slaps of butter melted against the deep orange centers of sweet potatoes. A crisp, fluted lettuce leaf held pale yellow apple sauce.

Luciano stole a sidelong glance at Juanita, his dark eyes full of merriment. When they both looked around, Mr. Palm was walking slowly toward the rear booth, shaking his head in wonder.

When they returned to Correo, Luciano pawned a bracelet for their supplies and then went out to the corral with Mr. Pentz to saddle the horses and tie the supplies into a roll behind each saddle.

"You look tired, Mrs. Pentz." Juanita sat on one of the stools at the small counter, glancing over their mail.

"I suppose I am. I haven't sat down long enough to tell." Mrs. Pentz was busy behind the counter scalding dishes. "Thank goodness no more busses stop this evening."

Juanita felt at ease with Mrs. Pentz. She was friendly and yet did not intrude by asking too many questions. Both she and Mr. Pentz seemed to have a genuine liking for all of their Navajo customers from Cañoncito. Often they stood around talking with some of the old people in Spanish, after the trading was over. Juanita knew from the number of old belts and necklaces Mrs. Pentz had shown her in the safe that the Navajos were heavily in debt to them this year.

Luciano beckoned to her through the door. Juanita buttoned up her leather jacket and drew on her gauntlets.

"See you next week," she called as she went out.

A bright half-moon illuminated the land; the trail lay plainly before them. They had ridden almost past the long line of mesas when the sorrel began to gain on the buckskin. As Juanita rode alongside, she could see that Luciano was having trouble. The buckskin was fairly staggering, its sides heaving, its head lolling as it made thick, wheezing noises.

"I knew Mr. Pentz gave this horse too much grain. These desert ponies aren't used to such rich food."

They slowed the horses and Luciano got off, talking gently to the buckskin as it wheezed and hacked and tried to lie down on the trail. He tightened the reins and pulled the horse to its feet.

"I know just how the buckskin feels. I'm beginning to feel a little that way myself." Juanita rubbed her stomach gingerly. "I think the duck was too rich for me."

"All this jogging on a full stomach has upset you. Walk a while, maybe you'll feel better."

They led the horses along the trail. "I'd much rather have this buckskin founder behind me than under me."

When Luciano's horse seemed steady on its feet again, they mounted and rode the rest of the way.

At the hoghan, Juanita helped untie the packrolls from the saddles. She hadn't realized how tired she was. During the last part of the ride home, the jerking motion of the trotting had been even more upsetting to her stomach. She was a little unsteady on her feet as she carried in some of the supplies. At last she sank down on a pallet of sheep pelts against the wall and removed her boots. Boots were not made for walking on cement sidewalks. Her legs ached, and her back ached too, and as if that wasn't enough, her stomach felt as though any moment it would turn within her. She stretched out upon the pallet. Once she smiled sleepily at Shimah, and that was all she remembered.

Juanita was awakened by Shimah's voice, pitched higher and louder than usual, as if she were scolding someone. She was. Looking about her, Juanita could see Luciano sitting on the edge of her pallet, his face grave and perplexed. Shimah continued to upbraid him, shaking her head as if to make her words more forceful, drawing her eyebrows together in a frown. And then Luciano began to laugh—deep, rippling laughter. Shimah paused in her tirade to stare in amazement at him. He continued to laugh, clutching his sides.

"What on earth is the matter?" Juanita raised up on one elbow. Her face was flushed, the dark coil of her hair had loosened and hung low on her neck.

"Shimah is very angry with me. She says I should be ashamed, treating you this way when you're so far from your own people." He looked over at Shimah, and his eyes began to crinkle with laughter again.

"What way?"

"Getting you drunk. Taking you to town and filling you with whiskey."

Juanita sat up straight. "Drunk?"

"Yes. I brought you home, and you could hardly walk. Right away you fell over and went to sleep. I should be ashamed."

"But Lu, tell her the truth."

Luciano's mother was still muttering with indignation when he began to explain how Juanita had gotten sick on the way home. "I had a sick horse and sick woman to take care of. You know I didn't give the horse whiskey."

Shimah smiled faintly, and the frown left her forehead. Il-tha-bah and Yee-ke-nes-bah began to giggle. Shimah covered her face with her hands and laughed, her shoulders shaking. Then she wiped her eyes with the back of her hand.

Her face was serious again as she questioned her son. Was her daughter-in-law's sickness like the last time?

Juanita nodded.

The older woman pursed her lips thoughtfully. "It's been a long time since we've had any fresh-killed meat."

The sickness seemed to return each morning. Juanita had no appetite and her stomach would not hold what she ate. On days when her husband went into Albuquerque, she stayed at the hoghan. After one short trip to the spring, she stayed at home even when Luciano was riding someplace nearby. The weakness in her legs, the uneasiness in her stomach, the unexplainable listlessness that pervaded her whole body made her wish to go nowhere and to see no one.

Shimah went about with a wise look upon her face, fixing pallets by the fire for her daughter-in-law, brewing herbs into tea. Juanita guessed, as well as the older woman did, that her illness was a natural thing—nothing new to womankind; and yet she was reluctant to admit it to herself, or to put it into words when she was alone with Luciano. She would wait until later. Perhaps Lu would drive her into Albuquerque in the wagon, and she could go to the government doctor.

Juanita spent whole days reading, mending, and answering letters until she could bear the inactivity no longer. Then she would walk up over the rim of the compound and start off toward one of the smaller, tree-dotted mesas or follow the arroyo as it cut down through the pasture land. As always, when she walked off like this, she could look back over her shoulder and see Il-tha-bah and one of the children following her, or perhaps Shimah, padding along behind at a discreet distance.

And then, as suddenly as it came, the sickness was gone. Her appetite returned and she felt strong again—triumphant over the vagaries of her digestion.

Luciano had ridden away to visit at one of the hoghans, hoping to hear of work somewhere on the reservation. Perhaps it was the feeling of returned strength, or perhaps it was the pressure of all the days of inactivity, but Juanita found herself planning ways to get away from the hoghan without the usual family surveillance. She wanted for once to walk somewhere and feel that she was completely alone.

She put the blankets out in the sun on the huge flat rocks at either side of the little house. She helped her sisters-in-law about the hoghan most of the morning, then she gestured that she was going to the rock house. She walked leisurely enough to her door and turned slowly; no one was watching, then she slipped around the corner of the house and down over the edge of the compound. If anyone had come from the hoghan before this moment, she had planned to begin folding up the blankets as though she were out there for that express purpose.

But she was out of sight now and running across the flat land until she reached the other side of a long ledge of rock. She followed the ledge until she could safely circle behind one of the mesas. Once behind the mesa, she slowed to a walk, thinking that it had been rather clever of her to slip away from her sisters-in-law, and, at the same time, rather foolish to have allowed their well-meant watchfulness to annoy her to this extent.

Juanita walked on and on, swinging her arms, tilting her head back and breathing deeply, enjoying to the fullest her first moments of complete privacy. Lizards darted across the rocks at her approach; long-legged, black beetles waddled into the shelter of dry grass clumps; from beyond the mesa came the notes of meadowlarks calling. But the rest of the earth, for as far as she could see, seemed to drowse beneath the warming sun. She wondered if her sisters-in-law had missed her. Perhaps they were searching already.

Another larger mesa was ahead. Instead of walking behind it, she climbed the sloping side and, reaching the top, sat down against an up-thrust ledge of rock. She could see the hoghan and the rock houses below her at a distance. It wasn't long before a full-skirted figure came from the hoghan, went to the smaller rock house and to the larger one, then returned hurriedly to the hoghan. Two full-skirted figures emerged; they walked all about the compound, pausing at the rim to look out across the country. Juanita felt a small pang of conscience at the trouble she was causing, but she quickly smothered it. The past weeks had left too many things unanswered in her mind. She needed this time alone.

Now the thoughts that she had been pushing aside each day came crowding into her mind. Their money was gone and they would soon run out of things to pawn; what would come after that? There was no answer, unless waiting was an answer. Somehow waiting and inactivity had made the small annoyances of camp life loom large, out of proportion. Things that she and Lu usually laughed off together, had, the last few days, become almost unbearable: washing clothes a few at a time in a niggardly amount of water; smoothing and straightening them as they dried, for there was no way to iron them; trying to take a satisfactory bath in the water from a lardpail. All her efforts toward order and cleanliness seemed at cross purposes with camp life.

There were other things fast becoming unbearable: the monotony of the food when supplies began to run low: fried bread and coffee, coffee and fried bread, perhaps a few potatoes cooked with bacon rind; the sickening, strong odor of goats when she passed the sheep and goat corral; no one to talk to, no one to exchange ideas with, except Lu, and hunting for a job had made him moody and uncommunicative most of the time.

Perhaps if she could have been by herself before, as she was now, she could have thought these things through a few at a time, and they would not have accumulated until they weighed upon her and made her doubt her own courage and strength to see things through. Yet how could she have been alone without running away like this? That was another thing: the family's strict vigilance over her. What was behind it? There must be something behind the concerted effort of a whole family watching her, following her. Thinking back—it had begun the night of her arrival. Not once since then had she been out of their sight.

Juanita leaned against the rocks wearily. What was the use of thinking when there was no answer? Gradually she was aware of the warmth of the sunshine on her head and shoulders, on her legs. It seemed to go deeper than her skin, and to warm the flesh and bones beneath. A family of rock squirrels, unaware of her motionless figure, quarreled noisily on a nearby ledge. The junipers were heavy with the dull yellow-green of new growth. Across the mesa top new green was pushing upward through the faded yellow mats of grass. Wisps of white cloud hung almost motionless in the very blue sky. In the distance, the mesa Des Jin seemed to brood over the little canyons below—Des Jin, with ledges of rose and purple rock, warm-colored in the sunshine.

This was Lu's home, the country that he loved. Before she'd ever seen it, she'd seen it through his eyes. And the other things, he'd told her about them too. She'd known those things and more, and she had wanted to come to Cañoncito. She hadn't known that Lu would find it so hard to get a job. She hadn't known about his family's watchfulness.

She sat up suddenly, in full possession of something which she had almost forgotten. Had there been some way to see all of this ahead, she would still be here now. She knew that. Blind faith would have blotted out uncertainty—faith that she and Lu together could surmount any difficulty.

Juanita felt reassured. She had needed this time alone. That faith had been almost buried beneath her own weakness and doubt.

From far off, she could hear the tinkle of sheep bells—Shimah coming in with the flock. Juanita could see the low-hanging cloud of dust. Shimah would be worried when she found her gone. Suddenly, Juanita was ashamed when she saw her mother-in-law walking around the edge of the compound, peering into the distance, ashamed that she should be causing anxiety to this older woman who had been nothing but kind and thoughtful toward the daughter-in-law in her household.

Juanita started to rise; she would go back now so Shimah would not worry. Then she saw a rider in the distance. A buckskin horse—Lu returning home. She had expected to be home before he was. He would be provoked . . . he'd think that running away like this was childish. And when he found his mother and sisters searching for her, he would probably be angry.

The rider didn't dismount. The women clustered about his horse for a moment and then stood back. He rode half way around the compound before he picked up the trail—the trail that was plainly marked in the sandy soil behind the rock house. He followed it easily to the long ledge, behind the mesas, and to the mesa that Juanita had climbed.

Juanita got up self-consciously and walked across the mesa top to meet her husband.

"What possessed you to do a thing like this?" He looked down at her from the saddle, his face inscrutable, his eyes clouded darkly.

"I wanted to walk without someone following me. You don't know what it is like to have someone behind you every minute."

"Promise that you won't do this again."

"But why, Lu? Why can't I ever go anyplace by myself? Won't you tell me?"

Luciano bent toward her, his voice softening. "When we came here I told you there would be things you weren't accustomed to. This is one of them."

"If you weren't so evasive. If you'd only give me a reason for these things."

She was pressing the question further than she should. She knew that now. Lu's face was set with anger again.

His voice was too low, too steady, as though he had to force it to be that way. "Juanita, you must accept my judgment in this." He kicked his foot loose from the stirrup and held out his hand. "Now, up behind me."

SIX
Three Shriveled Potatoes Left

They were drinking boiled-over coffee. The clatter of horse's hooves broke the stillness of the compound. Pulling the blanket aside, Yee-ke-nes-bah looked out and then turned to Shimah, talking excitedly. "Il-tha-bah's husband has come home."

Shimah set her coffee cup down with a splash, gathered her Pendleton about her so that one fold of it shielded her face, and hurried out the door. Luciano caught the question in Juanita's eyes. "It's still the custom here that a mother-in-law and son-in-law do not meet. My mother is being polite; she's leaving so that Il-tha-bah's husband may be welcomed inside."

Yee-ke-nes-bah and Il-tha-bah began to giggle as, all in one moment, the older sister tried to straighten her clothes, smooth her hair, and wipe a smudge of dirt off little Bijo's face.

When Il-tha-bah's husband appeared in the doorway, there was much confusion. Wudy and Phillip turned suddenly shy and edged close to Juanita and Luciano. Il-tha-bah smiled, hiding the smile behind her hand, as her husband lifted Bijo from her lap and swung the child up to his shoulder. Bijo cooed and squealed. Luciano arose to shake hands with his brother-in-law and to introduce Juanita. Yee-ke-nes-bah moved silently to the fire and shoved the coffee pot back among the coals. When everyone was seated again, all was quiet. There was so much to tell, so much to ask, no one knew where to begin.

Il-tha-bah's husband was tall and slender. He was young and good-looking. Just now he was occupied with making a series of grimaces for his daughter's amusement. This seemed to interest Phillip and Wudy too; they forgot their shyness and were soon standing in front of him, laughing with Bijo.

The conversation had touched on Luciano's marriage, on the hard year that everyone was having in Cañoncito, on the health and well-being of the relatives that Il-tha-bah's husband had stayed with in Crown Point, when Luciano asked his brother-in-law if there was any work near the Agency. His brother-in-law shook his head. "I worked a few weeks for a trader, cutting wood while the man who helps him was away piñon picking. But there was nothing around the Agency. 'Maybe a little work this summer,' the Agent said."

Il-tha-bah poured coffee for her husband. He tasted it, then drank sparingly. "I'd better unload my pack and turn my horse loose."

He came back in with a twenty-five pound sack of flour on his shoulder, a small sack of sugar under his arm, and two packages of coffee. Placing these beside the doorway, he said, "Tell my mother-in-law these things are for her." Then he began opening one of the packages of coffee.

The hoghan was soon filled with the aroma of fresh boiling coffee. Juanita thought that she had never smelled anything so good. Strange how life out here made such a simple thing a luxury. Before everyone had emptied their cups, Il-tha-bah began to carry her things from the hoghan to the long house. Her husband helped her with the bedroll and then busied himself unpacking the remainder of the food he'd brought. Bijo rode gleefully astride her father's shoulders as he carried the saddle to their house. Il-tha-bah returned one last time to set a bag of potatoes and two precious cans of tomatoes beside her mother's supplies.

When Shimah came back to the hoghan, she exclaimed over the things in the doorway and began busily to put them away in the cupboard. Luciano touched the two remaining bracelets on his wrists. "These will jingle together a little while longer."

But twenty-five pounds of flour didn't last long when it was made into slapped and fried bread for Shimah and Luciano and Juanita, Allen, Yee-ke-nes-bah, Khee, Phillip, and Wudy. It might have lasted much longer, and the coffee too, had not one of Shimah's women relatives visited her.

On that day Juanita and Luciano were returning from the spring with the wagon. Shimah was outdoors, carding wool, on the sunny side of the hoghan. An older woman was with her.

"That looks like old Seraphina." Luciano jumped down from the wagon seat to unhitch the team. "I'm surprised that she hasn't been here sooner."

"And who is Seraphina?"

"One of my mother's clan relatives. And . . . a meddlesome old woman."

Seraphina was more frail than Luciano's grandmother, and her shrewd little eyes were set in a face as wrinkled and puckered as a withered apple. Even her voice had shriveled. She was piping in a thin whine when Juanita and Luciano rounded the hoghan. "How do you have wool left for weaving? Ours was gone long ago."

Shimah took the white fluff of combed wool off one of the wool cards and laid it with the others on an outspread floursack. "There isn't enough here for even a small rug. I'm just preparing it for the spindle since there is nothing else to do."

The older woman's eyes brightened with curiosity as Luciano introduced his wife. Her voice rose even higher as she turned to question Shimah. Juanita smiled and sat down beside her mother-in-law, taking a handful of wool to loosen with her fingers before Shimah carded it. Seraphina asked question after question. Sometimes Shimah answered, sometimes she didn't. And when there was an opportunity, Luciano's mother turned the conversation back to the sheep.

"You have Seraphina's approval with one slight reservation," Luciano told his wife. "She said you are a good-looking woman but it is too bad you aren't Navajo."

Shimah and Seraphina were discussing the hard winter and how difficult it was to keep their small flocks intact. The older woman told a long and involved story about her family's hardships during the winter, and when there was a pause, Shimah made the proper exclamation of surprise or sympathy.

"What is she saying?" Juanita asked her husband.

"Not much, except that her family has been living for several days on tortillas made from cornmeal and a little water, rather than kill one of the ewes which will be lambing in a little while. Their coffee has been gone for a long time and the corn, now, is almost gone."

"I guess we aren't the only family tightening up the belt."

"No, it's much worse this year for everyone, but even in good years, a family will get along on most anything rather than kill one of the ewes before lambing time."

Old Seraphina was drawing her worn blanket about her shoulders and rising stiffly to her feet. She smiled at Juanita, her worn stubs of teeth showing, and told Shimah that she would be going since she wanted to visit another relative before returning home.

Shimah followed her around the hoghan and then beckoned her inside, where she divided half of the dwindling sack of flour and gave her part of the last package of coffee. Old Seraphina thanked her relative over and over and hobbled off across the compound, clutching the bundles of food in a fold of her blanket. Juanita raised her eyebrows and looked helplessly at her husband.

"There was nothing else my mother could do. It would be the same if we went to her hoghan and they still had flour."

And so they rode to Correo a few days sooner and pawned Luciano's last two bracelets.

Luciano stood at the counter, gazing long at the canned goods. With his feet spread wide apart and his hands deep in his Levi pockets, he read the labels: "Hand-packed tomatoes, cream style, golden bantam corn, sliced breakfast peaches, satsuma plums in heavy syrup."

Juanita nudged him. "You'd better be deciding whether it will be red beans or pinto beans this time."

When Mrs. Pentz came to wait on them there was no hint that the last of the Platero resources had been traded for these supplies. Luciano ordered a small sack of flour casually, two pounds of sugar, three pounds of coffee, and three pounds of pinto beans. He pursed his lips and studied the brands of lard carefully, then decided there was enough at home. He ordered part of a slab of bacon instead.

Juanita watched as Mrs. Pentz stacked the supplies on the counter and totaled the prices. There was twenty cents left over. Luciano bought twenty cents worth of long, green chilies.

Stacked all together it seemed like a lot of food, but give a portion of it to Il-tha-bah's family and divide the rest among eight people, and there was all too little. Would it last four days or even three? And after that?

Juanita had told herself that she wouldn't worry. She would let each day take care of itself. They had food enough for perhaps four days. Something might turn up in those four days. But what? She didn't know, and somehow she felt that Lu's easy manner was masking feelings the same as her own.

As her husband took some of the supplies out, Juanita asked Mrs. Pentz for a pencil and paper. She had thought of this before and knew that it was one way she could turn in an emergency. But she had hoped it wouldn't be necessary. She wrote hastily:

Dear Nadine:

We are flat broke and still no job. Have you any extra money you could send to tide us over?

As ever,
Nita

Two days there and two days back . . . allowing for delay . . . a week. Juanita lifted a handful of green chilies from the paper bag. "Trade you these for an envelope and a stamp."

The mesas were purpling in the evening light. A strong wind arose out of the west to pile the clouds higher and higher above the mesas. It was a long ride from Albuquerque to Cañoncito in the spring-wagon. The high hind-wheels squeaked a queer sing-song, turning over and over in the well-worn ruts of the narrow road. Juanita and Shimah huddled in the bed of the wagon, drawing the blankets about their heads. The wind was cold, piercing. Luciano rode alone on the driver's seat.

The day had been a long one. They had driven first to the Indian Hospital on the edge of town, and Lu had insisted upon going in with her. The doctor had looked tired, but he'd managed a smile when he told them that from all indications the Navajos were on the increase. Lu was jubilant. Nothing could stop him today. He'd get a job somewhere. Watch his smoke! By evening he was less jubilant; the day had been only the same as any other day in town.

It was dark when Luciano pulled off the road and stopped the wagon in a sheltered place beside a mesa. He lit a juniper branch for a torch and held it high while Juanita and Shimah stirred sleepily among the blankets.

"We'll camp here and eat. Perhaps the wind will die down soon."

Juanita followed him to gather wood for a fire. By the flare of the torch, she could see the taut lines of his face—the unhappiness.

"Don't worry so, Lu, you can't get a job when there's no job to be had."

His lips traced a smile but there was nothing behind it. "The only sure thing is the sheep camps this spring. But how can we get along until then?"

"We'll get along somehow." It was in her mind to tell him about the letter to Nadine, but she didn't. His pride would not have allowed her to send it. But perhaps when the money arrived, he would see things differently. So she closed her lips over the inadequate words, "We'll get along somehow," then locked her arms about the dry branches she had gathered, and walked beside him to the wagon.

The fire burned hot, and in a little while Shimah had the coffee boiling and strips of bacon sizzling to eat on cold fried bread. As they ate, Shimah sometimes glanced at her daughter-in-law, a smile far back in her eyes, and Juanita knew that it was only with pride and anticipation that she thought of the coming grandchild. If she was worried about how they would get along or what they would eat, it didn't show through the composure of her strong, gentle face.

The wind was dying away in the darkness when they kicked sand over the fire and climbed back into the wagon. Although Luciano protested that it would be too cold and windy for her, Juanita, wrapped to her nose in a blanket, rode on the seat beside him. After what seemed a very long time, he took the reins in his left hand and with the other found her hand beneath the Pendleton. Worries and uncertainty seemed to slip away, and there was nothing but the two of them and this moment.

"I am happy enough about the baby to sing," he told her.

Juanita remembered the wild, high songs he used to sing when they were first married.

"But somehow I can think of no song for it."

Yet there was a song: the far-off voice of the wind, the queer sing-song of the wagon wheels.

In four days the supplies were gone. There was flour left, and coffee. Only by eating small amounts and then tightening up their belts had they managed to make the food last that long. Already Shimah had killed many more sheep than the spring increase would replace, and so the straggly remainder of her flock grazed in peace while the family drank unsweetened coffee and ate plain fried bread.

In three more days there was no fried bread; the lard was all used up. Shimah was boiling over twice-boiled-over coffee grounds to get the pale amber liquid they drank. There was a little flour left, and Luciano announced that he would make white flour tortillas for the evening meal.

Juanita surmised this was a little game to keep up her spirits. She felt weak and light-headed, and the gnawing sensations in her stomach were very real. Hunger was a new experience. Never before in her life had she been so hungry. Probably Lu worried more about the short rations than she did. The thought that there was money on the way—money to buy potatoes and meat and the staples, flour, sugar, and coffee, was often in Juanita's mind. In fact, she caught herself naming over the different foods they would buy just for the pleasure of repeating the words. She pushed the alien thought away: that Nadine might not have the money to send.

Phillip and Wudy followed Luciano around as he built the fire carefully and set the flat piece of sheet iron on two rocks, just the right distance from the flames. One little mistake and the tortillas would be no good, he told them. They nodded, round-eyed and serious.

Juanita leaned back against the wall of the hoghan, her feet tucked under her. Slowly she raised her hand to replace a pin in the heavy coil of her hair. At that moment Luciano looked up to see her dark, poised head outlined in the curve of her arm. They exchanged a long glance, and then Luciano went back to the exacting business of tortilla-making while a smile tugged at the corners of his wife's mouth.

With a flour sack tied about his waist, he began to mix the dough of flour and water. Allen and Khee groaned that he was taking too long—hunger would overcome them before his tortillas were ready. But Luciano ignored them as he added imaginary pinches of dust from the floor and pretended to spit upon his hands as he took a piece of dough to be pulled and patted, stretched and slapped into a tortilla.

While the first flat piece of dough was baking on the sheet iron, Shimah went quietly to the big trunk at the back of the hoghan and searched among the things stored within its depths. She brought out three small, shriveled potatoes. Turning them over in her hands before Juanita, she gestured that they were for her. Then she buried them in the hot ashes of the fire.

"But, Lu, I won't sit here eating three whole potatoes while the rest of you have nothing but tortillas and weak coffee."

"My mother says that she put those potatoes away for you when the supplies first began to run low. You must eat them. We are all accustomed to going days with little food. You are not."

Luciano's tortillas were a great success. He inquired anxiously about their texture, their flavor, and received flattering words of praise. Finally he settled himself beside Juanita with a cup of coffee and a large, round sample of his own cooking.

When Shimah raked the potatoes from the ashes with a stick, they seemed even smaller and more shriveled than before. Brushing the ashes from them with her skirt, she insisted that her daughter-in-law take all three. Juanita made vain attempts to divide them with the rest of the family. But even little Phillip and Wudy bit deeper into their tortillas and backed away from the proffered food.

Luciano cut the potatoes open with his pocket knife. Wisps of steam rose from the white, mealy insides. Juanita ate the first one plain, refusing even salt. Nothing had ever tasted so good. She reached hungrily for another.

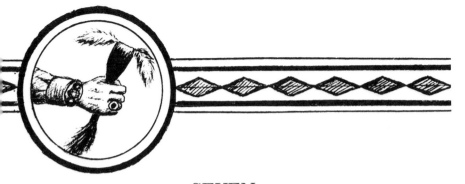

SEVEN
The Sing

Convincing Lu that she wanted to go horseback riding was a little difficult. He argued that she had not been feeling well enough to ride. But once they were in the saddle and loping along the trail which followed the long line of mesas, it was simple to suggest that they ride on over to Correo for the mail.

The midday bus was just arriving at the trading post, and Luciano had trouble getting the buckskin past the large gray coach. The horse kept rearing on its hind legs and, as Luciano tried to quiet it, pranced sideways, tossing its head nervously, rolling frightened eyes. Juanita stood at the hitching rack as her husband dismounted and knotted the reins securely.

"Trying to give the tourists a thrill?" she teased him.

Luciano bent to tuck the bottoms of his Levis into his western boots. He straightened up, grinning. "There, now I look like a real cowboy."

They stood beside the horses as the bus passengers alighted. Two women in wrinkled slacks led their children toward the rest rooms, children whose faces and clothing were stained by fruit and chocolate candy. Several passengers followed the bus driver into the trading post, and a few remained outside, walking along the driveway to stretch their legs.

When most of the passengers were seated at the lunch counter, Luciano and Juanita went inside and directly to the post office window. Mrs. Pentz stopped long enough from making sandwiches and pouring cups of coffee to get their mail for them. There were several letters, one from their friend Chief Standing Bear. While her husband leaned against the post office window reading it, Juanita opened a flat envelope from Nadine. The blue paper showing faintly through it was a money order for twenty-five dollars.

"Standing Bear says there's no picture work for Indians right now. Some of them are having a tough time."

Juanita took the sheet of letter paper he handed her and read the fine, slanted handwriting.

All your friends here think that you made big mistake going to reservation. They say you will tire of that life. When I hear them talk like that I stand up for you. I say: they know what they are doing. And it is right.

Your Sioux friend,
Mato Najin

"I wish Standing Bear could see this country out here."

Luciano smiled. "He'd still say the Sioux country was better." He reached for Nadine's letter.

Juanita took a deep breath. "There's nothing in it but a money order and a note saying she'll write later." Unfolding the blue strip of paper, she watched his face anxiously.

"Nadine didn't owe you any money."

"No, but now we'll owe her some. It's to buy supplies."

"You wrote her that we needed money?" Luciano asked incredulously.

Juanita nodded.

Luciano's expression didn't change. He walked to the counter, his boot heels drumming a deliberate rhythm against the wooden floor, and stood looking at the shelves of groceries.

Mrs. Pentz was still busy at the lunch counter. "Just help yourself to what you can reach."

Juanita began taking packages of coffee from the shelf. "Shall we splurge and get some of these plums?" She looked back over her shoulder. Luciano was going out the door.

Mechanically, Juanita continued to select supplies, half of her mind checking over the staples which Shimah would need, the other half struggling with the realization that her husband was more deeply affected by her sending for money than she had expected. She heard Mrs. Pentz clearing dishes from the counter, ringing up the checks as the bus passengers began to leave. She heard the powerful motor of the bus and the scratching of heavy tires on gravel as the coach pulled away.

Juanita bought as much as she thought two horses could pack: two sacks of flour, sugar, lard, baking powder, salt, coffee, potatoes, beans, salt pork.

"You may have to loan us some strips of canvas or gunny sacks," she told Mrs. Pentz. "We didn't bring anything in which to pack this home."

Juanita looked at the bright labels of the canned goods, finally selecting tomatoes and peaches and plums. Although the small red apples were expensive, she ordered a large sack of them. It had been a long time since they had eaten fresh fruit.

When Mrs. Pentz cashed the money order and deducted for the supplies, Juanita went outside. Luciano was at the hitching rack, standing close to the buckskin, rubbing its nose. Juanita did not need to look into his face to know that he was terribly hurt and trying to hide it. She walked toward him, scarcely knowing what to say. "I should have told you when I wrote to Nadine, but if I had, you wouldn't have let me send the letter."

"No," he answered almost inaudibly.

"There had to be money from somewhere for food, not just for us, but for the rest of them at the hoghan. We couldn't let pride interfere in a situation like that."

Luciano dropped his arms limply to his sides. "It isn't being proud about borrowing money, it's my failure. You shouldn't have to do this. In my own country among my own people I should be able to take care of you."

The buckskin stamped its feet restlessly and tossed its head.

"I have a deal with one of the fellows for my silver tools. I was waiting until he offered something close to what they are worth. I guess I should have taken his last offer."

"No, Lu, you can't sell your silver tools. That's your trade."

"I don't seem to be working at it."

Brooding had made him this way. All those days in town, walking from one shop to another, had made him doubt himself. Now she had increased that doubt by asking for outside help. "My husband, it isn't you. It isn't us. This is something beyond our control . . . economic conditions which we can't alter affect us."

"I tell myself that. But still my own failure seems real."

Juanita stood very close to him. "There have been times when I doubted my own strength to see this through, like the day when I ran away to the mesa top. I was ready to give up trying that day, so many little things had piled up together and I had even lost sight of why we had come here. But I know now that nothing is as important to us as building our own life here, the sort of life we want together. Lu, we mustn't lose faith in ourselves."

Luciano began unbuckling the pack straps behind the saddle. "My mother will be glad to see what we are bringing."

That was all he said but Juanita knew her words had reached him. His mind was free to look ahead again. She started back into the trading post, her husband following, then turned and said softly to him over her shoulder, "But whatever comes after this, I promise we'll see it through somehow by ourselves."

Shimah traded some of the new flour for blue corn. She ground this into fine meal on the metate and baked it into strips of paper-thin bread. Juanita watched as her mother-in-law deftly spread the thin batter on the flat hot stone, waited until just the right moment, and then, with one quick movement, peeled it from the stone. When the thin blue bread was finished and tied into a flour sack, Juanita went with Luciano and his two sisters and Allen to a Sing at Mary Chavez's.

A coyote had followed Mary's wagon when she was driving home from Correo. A Sing was being held to forestall any evil.

Shimah was related to the Chavezes, and was sending what she could to help feed the people who would attend.

The Chavez's hoghan was on flat land. No trees, no ledges of rock were in that open sweep of country between mesas. The fire in the cook-shelter blazed brightly in the fading light of evening, illuminating the many colored skirts, the glossy, yarn-tied black hair, and the animated dark faces of the women who sat around it. Beyond the hoghan and about the corral could be seen the shadowed outlines of spring-wagons and restless, hobbled horses.

Juanita went with her sisters-in-law into the shelter while Luciano and Allen joined a group of men beside the hoghan. The gnarled and twisted cedar branches in the long-shaped fire gave off a tremendous heat, but the older women who sat nearest, keeping the big coffee pots filled, stirring the kettles of beans, making fried bread and slapped bread, didn't seem to notice. Juanita recognized many of them as relatives whom Lu had introduced her to at the Chapter House meeting. They nodded to her, some of them extending their hands.

The old woman patting round, flat cakes from cornmeal was Seraphina. When she looked up to take the flour sack bundle from Il-tha-bah, she saw Juanita and her face brightened with a puckered grin. She moved a lardpail of water and made more room close to the fire. Juanita was grateful, for already her black skirt and leather jacket had begun to seem inadequate against the chill of the night air.

Men and women drifted over from the hoghan, drank coffee, ate beans and hot bread, and then drifted back. It kept the women busy ladling beans, filling coffee cups, passing the various kinds of bread. Juanita noticed they served only one group at a time, and while that group ate, more bread was made, a coffee pot refilled, and one of the younger woman was sent for more wood or perhaps a pail of water. One group finished eating and passed their cups to the young girl washing dishes before the next group came in.

Sitting quietly, Juanita was acutely aware of everything about her: a dog barking in the distance, the thud of a horse's hooves as someone rode across the compound, and in the shelter, the hum of many soft voices and the fragrance of cedar smoke from the fire mingling with the pungent odor of freshly cut juniper boughs. The uneven circle about the fire became larger as the hour grew later. Women came in with their families to eat, then stayed behind to sit about the fire and exchange the latest news and gossip.

When Luciano came to the shelter for coffee, he told Juanita that the Sing would soon begin and if she wanted to go in she must be ready to sit for a long time, as no one left the hoghan until the proper pause between songs.

In the doorway of the hoghan they separated. Luciano went to sit among the men on the south side, and Juanita followed her sisters-in-law and sat between them, leaning back against the wall on the women's side, the north. More and more people came in until the half-circles of men and women were three to four rows deep.

Juanita could just see the Medicine Man at the back of the hoghan. He was large and dressed in Levis, a faded purple shirt, and a red headband. Sitting cross-legged, gazing into the fire, occasionally looking up to the smoke hole, he seemed to be waiting. Presently he poised a gourd rattle decorated with eagle down in his hand. To his left on a sheep pelt sat Mary Chavez. On a strip of new print material before her was a small heap of silver and turquoise jewelry, her own and those of others who wished to share in the benefits of the Sing.

The "big star" had come into view through the smoke hole and the Medicine Man was ready. The rhythm began with the rattle and the first few notes of his voice. Then the men and women joined in, their voices rising as one voice, soaring. The power of the chant filled the hoghan—a positive power stronger than any evil. Dark eyes and dark faces were intent in the firelight. As each song ended, the Medicine Man's voice trailed off last, the rattle beating the rhythm until he began a new song and the other voices joined his again.

It didn't seem true that a modern city was near here, with theaters and shops and factories, busses and automobiles. It couldn't be true. Juanita sat through pauses in the chant when some of the people walked outside, and those inside turned to each other to talk, to share a cigarette. When the chanting began again she caught the questioning glances of her husband: Was she tiring?

The night had turned toward morning. More of the men lounged against the wall, half-reclining; some were singing, others resting. Those resting sat with their hats down over their eyes, as though asleep, but the chanting was as strong and as rhythmic as ever. The women changed positions now and then, raising a knee under a full, bright skirt, clasping it with their hands, wrapping their Pendletons about their shoulders as the fire died down, turning sleeping children more comfortably in their laps.

A buckskin bag of pollen was passed from the Medicine Man to Mary Chavez and then around to the women's side. Juanita could see approval in Luciano's eyes when she took the bag and repeated the motions of her sister-in-law: A pinch of pollen between the thumb and forefinger, touched to the tongue, touched on top of the head, and then released upward to the heavens.

When they met outside, he asked, "How did you like your first taste of pollen?"

"It was sweet and a little bitter."

Walking to the cook-shelter, she yawned. "I don't believe I can stay awake if I go back into the hoghan."

"I noticed your eyes were getting heavy. My aunt will fix you a place to lie down in the shelter."

Not one relative, but three, heaped sheepskins into a pile and covered them with a blanket. As Juanita went to sleep, she was vaguely conscious of more shawls and blankets being piled on her.

When Juanita awoke, dawn was a gray streak in the sky. Her husband stood beside her. "Come on, sleepy-head, the Sing is over."

They drank the scalding coffee that Luciano's aunt poured for them and then started home. The ground was covered with frost; trees and bushes were heavy with it. People were scattering toward their hoghans, bright Pendletons drawn tightly over dark heads, bright skirts swinging. Wagons passed them with old people and sleeping children huddled in the back. Men on horseback rode away singing, the horses' and the singers' breath white against the frosty air. Lu's sisters and brother were far ahead. Juanita and Luciano walked faster to catch up with them.

"No one seemed very dressed up at this Sing. I expected to see more jewelry," Juanita said as she tried hard to match her stride with her husband's.

"People seldom dress up for a one-night Sing. And you forget that this has been a hard winter. Most everyone's jewelry, like ours, is in pawn."

Something of the Sing, perhaps the rhythm of the chanting, still clung to Juanita as she walked along. Many things had not been as she expected. There was no discomfort, no unpleasantness in the crowded hoghan. The people were quiet and slow-moving as they got up to walk outside or returned to their places. Their voices, as they talked together, were low and soft. From the bodies crowded in half-circles about the fire, there emanated only the strong odor of wood smoke; not just the wood smoke of tonight's campfire, but of a hundred campfires before—wood smoke which seemed as integral to Navajo garments as the color or the weave. It was possible to be in the crowded hoghan and yet turn her thoughts inward and be alone. No personality intruded itself upon her consciousness, only the chanting, which at times seemed like one great distant voice.

When they arrived home, the hoghan was swept out and in order. Shimah must have awakened before dawn. There was a pot of backbone soup bubbling over the fire.

Shimah asked about the Sing. Who was there? Did her daughter-in-law get sleepy? Was there enough paper bread? Did they see Wounded Head's family? Allen had unrolled his blanket and was taking off his boots. Yee-ke-nes-bah began to fill their bowls from the bubbling pot of soup. They named a few of the families who attended the Sing. No, Wounded Head's family had not been there. Shimah tilted her head to one side. "That is strange", she said. "They stopped here last night after dark. I thought they were on their way to the Sing."

"Soup for breakfast, and I liked it." Juanita laughed as they stumbled sleepily into the rock house.

"Nothing like backbone soup and a siesta when you've been out all night." Luciano stretched full-length on their blankets, one arm outflung. His eyes closed wearily.

Juanita began to pull off her shoes, then stopped to scratch her neck vigorously. The crawling sensation continued down her back. "Lu, something's biting me."

Her husband sat up and pulled her blouse up over her shoulders. He began to laugh. "You not only have a bite, you have a bug." He held the leggy brown object between his thumbnails for her to see, then crushed it. "I thought when I found you burrowed under all those strange Pendletons this morning that you'd probably pick up something."

"I feel itchy all over now." Juanita removed her skirt and blouse, then slipped into a flannel robe. She and Luciano examined minutely the clothing she had worn to the Sing. Then Luciano loosened her hair and began to comb through it with scrupulous attention to each dark strand.

Juanita shuddered to herself; bugs . . . lice. She remembered her mother's horror, when as a child, she had caught head lice from someone at school. All the hair washing and all the combing with a fine tooth comb had not rid her of them. Her mother had hated to ask at the drug store for a bottle of Larkspur Lotion. Nice people didn't need such things. And yet, from what her husband told her, out here bugs were the rule rather than the exception. People remained free of them only by watching their clothes carefully, and washing their hair frequently. But among the very old, and the very young, and the very lazy, bugs were always present.

When Shimah passed the rock house on her way to the sheep corral, Luciano called out the window to her. Once she was inside, he confided in a whisper, "My wife is lousy."

His mother was quiet for a moment and then she began to giggle softly as she was told about Juanita sleeping under the Pendeltons. She nodded her head. That was how to get them. Then she picked up Juanita's outer garments and ran her fingers along the seams with practiced care. "The bugs get in the seams and gathered places to lay their eggs" she said. Tomorrow we'll go over all your clothes."

Juanita sat on the edge of the bed, her dark hair loose and hung about her shoulders. For just one moment she had been horrified. Now the incident was dwindling to its actual importance as she remembered her husband's words. "You don't have to keep 'em when you get 'em, unless you want to."

EIGHT
Yellow Pollen

The sun was warm. Juanita sat on the flat rocks at the edge of the compound drying her hair. She watched a flock of sheep, a gray patch, moving slowly across a distant slope of green. From the trail alongside the mesas stretching toward the Chapter House came the wild soaring song of a young man driving a wagon piled high with juniper boughs.

Shimah brought a blanket and spread it over the rocks. Braiding her hair loosely, Juanita went inside to help carry out the clothing. Her mother-in-law went over each garment carefully, examining the linings and where the sleeves were set in. She talked quietly to herself and occasionally glanced up at Juanita, chuckling softly.

It was on Luciano's dark blue suit that they first discovered the yellow pollen, fine yellow powder dusted over the shoulders and down the back of the coat. Shimah stared at the coat; her feet seemed rooted to the ground for that moment. Then she grabbed the coat and brushed and shook it until there was not a trace of yellow dust left.

Shimah carried the remainder of the clothing hurriedly into the sunlight. Other garments were marked with the yellow pollen, among them Juanita's white summer coat. Hunting for bugs was forgotten, and Juanita could tell by her mother-in-law's face that this was infinitely more serious. And yet what could it be? Fine yellow dust . . . as fine as the pollen in the Medicine bag at the Sing. Then she remembered: A ride down off a mesa top . . . evening . . . Luciano shaking his Stetson carefully . . . small puffs of yellow dust.

A rider was coming across the flat land. That might be Lu. Perhaps he could explain this. The horse and rider rounded the last mesa and galloped across the pasture. But the horse was not a buckskin and the rider was a stranger to Juanita. He dismounted and dropped the reins over the horse's head.

The strange rider was shorter than Luciano, heavier, and perhaps a little older. Large turquoise pendants hung from his ears, and his uncut hair was bound with a purple band. Shimah was glad to see him. She and Juanita followed him into the hoghan. Yee-ke-nes-bah paused in her sewing to greet the stranger. He might be a near relative, Juanita thought, as he sat down easily against the wall. When Phillip and Wudy came running in, the stranger lifted Phillip to his knee. And he might be Lorencito, the oldest brother.

Whoever he was, he seemed interested in Juanita's presence in the hoghan. Even after Shimah explained that she was Luciano's wife, he continued to watch her, curiosity and friendliness mingling in his dark eyes.

Shimah told him about the yellow pollen. Juanita could almost follow the story by her mother-in-law's excited gestures. Shimah's face was strong and tense, and her voice carried an undertone of fear. Only her hands seemed like her real self, although they moved excitedly as she gestured. Strange that Shimah should tell the stranger about the yellow pollen, rather than ask the rider about himself, about news which he was surely carrying. Of what interest could the yellow pollen be to him?

But he was interested. He leaned forward to better hear her words; his eyes narrowed and his face looked very grave. He asked many questions. Sometimes Shimah answered and sometimes Yee-ke-nes-bah answered. Through their conversation one word seemed to repeat itself until it began to echo in Juanita's mind: *ma-itso . . . ma-itso.*

When Luciano came home, he confirmed what Juanita had guessed. Their visitor was Lorencito, his elder brother. The brothers greeted each other heartily and Luciano laughed as Lorencito told him of his surprise to know that he had a sister-in-law. "But I suppose all younger brothers grow up and marry."

There wasn't as strong a resemblance between Luciano and his older brother as there was between Luciano and Allen. Lorencito's face was broader, and his features were less sharply molded, his face and his gestures were more dignified, perhaps because he was older, or perhaps because he was a Medicine Man.

Lorencito began to talk seriously to Luciano. Juanita heard the word *ma-itso* repeated again and again. Shimah sat nodding her head as her oldest son talked, occasionally adding a word to what he was saying. Luciano turned to Juanita. His face was as grave as his older brother's. "Lorencito says that it is not safe to keep this from you any longer. I should tell you now."

Juanita waited. Her mouth and throat suddenly felt dry. She could not have spoken. Her thoughts raced: They are in some way connected, *ma-itso* and yellow pollen. Perhaps it's all connected, the puzzling and unexplained surveillance too. The looks on the faces around her, were more than a little bit frightening.

"Before we came here," her husband began, "when I tried to tell you about everything which might seem strange to you, I didn't tell you about *ma-itso*, the wolf clan.[2] It no longer seemed as believable to me as it once had. Perhaps all the years in school did that. Anyhow, in Hollywood I seldom thought of it. When we came here, my mother told me the wolf clan was still strong in Cañoncito. I didn't tell you then because I could see no reason why they would try to harm us. But to be sure you were safe, my mother and sisters watched you every minute.

"There were times when I almost told you, those times when you were upset about things you didn't understand. And yet I hated to frighten you needlessly. Already there was so much for you to worry about. It seemed better to wait until I had a job, until we were living in town and then tell you.

"But now two things have happened which make me sure the *ma-itso* is for some reason after us. I found yellow pollen in an X mark on my hat brim, and today my mother found pollen on our clothes. That is their warning. Lorencito thinks you will be safer if you know about this evil thing."

A hundred questions sprang to Juanita's lips, but her husband went on talking, interrupted now and then by Lorencito or his mother.

2 Every Navajo belongs to a clan which is passed down from his ancestors. *Ma-itso* means "wolf," but *yaa nal gloshi* is the word used for "skin walkers." (Artist's note)

"The wolf clan is as old as the Navajo tribe. From the beginning, some men turned certain powers, which should have been used for good, toward evil things. Corn pollen, used for blessing, is used by the *ma-itso* as a warning to a person marked for death. And death does not come in a usual manner; it comes in a round-about way which cannot be easily traced. The victim sickens suddenly, or sometimes his mind leaves him. Sometimes the victim meets with a mysterious and fatal accident.

"They bring about most of these deaths by witchcraft. They try to get some part of your clothing, or fingernails, spit, a strand of hair, so their evil will more easily affect you. That is one reason you were always followed when you left the hoghan, so you would leave nothing behind, not even a button or a raveling from your dress which the *ma-itso* could use against you."

It doesn't seem possible, Juanita thought. The last witch was hung at Salem. Witchcraft may have existed long ago in Europe, it may still exist in some parts of the world today, but this is America and the twentieth century. And then she said aloud, "What good does it do the wolf clan to kill people?"

"Sometimes they kill a person who discovers their meeting place. Sometimes they kill very wealthy people and rob their graves of clothes and jewelry. They have no fear of the dead. They even use a dead person's skin, chopped fine, to put into the food of intended victims. That is supposed to poison them. And sometimes they try to do evil to a whole family that is powerful in their part of the country and has aroused their jealousy."

"Why don't the rest of the Navajos bring the members of the wolf clan to justice?"

"They do. When they catch one in his wolf skin they kill him right then. But the *ma-itso* is a secret organization. No one knows who belongs to it. And it would be serious to accuse anyone without proof."

"Catch one in his wolf skin?"

"Yes, that was how they got their name. It is said they dress in their best clothing, put on all of their jewelry, paint their faces, and then lace themselves into large wolf skins. Long ago, people believed they chanted something which actually changed them into wolves. Lorencito says it is believed now the chant only gives them the cunning and swiftness of wolves, but they are still just men inside wolf skins. They run almost upright with sticks held in their hands pushed into the forepaws of the skin. From a distance they look like very large wolves, and of course the only tracks they leave are wolf tracks. Some of them are very clever, and are seldom caught.

"My mother and sisters have been finding wolf tracks close to the hoghan since you and I have been here. I thought at first it was one of them after the sheep. That was why someone always followed you at night; you might have run into one of them prowling around here."

Juanita's mind recoiled from the thought of an encounter with one of the creatures her husband had described. It took little imagination to see the pointed ears, the shaggy wolf hide, and the cruel and cunning man-animal crouched beneath it.

Shimah spoke, breaking the silence. "Tell my daughter-in-law there are few of them now. Long ago there were two men at the head of it. They ran in packs like real wolves. No one was safe. But those two men were killed and now the members work alone or a few together. There are not so many now as there were long ago."

Lorencito added, "There is nothing to be afraid of if my sister-in-law is careful and leaves them nothing to work their evil over."

Juanita was not afraid. Rather, she was confused by the sudden knowledge of strange things and strange ideas which could not easily be assimilated. Men disguised as wolves, men who made their living by stealing, killing, and robbing graves—an underworld on the reservation. She respected the intelligence of her husband's people too much to dismiss the whole thing as superstition. Yet she could not believe that these men—this wolf clan—could in any way alter her life or that of her husband.

Luciano was speaking again. "It was the wolf clan which caused my father's death. His power was as strong for good as their's is for evil. But they finally killed him. They poisoned something he drank."

Shimah touched his arm and spoke quietly, then pointed to the north.

"My mother says we must not climb the mesa Des Jin. It is thought that somewhere on the mesa the *ma-itso* hide their wolf skins."

The next time the family talked together about the wolf clan was when the old grandfather came to visit. He walked to their hoghan, and it seemed he was even more feeble as he leaned on the crude walking stick. Yee-ke-nes-bah built up the fire, while Shimah hurriedly filled the coffee pot and set it in the flames. The old man settled himself heavily at the back of the hoghan to talk with his grandsons.

It was Lorencito who told him about the pollen on Juanita's and Luciano's clothing. The grandfather shook his head and muttered, "Yes, we still have evil ones among us. This family has always had trouble with them. . . ."

As the grandfather talked, strange new things about the *ma-itso* began to unfold. The evil ones would not be taken alive if they could help it. Dead, they would reveal none of the secrets of their clan. But occasionally one was caught and information tortured from him before his captors finally killed him. If a person surprised members of the wolf clan at their meeting place, he was given the choice of death or joining the clan in their evil work. Becoming a member was not easy. To prove his loyalty, each new member had to kill a near relative, someone in his own family.

Medicine Men sometimes secretly belonged to the wolf clan and no one suspected when they brought about the death of a patient they had been paid to cure. Shimah agreed with this. She and her sister had always believed that the Medicine Man singing over their mother had killed her, as her death had been sudden and mysterious. Lorencito pulled at one of the turquoise pendants in his ears as he told them of a woman near Crown Point who was suspected of practicing witchcraft. The grandfather nodded his head. Yes, women sometimes became members, usually a woman whose father, husband, or brother already belonged to the *ma-itso*.

When the *ma-itso* were plotting a death, they sometimes drew the victim's picture on a rock or on a tree, or other times they made an effigy of clay or wood. But they always tried to get something belonging to that person, so their power over him or her would be stronger. At Laguna, the grandfather had seen figures made of clay and rudely carved sticks wrapped in cloth, for the Pueblos, too, had their evil ones. However a picture was marked, or wherever an image was pierced, that was where the pain started on the victim.

"It doesn't seem possible that a picture or a clay figure could affect a real person," Juanita whispered.

"Many wise old men like my grandfather say the same."

"Did you tell him about the pollen on your hat when you left Wounded Head's?"

"Not yet. But because we were at Wounded Head's doesn't prove anything. We didn't see him put it there. The *ma-itso* sometimes work in strange ways."

But what Luciano told him seemed proof enough to the old grandfather. He leaned forward gravely, one gray forelock hanging over his eyes. "Don't go there again, my son; Wounded Head is one of them. Many of the people here think so. We are just waiting to catch him in a wolf skin." For a moment he sat there blinking, then he began to sip his coffee.

Lorencito started to tease his grandfather. "His wife seems very nice and she is such a good cook, I will miss going there."

The old man snorted and almost spilled his coffee. This was no jesting matter. "Don't let good cooking blind you. A woman knows when her husband does not earn a living honestly." Then he saw the small bit of laughter in his grandson's eyes. He shook his head as though chagrined and set his cup down carefully in front of him. When he continued, his voice was lowered. "I have seen with my own eyes silver buttons on a blouse of hers—buttons that were on your father's moccasins when he was buried."

"I hope I'm there when they catch old Wounded Head in a wolf skin."

"Lu, don't think about it. The less we think about this, the better it will be for both of us."

They were alone in the rock house getting ready for bed by the yellow, flickering light of the lantern. Juanita stood by the improvised dressing table; she had taken down her hair and was brushing it.

"You don't believe any of it, do you?" her husband asked.

"I don't disbelieve," she answered. "I can see how the *ma-itso* could actually harm people who believed in it. And I can see also how anything unexplainable is blamed upon witchcraft." Juanita had read the legends of werewolves in northern Europe, in the Black Forest of Germany. She had read present-day accounts of witchcraft practiced by voodoo cults in Africa and the West Indies. It did not seem reasonable that it was all superstition; there must be some facts behind it. But in everything she'd read about witchcraft, the person harmed was always someone who believed he or she could be harmed. She explained this to her husband.

He nodded but did not answer.

"I still don't see why the *ma-itso* should single us out," she added. "We aren't wealthy. We own nothing worth stealing."

"Perhaps because we are of this family."

"Or, if witchcraft works as I believe it does, on the superstitious mind, too many educated boys and girls returning to live on the reservation would lessen the power of the *ma-itso*. Once their hold on the people is broken, their power will be broken. People have to believe that evil can harm them, as they have to believe that a Medicine Man can cure them. I think Wounded Head is trying to frighten us back to Hollywood."

"Perhaps." Luciano blew out the lantern. "Are you frightened?"

"No. The *ma-itso* can never touch us as long as we do not believe in their power. You said yourself that when you were away at school you didn't believe in it."

"Yes." Luciano's voice was not very strong against the darkness. "But that is like all other things. When you're at school you think one way. When you come back here you find yourself thinking in old ways."

NINE
A Summer Job with Mrs. Pentz

Spring winds blustered across the mesas and whistled noisily down the canyons. Blue jays swung on the juniper branches, scolding impudently. Everywhere the earth was covered with pale new green. In the distance, Walking Around Mountain stood cloaked in snow. As the horses picked their way up the steep bank of an arroyo, Luciano pointed to the smoke clouds billowing from the fields below where the arroyo widened. "Marhilde Chavez is burning the stubble of last year's corn."

Following the trail between upthrust ledges of rock, they came upon a small boy herding sheep. The bellwether, *baaing* shrilly, plunged across in front of the horses and clambered up the rocks on the other side. Luciano and Juanita pulled up on the reins and waited while the rest of the flock straggled after him. The boy made ineffectual shooing motions with a stick and ragged piece of cloth as the early-dropped lambs followed the ewes on wobbly legs.

There was no real reason for going to Correo. Letters perhaps from California, a spool of thread for Shimah, but it was mostly for the joy of riding on a day like this.

For once, Mrs. Pentz wasn't busy. She sorted through the stack of mail. No letters for them. Luciano went outside to the corral while Juanita chose a spool of thread from the notion cabinet.

"I've been hoping you would ride over this week," Mrs. Pentz began. "There's something I wanted to talk to you about."

Juanita could sense that whatever it was, the trader's wife was hesitant to mention it. She tried to ease the awkward silence. "It was such a beautiful day, all we needed was a small excuse to ride somewhere."

Mrs. Pentz dropped the spool of thread into a small bag and twisted the top. "My husband and I have talked of this for some time, but I didn't know how you would feel about it. I need someone to look after my house, since from now on we will be increasingly busy in the store. There is no one else around here I feel I could depend upon."

Juanita smiled, thinking: Mrs. Pentz is really kind, and she's so afraid that offering me a job will offend me. "You don't know what a help a job would be to us right now. But are you sure you aren't offering this because you know we need it?"

"No," the trader's wife assured her. "I have to have someone every summer. But of course I couldn't help knowing that Mr. Platero was having a hard time finding work and that you'd had to send for money." Mrs. Pentz paused. "And you're expecting a baby, aren't you?"

Juanita nodded. "Sometime this fall. But I've felt marvelously well so far."

"It won't be hard work, no harder than if you were keeping house for yourself and cooking three meals. No laundry. We always send that out. The water's too hard here to bother with it. I could pay you fifteen dollars a month, besides your room and board. Would that be enough?"

"It seems too much for what little I'd have to do, and for the amount I'll eat. You've no idea what an appetite I've developed."

Mrs. Pentz laughed. "You let me worry about that."

Juanita stepped back from the counter. "Would you mind if I go outside and talk to my husband about this?"

Luciano turned from watching the mare and the new colt in the corral. "Ready to start back?" Then his eyes darkened as Juanita told him about the job. He shook his head slowly. The ewes were beginning to lamb; he'd be needed at the sheep camps one day soon. Besides, he didn't want her to work.

Juanita explained that this might solve their problem. He would be free to go anywhere to look for work, and he wouldn't have to worry about her. This would be something certain during the summer, something they could depend upon until he got a job.

Luciano turned to watch the colt again, still shaking his head.

Then Juanita used an argument which would be hard for him to refute, an argument which seemed to her like taking a woman's advantage. "The next few months I won't be very comfortable anywhere, but I would be better off here than at the hoghan. I should have a more varied diet than I've been getting, foods that I'm accustomed to. I would have that here." She couldn't just say flatly: Lu, we'll need the extra money.

"All right," he said at last. "I can see it would be better for you here until I get a job." His knuckles were white as he clenched the corral post. He still kept his face averted. "Il-tha-bah's husband is home now; he can do the man's work around the hoghan for my mother. I think I'll go back to Crown Point with Lorencito. Perhaps if I sit on the bench at the Agency long enough, they'll give me a job to be rid of me."

The day at the trading post began at sun-up. Some of the tourists who had stopped overnight would need gasoline and road information before starting on their way again.

For Juanita, the day began before this. With the light of dawn coming through the front bedroom windows, she was out of bed, reaching for the clothes which lay folded over the back of the chair, slipping her feet into stockings and shoes. As she combed and coiled her hair, sometimes scarcely looking into the mirror, she wondered if Luciano was getting up at this time too; perhaps right now he was dashing cold water over his face from a basin outside his brother's wife's hoghan. While the water boiled for coffee, Juanita washed at the sink. She had breakfast ready and on the kitchen table when the trader and his wife got up.

Mornings, after the dishes were done, she cleaned house thoroughly and then thumbed through the cookbooks as she planned the noon and evening meals. Her business training had taught her to be systematic about any work she undertook, but bookkeeping in a bank, lunching at the corner drugstore, preparing dinner with the aid of a can opener in the apartment she shared with Nadine had not added to her experience for this job. Mrs. Pentz didn't seem to notice how often Juanita consulted the cookbook, at least she didn't mention it. The meals were well-planned and well-cooked.

Sometimes when they were having steak or canned peach pie, both of which Luciano was very fond, Juanita could scarcely eat for thinking of her husband. She wondered if Lorencito's wife's relatives were fairly prosperous or if the depression had reduced them to a diet of fried beans and coffee.

The afternoons were longest, especially the time between washing the lunch dishes and beginning the evening meal. There was nothing to do. To sit quietly and read or sew was out of the question. She needed to be busy. While she worked, pictures of Lu sitting on a bench at the Agency were often in her mind. Lu, pushing back his pride and asking the agent for any kind of work. Eventually Juanita added cleaning the tourist cabins to her duties. Mopping the linoleum floors and changing the bed linen filled the empty afternoon hours and left her weary enough that when night came she dropped off easily to sleep.

On her first payday, Juanita rode into town with Mr. Pentz. She asked him to leave her at the Indian Hospital, a few blocks off Fourth Street. Walking into the cool, semi-darkness of the entrance hall she was acutely conscious of how much she missed Lu, who in Crown Point seemed so very far away.

Dr. Richards was not busy. He smiled as he came into the large white-walled room at the front of the hospital and motioned Juanita to a chair beside the desk while he looked for her card in the files.

"How are you feeling?"

"Good," Juanita answered.

"Any nausea?"

A nurse came in with a memorandum for him. He scanned it hurriedly. One of the hospital attendants brought in several bottles and placed them among others on the shelves at one end of the room. She lingered for a moment, straightening the white towel on the examination table, adjusting the white-curtained screen which stood beside it. This must be the supply room, office, and examination room, all in one. None of the details of the room had impressed Juanita before. She remembered only the doctor's tired smile and the quick gladness in Luciano's eyes.

When the nurse left and the doctor glanced up, repeating his question, Juanita said, "Only a little, when I'm working at the cookstove."

"Getting plenty of exercise?"

"Oh, yes."

"But nothing too strenuous?"

Juanita shook her head.

The doctor listened to her heart, then took her pulse. "Everything is okay there." After checking his notes on her card, "Let's see, you're due about the middle of October, aren't you? We try to keep an account of the confinements ahead." The doctor pushed his chair back. "You'll be in about this time next month?"

"Yes," Juanita answered as she walked toward the door. It all sounded so matter-of-fact and certain when the doctor talked about it. She'd be in on this day every month. She'd come to the hospital some day before the middle of October to have the baby. Juanita started up Indian School Road toward Fourth Street, scarcely noticing the feathery lavender blossoms of the tamarisk which grew in the dooryards of the adobe houses. There was no way of knowing where she'd be in October. . .wherever Lu happened to get a job. And if he didn't get a job? But he would, she told herself firmly.

Walking past the trading posts and motor courts on Fourth Street, the grocery stores, lumber yards, and hardware stores, Juanita paused to look at display windows as she made her way toward Central. A woman passed her carrying a brown-eyed, curly-haired youngster, and at the corner she met someone wheeling a sleeping baby in a carriage. Strange, she'd never paid much attention to babies on the street before.

At the post office, Juanita sent five dollars back to Nadine. She planned to send the same amount each month until the debt was paid. At Montgomery Ward's, she ordered two gingham dresses, the adjustable kind.

Since it would soon be time to meet Mr. Pentz, Juanita started toward the parking lot where he always left the pickup truck. She passed a baby shop and then retraced her steps. She would just look in the window. Next month she planned to start buying a few things for the baby, but the ruffled bassinet and the dainty, lace-edged dresses drew her closer to the window toward the entrance. Once she was inside and a saleslady had come from the back of the shop, she couldn't just turn around and walk out again, so she bought a pink, ribbon-edged blanket.

Juanita had been working for Mrs. Pentz for six weeks when Luciano came down from Crown Point. He'd caught a ride with one of the agency employees in a truck. He seemed leaner, harder, and the brooding look was gone from his eyes. "I have only a little time. This fellow is going on to Albuquerque and will stop for me on his way back."

They sat down in the sun on a wooden step at the back of the store. There was as sudden shyness between them. Six weeks had been such a long time. They studied each other's faces for a moment and then Lu smiled slowly. "Are you feeling all right?"

"Yes, as long as I keep busy. When I have nothing to do, I'm lonely." Juanita was glad she'd put on one of the new gingham dresses that morning, the blue print with short, puffed sleeves. She linked her fingers across her knees. "What have you been doing?"

"I've been staying in camp with Lorencito and his wife. They're having a hard time, too. I don't like it as well as the rock house."

Juanita held his last words in her mind; this was as near as he'd come to saying that he missed her.

"I've been to see the agent. He talked to me right away, didn't keep me waiting outside to make me feel he was important. His name is Mr. Stacher, and all the Navajos at Crown Point like him. They call him 'Natahni Yazzi'—Little Chief."

Lu is talking around something, I can tell, Juanita thought. I'll just wait and see how long it takes him, Juanita thought.

He told her about Crown Point, the government buildings, the school. He'd seen his youngest sister Ha-nes-bah who was in school there. And then he said, without emphasis, as though it was really of no importance, "I have a sort of a job now."

"Oh, Lu, why didn't you say so."

"Well, it isn't much. It's just odd jobs around the buildings for this summer. They have me down on the payroll as a day laborer. One day I nail down a few loose boards on a building, another day I paint. Sometimes I dig a ditch for a water pipe, sometimes I mend the wire on the chicken pens."

"But you've never done anything like that before."

He looked sideways at her. "No one seems to notice. Of course, it doesn't pay much, but I think if I hang around there long enough I'll get a full time job."

They sat looking out across the country. Walking Around Mountain was hazy in the distance. Luciano pointed to a small, peak-shaped mountain close by. "That's Butterfly Mountain. The butterflies are thick there at this time of year. Medicine Men go there for a certain kind of little striped rock."

The Agency truck came all too soon.

"I'll write you letters when I can't come over. I have money for stamps now." He drew a thin sheaf of bills from his billfold. "I had a payday. You save these for us."

As she took the bills, he held her fingers for a moment and then ran lightly to the truck, not looking back.

His letters came surprisingly often, fine clear-cut writing on lined paper. It seemed strange to be getting letters from him. Before they were married, he had written when he was away on location; long letters, full of happenings around a location camp, letters that were a little swaggering, a little possessive. These letters were different. Most of them were uncertain and shy. They sketched briefly what he was doing, and that there might be an opening for him under the school disciplinarian. He asked if her work was getting to be too hard for her.

Juanita's letters to him were carefully written. Lu mustn't guess that on very hot days she kept herself going by force of will alone. She didn't write that when she cleaned the tourist cabins now in the afternoon, they seemed to have doubled in number, and the linoleum floor area seemed to have grown, or that she was increasingly conscious of the bulk of her body, the heaviness.

She wrote instead of some of the oddly clad tourists who came spilling out from the long busses as they glided to a stop in front of the trading post, or of the familiar people who arrived in spring-wagons to do their trading: George Abeyta's family, Toney Chavez's family, the Sandovals. The women usually came to the back of the store to visit, and Mrs. Pentz interpreted for them in Spanish and English, as Luciano's family could speak Spanish. Shimah drove the wagon over every two or three weeks. Things were better with her family since sheep shearing time. But always before Shimah left, Juanita added a sack of flour or potatoes, perhaps a slab of bacon, to her Mother-in-law's supplies, and paid for it from the money she and Lu were saving.

Juanita wrote her husband how Mrs. Pentz urged her to rest in the afternoons, to begin preparations for dinner later in the evening. She didn't write that she couldn't lie down for long, how the heat and the endless circle of her thoughts made rest impossible.

One afternoon Juanita stood at the front bedroom window watching a spring-wagon turn slowly onto the graveled shoulder of the highway. Even at a distance she could see it was her mother-in-law's wagon. Someone was on the seat beside Shimah. As the wagon rumbled closer to the trading post, Juanita watched with pride. None of the other women managed a team quite like Shimah; she could pull on the reins with the strength of someone twice her size.

Her mother-in-law leaned to the right, wrapping the reins securely around the brake handle. It was Il-tha-bah on the seat beside her. The two women got down from the wagon, using one spoke of the front wheel as a step. Juanita followed the bright flash of their skirts until they entered the trading post.

Juanita sat at the back of the store with her sister-in-law while Shimah stood before the counter, pursing her lips, choosing one thing at a time. The trading over, Mrs. Pentz came back to talk between them. Juanita told her relatives that Luciano thought he might get a steady job in Crown

Point. She repeated all the meager bits of news from his letters which might be of interest.

Shimah held her hand to show how high the corn was growing; in a little while it would begin to tassel. The yellow squash were forming on the vines she'd planted in a patch close to the hoghan. Then Shimah came to the important news she had been saving. Il-tha-bah and her husband were going near Crown Point to live. The husband's relatives had long wanted them to come and live close by.

"You'll be going through Crown Point? You'll see Luciano?" Juanita asked.

Il-tha-bah nodded.

They sat quietly for a moment, then Shimah put her hand to her mouth shyly. Had Juanita made anything new for the baby? She always asked this question and Juanita always brought out the long box which was fast becoming filled with baby things. Il-tha-bah's face softened and she made gentle noises of approval as she and Shimah fingered the tiny dresses and the soft blankets.

When they had loaded their supplies into the wagon and gone rumbling down the highway toward the dirt road, Juanita took the ink tablet from her dresser drawer and sat down to write to Lu. He would be glad to hear that his sister and her husband were coming through Crown Point. She sat a long time holding the tip of her pen against trembling lips. She told herself over and over how important it was to work one more month because they needed that extra fifteen dollars. Carefully, she shaped the beginning of a letter in her mind. There must be no mention of the heat and weariness and the loneliness for him that was becoming unbearable.

The day was sultry and windless; thunderheads were piling up behind the mesas on the far rim of Pueblo land. As Juanita washed the lunch dishes, perspiration formed in tiny beads across her forehead and gathered at the nape of her neck under the thick coil of hair. The blue print dress clung in moist patches to her back and shoulders.

After the dishes would come the cleaning of the tourist cabins. Days like this when she opened the door to one of the low-roofed cabins, the oppressive heat was a physical barrier against which she had to force her way inside. She needed only to tell Mrs. Pentz that she didn't feel like cleaning the row of cabins. There was the pride she took in asking no allowances for her condition. There was her determination through the past months to earn the salary paid her, and she hated to give up now. Perhaps all the cabins wouldn't need cleaning. There were fewer tourists with summer over and the fall school term beginning. Lu had written something about Crown Point School opening in another week. She hadn't heard from him since that letter.

Juanita poured boiling water over the stack of dishes, and reached to the line above the stove for a tea towel. She did not hear her husband come in.

"Are you ready to go to Crown Point with me?" he asked softly, trying not to frighten her.

She turned, disbelief on her face. "Oh, Lu!"

He put one arm about her, drawing her against him lightly, and brushed her flushed cheeks with his lips.

They stood together for a long time. Juanita spoke against his shoulder, "You should have written you were coming."

"Can't you get away?"

She pulled away from him gently so she could see his face. "It's only that you surprised me. My things aren't packed. I thought you'd write."

Juanita turned one of the kitchen chairs toward him. "It will only take a minute and I should finish these dishes for Mrs. Pentz. She knew I'd be leaving as soon as I heard from you. My month was up several days ago." She leaned against the draining board. "You really got the job at the school?"

Luciano nodded.

Juanita's hands were not very steady as she wiped dishes. "Why didn't you let me know?"

"But it just happened; I just got the job." Lu turned sideways in the kitchen chair, hooking one elbow across the back of it. "I did everything at once: stopped at the hospital and told the matron to have a room for you, borrowed a pickup truck at the agency, drove to my mother's for the things in the rock house, and then came here."

When the plates were stacked in the cupboard and the cups hung by the handles, Juanita went into the trading store to talk with Mrs. Pentz. The trader's wife laughed. "Don't worry about leaving so abruptly. I knew when I saw that truck I'd be cooking my own dinner tonight."

So to Crown Point, Juanita thought as she returned to the kitchen. I'll not try to look any further than that.

Luciano called to her from her room. He had the suitcase open on the floor and was awkwardly trying to fold her dresses to fit into it. She gathered up her sewing and stationery and toilet articles and began to pack them. Trying to hurry, she felt clumsy, heavy. Suddenly she sat down upon the floor and began to cry.

Luciano was alarmed; he knelt beside her. "What's the matter?"

Juanita leaned against him, sobbing, covering her face with her hands until she could find words to answer. "I don't know, I think it's just the relief that now we can see a little way ahead."

"I felt that way too, all weak inside, when Mr. Stacher and the disciplinarian finally decided to let me try the job." He began to tighten the straps about her suitcase.

Everything was packed and in the back of the truck. They said goodbye to Mr. and Mrs. Pentz. Juanita relaxed against the leather cushion of the seat. It seemed unbelievable now that they were actually leaving for Crown Point.

Luciano started the motor, meshed the gears, and pulled out slowly toward the highway. As they reached the curve of the road, he said resolutely, "I suppose I ought to tell you exactly what Mr. Stacher said. He said he couldn't make the appointment permanent until he saw that I was doing all right at the job. They've tried other returned school boys and it hasn't worked out. But don't let that bother you. It will work out this time. It has to."

TEN
Crown Point

It was a narrow canyon road which led up to Crown Point, a rough and rutted road. The rock formations were fantastic twisted masses like some of the ledges north of Cañoncito, but here there were more trees, piñon, cedar, and yellow pine. Only in places where the rocks rose in stark forbidding walls on either side of the road were there a few moments respite from the sun as it shone in one long blinding flash across the windshield.

Luciano drove the truck in a queer zig-zag fashion, trying to avoid the larger holes by hitting the lesser ones. "At the Agency, they say this road goes back to nature every year."

Juanita pressed her toes harder on the floor boards. "I believe it."

Her husband shifted into second gear as the truck began its whining pull against the grade ahead. For a time they rode without talking, Luciano occupied with keeping the truck on the rough steep road, Juanita allowing her thoughts to wander into what lay before them.

Lu had not been certain of her reaction when he told her there were no vacant houses at the Agency. He hurriedly assured her that the agent would provide suitable living quarters, somehow, as soon as she was able to leave the hospital. But, temporarily, Lu would stay at the boys' dormitory while she had a room at the hospital. She'd be going to the hospital in another month anyway. The uncertainty of where they would live was of small concern to her. The important thing was that they were together again.

Lu's salary of fifty-five dollars a month didn't seem like much when you first thought about it. But considering that there was no rent to pay, she felt sure she could stretch it over their expenses and even save a little. Certainly she could manage on his salary if Lu could fulfill all the duties of an assistant disciplinarian to earn that salary.

He had not even seemed worried when he named the various duties he would be undertaking—duties which would be strange to him at first: seeing that the boys in both dormitories were up on time, washed, dressed properly and in line for breakfast, supervising their meals in the dining room, supervising their play on the schoolgrounds, overseeing the boys as they cleaned their washrooms, checking through the dormitories at night to make sure the matrons were understood and obeyed, and that everyone was in bed before "lights out."

Then there would be the interpreting for the little boys newly enrolled in the school, and the role of elder brother whose comforting words would explain some of the strange things and help to put them at ease in a strange place. Between times, he would help repair shoes in the school shop, help issue new clothing to the boys who needed it, and handle the comb and scissors when their hair needed cutting. Those were the duties of the assistant disciplinarian, and Lu was not dismayed. He would do all of it and do it well. The agent would be looking for no one to replace him. Lu said so.

The long, tiring ride was over; the road leveled off and there was Crown Point. Luciano pointed out the employees' houses, surrounded by neat grass plots, to the north of the road, and the government building which faced three sides of a square to the south of the road. The square was outlined with large shade trees, and the end nearest the road was planted with flowers.

As Luciano parked the truck beside the Agency office, he indicated two stucco residences. "Those are the agent's and the doctor's homes." Walking south along the square, Juanita looked from one to another of the old-fashioned buildings her husband pointed out. The dormitories, the Employee's Club, the dining room, and the sewing room. Some were frame, two story buildings, with long broad porches. A few were made of stucco, and all were newly painted and in good repair. Lu told her that the hoghan made of logs between the girls' dormitories had once been used as a club room for the older girls. Dominating the south end of the square was the large brick school, the playgrounds of hard-packed earth spreading from it. They stood in front of the white frame hospital now. "And that's all there is to Crown Point, besides the trader's down the road and the post office," he said.

"It looks barren, doesn't it, in spite of the grass plots and shade trees and flowers?"

"Government buildings always look that way in this country."

The front hall of the hospital was cool and quiet. Juanita and Luciano stood for a moment in the semi-darkness before the matron appeared from a small side office. The matron was slender and pleasant looking. She squinted her eyes to see Juanita better in the gloom of the hallway.

"This is my wife, Mrs. Platero."

The matron continued to stare curiously at Juanita. "Why, you have long hair, haven't you?" she said at last. Then, apparently recovered from her surprise, she led the way to Juanita's room.

Luciano left them and returned to the truck for Juanita's suitcases. The matron chatted pleasantly. "We've moved the other bed out so unless the hospital becomes suddenly crowded, you'll be by yourself." She raised the shades, adjusting them evenly, smoothed the plain white spread on the bed, then paused in the doorway. "It's past the dinner hour, but there's usually something left. Would you like a tray sent from the kitchen?"

Juanita nodded. "If it isn't too much bother. I believe I am a little hungry." She sat down on the bed, looking about her; she could hear the rustling of the matron's starched uniform as she went down the hall. It was a corner room. The hardwood floor had recently been scrubbed and waxed. The walls were white and so were the high, narrow bed, the chairs, and the small table. Two large windows looked out on the tree-shaded square, and a smaller window faced the sewing room. The curtains added to the severity of the room; they were plain and white and stiffly starched.

When Luciano brought the suitcases, he helped Juanita unpack and hang her clothes in the shallow closet.

"Why do you suppose the matron was so surprised at my hair?" she asked.

Luciano grinned, while straightening a dress on a hanger. "I guess I was trying to impress her this morning so that she'd give you a nice room. I told her my wife was an educated woman and that we lived in Hollywood before we came here. Perhaps she expected a flapper."

There was nothing to do now but wait, and waiting was a hard thing. The days passed slowly, as slowly as the leaves changed color in the trees around the square.

The first few days, Juanita had reveled in the leisure. She'd slept late in the morning and sometimes for an hour or so in the afternoon. The hospital attendants cleaned her room and brought her meals on a tray from the kitchen. There was nothing to do, and she loved it. But only for a few days.

There was no more sewing for the baby; everything was finished and neatly folded in the long box on the shelf of the closet. She reread books she'd brought from California, wrote letters to her family, to Nadine, and to other friends in Los Angeles. It took time to write the letters, to compose half-truths which seemed to cover their daily lives and yet did not tell about the expected baby. She had decided to wait and do all of the announcing afterward. No reason to have people worrying about her needlessly.

Luciano came in at odd moments several times a day. Sitting at the window, watching the children on the playground, he would point with pride, "There goes one of my haircuts." Evenings they walked together around the square and a little way down the road. This evening the wind was sharp as it swept down the canyon road. Juanita pulled her coat about her. A crescent moon hung in the western sky. "Standing Bear told me once that the Sioux women believed if they looked over their left shoulder at the new moon, the baby would be a boy."

"No use bothering about that." Luciano shrugged his shoulders. "The baby's certain to be a boy anyway." Then he began to tease her as he had the past few evenings. "I think Francisco would be a good name for a son, or perhaps just plain Pablo. Something easy for our relatives to pronounce. I hope you haven't planned on a girl all this time!"

Juanita could see his teeth flash white as he laughed. "It doesn't matter whether it's a boy or girl," she said agreeably. "I haven't planned on either. I only want it to be born perfect and very soon."

Luciano linked his fingers with hers as they walked back to the hospital. They sat for awhile in the long swing on the hospital porch, watching the lights in the other buildings wink out, then she went inside to bed and he returned to the boys' dormitory.

The next afternoon when the nurses weren't busy, two of them stopped in to talk with her. Juanita was glad for their afternoon visits; they helped break the monotony of a long day, but she always found herself strangely shy with the hospital employees. It was as though she sensed the curiosity behind their friendliness, the unspoken questions.

The matron came in, bringing two current magazines to help Juanita pass the time. "Just saw Mrs. Tsosi in the hall," she told the nurses.

"Another baby?" one of them asked.

"Looks like it."

The matron turned to Juanita. "She always waits until the last few minutes, comes in, lies down on a bed, has the baby, and then wants to get up and walk out with it."

"She has a large family," observed one of the nurses, "and it's been that way with every baby."

"I've heard that Indian women have an easier time, but not that easy," Juanita protested.

"She's an exception," the matron spoke up. "I've been in other Indian hospitals and I've seen plenty of Indian women have a hard time with their babies. Birth is still a strenuous method of production, whether it's Indian babies or white."

They all laughed at this.

"Waiting is almost as hard, isn't it, Mrs. Platero?" one of the nurses asked.

"I wish there was something for me to do, the time might pass more quickly."

"We can put you to work folding bandages," the matron suggested.

Folding bandages helped, and so did reading, answering letters, getting trays at mealtime, and unfolding and folding the baby clothes. Seeing Lu for a few moments in the morning and a little longer at noontime, together with all of these things broke up the waiting, but didn't end it.

Then one morning Juanita felt too ill to get up. She sent the breakfast tray back untouched. Her body had never felt so heavy, so overfull.

The matron came in quietly. "Don't you feel like eating anything, Mrs. Platero?"

Juanita shook her head.

"When did the doctor tell you to begin to watch for this?"

"Anytime, now."

"Then this is probably it. If you'll get up and walk back and forth across the room it will hurry things a bit."

Juanita tried to walk and found that she could hardly force one foot before the other. Feeling weak and sick, she staggered back to bed.

When Luciano stopped by at noon, the first throbbing pains had seized her. "We won't be waiting much longer," she murmured. Tossing her head had loosened the heavy strands of her long thick braid; pain had darkened her eyes.

The school bell rang in the distance and Luciano did not get up to leave.

"Do they know where you are?"

"No."

The pains were becoming sharper, more breathtaking, and when they subsided, the relief was great in contrast. In the periods between, her body seemed to gather strength to meet the next onslaught. She could think more clearly.

"Shouldn't you be getting back?"

"No, I'm staying here."

After that she didn't question. Pain washed over her in great waves, then receded. She knew that she reached for his hand and found it. There was strength and endurance in the warm pressure of his fingers.

Being wheeled down the long, dim hall was a vague experience. She knew only that Lu walked beside her. The roaring in her ears was like an angry surf beating against jagged rock. Through it she could hear the doctor. "Mr. Platero, your wife is coming along fine, why don't you wait outside in the hall . . . more comfortable." The roaring in her ears distorted sounds and the doctor's and the nurses' voices came as from a distance. Their figures were blurred, unreal.

Juanita's whole being was intent upon meeting the waves of pain which came increasingly fast. Then suddenly the waves were no more and she was struggling in a sea of pain. She thought she heard her own voice crying out, but that could not be. The only real thing was her hand in Luciano's.

Gradually she was conscious that the struggle was over. She asked for water; never had she been so thirsty. Luciano held the cup so she could take but one short sip at a time. She relaxed. Her world was quiet and peaceful again save for the welcome piercing cries of a newborn baby.

"Lu, is that our baby?"

Luciano nodded.

"Is it all right?"

All the names Luciano had chosen were for nothing. The baby was a daughter and as perfect as Juanita had wanted. She was beautiful from the very first. Large dark eyes, dark hair in soft wisps about her ears, a button nose, an almost rosebud mouth, skin smooth and faintly tinged with olive. They named her Rosita after a song they both liked.

Luciano invented errands to the Agency office so he might stop at the hospital during the day. As soon as Juanita was strong enough to sit up, the nurses were thoughtfully forgetful about getting Rosita after feeding times.

Luciano was holding the baby carefully on his lap while Juanita balanced a tablet against her knees. "I've written my folks, Waano-Gano, Nadine, and Standing Bear. They'll tell the others. To appease them for our keeping it a secret, I've promised to send pictures as soon as we can take some."

"Did you write to Mrs. Pentz and ask her to send word to Shimah?"

Juanita nodded. "And to your sister Lupe."

The attendant came in with Juanita's lunch tray and straightened the pillows behind her. Luciano looked enviously at the broiled meat, the salad, and the fruit jello. "Guess I'll start eating with you. All I can say for the food in the school dining room is that it's plain, substantial, and there's lots of it." He held the tray firm while she cut her meat. "Mr. Stacher stopped me today and asked about the baby."

Juanita laid the fork on the edge of the salad plate and waited.

"There's still no house for us, but he said if we wanted to take the log hoghan which used to be a club room, the Agency would furnish material and labor to fix it the way we want."

"It might be fun to modernize a hoghan. Does that mean you're doing all right at the job?"

Luciano looked sideways at her. "I guess I forgot to tell you. I've been appointed for the duration of the school term. All Indian appointments are like that, for one year, and if your work continues to be satisfactory, you are reappointed each year."

Rosita began to squirm and pucker her face. Juanita slid the tray to the small table. "Here, I'll take her before she cries and someone hears her."

"I have to be getting back. Will it be all right to bring Lorencito over this evening? He wants to see the baby."

It was just after the six o'clock feeding. Juanita would always remember the two of them as they came into the room: Lorencito, the Medicine Man, walking softly across the hardwood floor, his large-brimmed, weathered hat in his hand; Luciano in clean Levis and a blue shirt, his black hair smoothed with water, his face aglow with pride.

Lorencito shook hands with Juanita and then touched the baby lightly on the cheek with his forefinger. Smiling, he turned and spoke to his brother. Juanita could tell he was teasing by the tone of his voice and the way he made Luciano laugh. "Get Lorencito a chair; there are usually some extra ones in the hall."

When they were seated, her husband tilted his head toward Lorencito. "He says she's a fine baby not to be a boy."

"Will all of the family be disappointed because we have a daughter instead of a son?"

Luciano repeated the question.

Lorencito's eyes held the smile which had been on his lips. He shook his head, the heavy turquoise pendants swinging from his ears. "All men talk of having sons, I think, but they love their daughters." He rubbed his hands against the knees of his wrinkled trousers, bent forward a little and gazed intently at the toes of his moccasins, then continued. "Shimah planned long ago if this baby was a girl she would give it her mother's name, 'Yee-ta-ne-bah.'"

"Yee-ta-ne-bah," Luciano repeated. "What a name for a daughter. That means, 'she gets into it.'"

It was Sunday afternoon. Luciano and Juanita walked from the hospital past the dining room and one of the dormitories to the log hoghan. Lu carried Rosita carefully in the crook of his arm; only the tip of her nose was visible from the folds of the baby blanket.

Drying leaves rustled underfoot. Overhead, the sun was traveling the southern path to the west.

The hoghan was of square-hewn logs, weather-stained to darkest gray. It was squat, six-sided, with a stone chimney rising from the east side of the roof. Luciano fitted a key into the heavy door and pushed against it with his shoulder. The hinges complained loudly as the door swung open.

"The fireplace smokes," Juanita said with disappointment, as she saw the black smudge which spread over the stone to the mantle. Smoke had left a gray coating on the wallboard panels of the room. Dust had sifted in and lay in ridges along the sills of the square-paned windows. The floor boards were rough and cracks yawned wide between them. From the exposed rafters of the ceiling hung an empty electric light socket.

"A kitchen could be added out this way." Juanita indicated the second panel over the fireplace. "The ceiling should be sealed in with wallboard, the floor fixed and covered with linoleum, and something done about the fireplace. Outside of those few things, there's nothing here that cleaning and a little paint won't fix."

"Mr. Stacher wasn't certain how soon a carpenter could get to this. But in another month we should be able to move in."

"Another month," Juanita echoed. Another month of living apart, Lu at the dormitory, she at the hospital, seeing each other for a few snatched moments during the day, a while longer in the evening.

"I don't like waiting that long either. But we couldn't move into this place as it is."

"We could," Juanita said resolutely. "And I believe I'd rather. We'd manage somehow while the place was being repaired."

Lu made a shrugging gesture. "That's up to you. It will be harder for you than you think. But I'll admit I'd much rather move here now than spend another month as we've been living."

"First thing in the morning I'll see what furniture we can get from the commissary," Juanita said half to herself as Lu closed the door behind them.

Walking back to the hospital she was already planning how she would send to California for her cedar chest and wedding gifts stored there. She would begin cleaning the hoghan tomorrow. Lu could hire one of the school girls to help her. Juanita was so deep in thought that she scarcely noticed the woman coming toward them. Lu touched her arm. "Here comes someone you'll like—Mrs. Skinner. I worked with her husband this summer. He's in charge of building maintenance here."

Mrs. Skinner appeared to be Juanita's age, perhaps a little older. She was plump and very fair. Her light brown hair was short and curly, and her blue eyes were friendly, the corners marked with lines of humor. "I guess I can see this baby now," she said when Juanita and she had been introduced. "I wanted to visit you at the hospital, but I hated to come barging in like an old busybody."

Juanita lifted the blanket from Rosita's face. She was still sleeping, her pink mouth puckered a little, her dark lashes like tiny shadows on her cheeks. Mrs. Skinner said sincerely, "She's a beautiful baby." Luciano smiled proudly and shifted Rosita carefully to the other arm. Juanita told Mrs. Skinner about moving into the log hoghan and invited her to visit them when they were settled. As they parted, Mrs. Skinner said, "Better let me come before you're settled. There might be something I can do to help."

In the days which followed, Juanita supervised the cleaning of the walls and the washing of the windows, and helped repaint some of the furniture from the commissary. She rode into Gallup one morning with Mrs. Skinner and bought red and white checked material for curtains. The result was clean, livable, and cheerful, but the commissary furniture was definitely out of place in the one-room hoghan.

"I suppose it is too late in the year to expect much of a selection at the commissary," she told her husband as they moved the iron bed from one wall to another. Any way it was set, the bed took up too much space and contributed nothing decorative to its side of the room. The old-fashioned chest of drawers was too tall; the white breakfast table, the odd chairs, and the barrel-shaped woodstove all looked out of place in the low-roofed hoghan.

As they unpacked the cedar chest, Lu assured her, "It will make a difference with our own things about."

Navajo rugs on the rough floor, books between bookends, pictures on the walls, Chimayo scarves across the chest and table. "I'm not so sure," Juanita answered.

Rosita began to fuss in the wicker basket. Juanita took her up and held her against her shoulder as she walked about the hoghan. "Of course, the remodeling will make a difference. With the fireplace fixed, we won't need the woodstove in the center of the floor. With a kitchen, we won't be so crowded in here. But still . . . we might live in Crown Point quite a while, two or three years, mightn't we?"

Lu sat down on the edge of the bed. "There's no way of knowing."

"But anywhere we live on the reservation we'll need furniture."

Luciano knew what was in her mind. "Furniture takes money," he reminded her.

"We've saved a little, perhaps this winter we could save more. By spring we could buy the few things we'd need: a studio couch, a smaller chest, a smaller table." She sat down by Lu. "But perhaps I'm going too fast. It's just that it would be so nice to have the hoghan the way I picture it." She wrinkled her forehead a little. It would take figuring and saving, but it wasn't impossible. None of the things that she and Lu wanted were impossible. The years stretched ahead of her as she sat beside her husband. She could see them plainly: Each year a step nearer to all the things they'd planned.

Luciano's voice broke in upon her thoughts. "We could buy furniture, though it might take longer to save the money than we think. But nothing comes suddenly in this country except the summer thunderstorms."

ELEVEN
A Hard Winter

The first snow came in the middle of November, falling silently from the low gray dome of the sky. It fell silently in large white flakes, through the day, through the night, until the surrounding country was white-blanketed and the buildings at the Agency were half-buried in drifts. The drifts on the north side of the log hoghan were as high as the roof.

Then the cold came. Bitter winds whipped across the snow, driving it into higher and higher drifts. The barren square was deserted. The school grounds no longer rang with the shouts of children; not many of them ventured outdoors to play. Only when absolutely necessary did Agency employees attempt to drive to the settlement of Thoreau or on into Gallup; the narrow canyon road leading down from Crown Point was almost impassable. More snow fell and for several days the road was blocked; no mail or supplies came through.

"It's useless to think of having any work done on the hoghan now," Juanita told Mrs. Skinner. "We'll have to wait for a break in the weather."

"Or until spring. Mr. Skinner said he doubted they would attempt any carpenter work around the Agency *this* winter."

Mrs. Skinner had come to spend the afternoon and help Juanita shorten an evening dress to wear to the dance in the school dining room that night. "There hasn't been snow like this in all the winters we've been here."

Juanita turned slowly as Mrs. Skinner pinned up the hem of the black taffeta. "When I brought this dress with me, I wasn't at all sure I'd ever wear it."

Mrs. Skinner mumbled through the pins in her mouth. "You'll be surprised at how we deck ourselves out at Agency parties. That's the only chance most of us have to dress up."

"I feel a little nervous about this evening. You're the only one I really know here at Crown Point."

"No need to be nervous. The people here are easy to get acquainted with. But I can remember how I felt when we first came." Mrs. Skinner sat back on her heels. "There, now all it needs is sewing and pressing."

Rosita awakened and lay blinking up at them from the wicker basket. Mrs. Skinner picked her up, saying apologetically, "I know this spoils her."

Juanita laughed. "If that spoils her, Luciano started spoiling her long ago." She bent her head over the taffeta dress and concentrated on stitches which would not show through on the "right" side.

Mrs. Skinner watched her. "You really should have a new hairdo with that dress."

"For instance?"

"You might wave it."

"I've never had any luck fussing with my hair."

"I could do it," Mrs. Skinner offered. "I do my own."

When Mrs. Skinner had returned with the curling iron, Juanita sat very still at the table, watching the progress of the dark waves in the hand mirror. "Lu will be surprised; he's never seen me with my hair curled." When Mrs. Skinner had finished and pinned her hair in a low knot on her neck, Juanita said, "It makes me look like a different person, doesn't it?"

They were quite pleased with their afternoon's work. Mrs. Skinner went home to prepare dinner. Juanita finished pressing her dress and pressed the trousers of her husband's good suit.

Luciano came home after the evening meal in the school dining room. "*What* have you been doing this afternoon?"

"Getting ready for the dance." Then she saw the incredulous look on his face. She raised her hand to her head self-consciously. "What's the matter? Don't you like my hair?"

"You don't look like you."

Juanita smiled and continued to lay his clothes out on the bed. "Rosita's asleep; you can dress while I eat."

She put on her coat, pausing at the door to cover her head with a scarf. He spoke: "I'm not going to any dance with you looking like a strange woman." Her husband's words made little impression upon her.

She cut across the square to the Employee's Club where she ate dinner every evening. Until they had a kitchen, there was no other way to manage. The top of the woodstove might serve for cooking breakfast or an occasional Sunday pot of stew, but it was necessary to eat most of their meals out. To stay within the budget of their living expenses and still save money toward furniture, Lu ate at the school where his meals were furnished and Juanita ate dinner and sometimes lunch at the Club.

When she returned to the hoghan, Luciano was sitting just as she had left him.

"Lu, you aren't dressed."

"I know it." There was a hint of laughter in his eyes. "I said I wasn't going to the dance."

He's teasing like he always does, Juanita thought as she got the baby ready for the night. When the blankets were pinned securely across Rosita, Juanita put on her black suede pumps, brushed them, and slipped into the taffeta dress. She smoothed out the long full skirt, and fingered the narrow ruffle of the square neckline. This was the first time in over a year that she'd really dressed up. She'd forgotten it was fun, exciting. Carefully, she touched the powder puff to her face and throat. Carefully, she applied bright lipstick while she held the hand mirror close to the single electric globe.

But Lu made no gesture of getting ready for the dance, even when she warned, "We're going to be late."

"I'll go if you'll comb the curl out of your hair." He tilted the chair back on two legs and grinned at her.

"Lu, quit teasing and get dressed. You know that combing my hair won't take the curl out."

Luciano walked over and picked up the wash basin, went outside and filled it at the faucet. "Here, this will."

"Are you serious? Don't you really like my hair curled?"

Her husband shook his head. "Makes you look different—sort of frivolous. I don't like it." He put a towel around her shoulders.

"I guess this is better than going to the dance alone." Juanita dipped her brush into the water. It took much brushing and two applications of Lu's hair oil before Juanita's hair was almost as straight and smooth as usual; but not all of the wave could be erased.

"Looks better anyhow," Luciano commented and began to whistle as he finished dressing.

The schoolgirl who was to stay with Rosita came at eight o'clock.

"We'll run over every hour or so to see if everything's all right," Juanita told her as they left.

The tables had been removed from the dining room, the chairs arranged along the walls, and powdered wax had been dusted across the floor. People stood in groups talking, or sat in the chairs around the room, watching the late arrivers come through the double doors. The dance had not yet begun. Most of the men wore dark suits, white shirts, and bow ties; the women were in evening gowns, with costume jewelry against their bare arms and necks and artificial flowers in their carefully dressed hair. Mrs. Skinner had been right: an Agency party was an event.

"That's the agent and his wife over there." Lu led Juanita toward them.

Mr. Stacher was not a large man. He was a little shorter than average, middle-aged, and active looking. Glasses gave his face a business-like, dignified appearance, but his voice and manner were friendly as he shook hands with Juanita. Were they going to be comfortable in the log hoghan? Mrs. Stacher was shorter than her husband, rather stout and very pleasant. She wanted to know how they liked Crown Point by this time. And how was the baby? Both she and Mr. Stacher were anxious to see her.

Luciano told Juanita as the walked across the floor toward a tall, slender, middle-aged couple how Mrs. Stacher had suddenly gone deaf several years before. "The Navajos say that she tried on one of the Yei masks, which is forbidden, and her deafness resulted from that."

Mr. and Mrs. Hager were most cordial. Mrs. Hager was one of the school teachers. She invited Juanita to visit her. The Skinners joined their group and Mrs. Skinner gestured immediately to Juanita's hair, and started to speak. Juanita laid her finger to her lips. When the men were talking together, Juanita spoke quietly. "It seems my husband didn't like my hair curled."

Wreaths of smoke were beginning to form around the frosted bowl-like ceiling lights. In one corner the orchestra was tuning up. The first dance was a waltz. Luciano led Juanita out on the floor, holding her lightly. The music was good for the size of the orchestra. Four pieces: piano, violin, saxophone, and drums. "All home talent," Lu observed when Juanita asked if the girl at the piano didn't work at the Employee's Club.

Waltzing close to the windows, Juanita could see the square panes of light outlined against the snow outside. "You dance like a feather, Mrs. Platero," Luciano said. The laughter was far back in his eyes as it had been all evening.

"Chicken or turkey feather, Mr. Platero?" They waltzed close to the orchestra to see the name of the piece they were playing.

Mr. Hager asked Juanita for the next dance. He introduced her to several of the male employees. She met the Agency's policeman and Mr. Herrera, who was the disciplinarian over Lu. It was a long time before Juanita danced with her husband again.

During intermission they drifted with the crowd toward the two tables at the end of the room which held the punch bowl and trays of cookies from the school bakery. Mrs. Skinner joined them. Luciano said this would be a good time to run over to the hoghan to see if everything was all right.

Mrs. Skinner took Juanita's arm. "Come on, it's time you met some more of the ladies. If this snow keeps up, we'll all be seeing each other a lot this winter."

The dining room became noisy with talk and laughter. Everyone seemed friendly and congenial. It was confusing at first keeping everyone's name straight: the doctor's wife, the disciplinarian's wife, Mrs. Brown, Mrs. Purns, Laura Taggart, Margy Box. But the faces and names began to assemble themselves properly in her mind with things Mrs. Skinner had told her.

Mrs. Brown had charge of the kitchen at the Employee's Club, and Margy Box was the Ute girl who helped in the school sewing room; she had been there the day Juanita and Mrs. Skinner hemmed the new red and white curtains. Mrs. Purns was the cook at the school; she had offered Juanita the use of her electric washing machine.

After intermission, a Paul Jones was announced. "If there's ever any ice, this always breaks it," Mrs. Skinner said as they took their places in the large circle. The orchestra began a lively tune and the circle of dark-suited men and evening-gowned women revolved.

The tall, blond young man who called "Ladies on the inside, gents on the outside" was Theron Cupp. Luciano had met him at the Agency during the summer. They had become good friends. Theron's people were traders. Sometimes he brought his wife, Grace, the pretty Navajo girl who helped in the school dining room, to visit at the hoghan. "Ladies to the right, gents to the left."

"Grab your partner and dance." Juanita found herself facing Mr. Herrera. She could see Lu across the room dancing with some lady in a blue lace dress, smiling and nodding as she talked to him.

"Everybody circle." Facing into the circle, Juanita could see all the people she'd met during the evening. A dark-haired woman in shell-rimmed glasses smiled at her. That was Laura Taggart, the head of the school sewing room. The slender woman in black satin was one of the nurses at the hospital. Almost everyone at whom she looked smiled and nodded to her: Mr. Stacher, Mrs. Hager, the disciplinarian's wife. This was her first Agency party and the faces were no longer strange. Everyone was friendly.

"Grab your partner." Someone almost swung her off her feet. It was Luciano. She was having a good time.

The deep snow and intense cold affected the Navajo families living near Crown Point. They began coming to the Agency for rations. Their flocks had been lost in the snow, their food supply was gone.

One morning an old woman came to the hoghan door. She pointed to herself. "Your husband, his mother," she told Juanita in Navajo, and walked past her into the hoghan.

Juanita tried to protest; this old lady was not Shimah. She must have come to the wrong place. But her Navajo was limited and the old lady did not understand or else was ignoring the protests. She seated herself on the floor next to the stove, allowing the worn Pendleton to slip from her shoulders. She sat there soaking up the heat, talking half to herself, half to Juanita, as her small bright eyes surveyed the inside of the hoghan and the furniture.

Coffee was left from breakfast; Juanita poured a cupful and offered it to her guest, who sugared it plentifully and drank it. Her bright eyes stared over the rim of the cup at one and then another of the pictures on the wall.

There was nothing to do but wait until Lu came home at noon and could explain to this woman that she was mistaken, that she had come to the wrong place. Juanita poured another cup of coffee for her and then went about her work.

When the water in the pan on the stove had warmed, Juanita poured it into the dish pan on the table and tested it with her elbow. She brought Rosita's basket close to the stove and began undressing her. The old woman made soft clucking noises and held out her gnarled hands for the baby.

Juanita's unwillingness to have this strange woman hold Rosita was apparent. The woman gestured to Juanita and to herself. "Your husband, Luciano, my son," she repeated and held out her hands for the baby again.

Juanita was thoroughly bewildered. She knew what the old lady was saying could not be true and yet here she sat saying it. When Rosita was bathed and dressed, Juanita placed her reluctantly in the outstretched hands. She could think of no answer to this puzzling situation, but certainly Lu would know what to do. Resolutely she finished the morning's work: washing the dishes and drying them, preparing Rosita's formula for the day, putting diapers to soak.

At noon, Luciano came home. He shook hands respectfully with the old lady.

"She says she's your mother, Lu, and I couldn't convince her that she isn't," Juanita said in a disturbed voice.

Luciano smiled. "She's a clan sister of Shimah's. I haven't seen her since I was a small boy. By clan relationship she would be called my mother."

Juanita remembered Luciano's attempt when they were first married to explain the clans to her. It had come about when he was telling how a man could never marry a woman from his mother's or his father's clan. The original clans were very old and dated back to the story of creation. Other clans had been added, far back in Navajo history, by adoption. Clan ties were still almost as strong as blood ties and clan rights were still powerful.

Luciano's "mother" stayed all afternoon. Juanita fixed coffee and bread for her and fried bacon on top of the woodstove. That evening Juanita asked her husband if it wasn't unusual for this relative to come to visit them in Crown Point. Luciano shook his head. "No, she probably came in for rations and heard I was here. Anyhow, this is a hard winter."

Luciano's "mother" was the first of their visitors but not the last. Clan aunts and uncles came into the Agency and stopped to visit with their relative, Luciano. Distant cousins, some of whom Luciano had never seen, came and brought their families. In the beginning Juanita didn't mind. They brought news of interest from the camps around the Agency. She juggled pans on and off the top of the small woodstove trying to keep the coffee hot and at the same time fry bacon and potatoes for them. They always stayed through a mealtime and often stayed all night, making pallets of their blankets and sleeping on the floor of the hoghan.

But when the distant cousins began to repeat their visits and sometimes stayed two or three days, Juanita appealed to her husband. "What can we do? Isn't there any way we can stop them?" Not only was it difficult to prepare meals for them, but it was expensive. Juanita had been unable to save anything from Lu's last two paychecks.

Luciano was puzzled, and upset. "I know of no way, except asking them not to come here. I hate to do that. Being hospitable to relatives is an old custom. Right now most of them are living on a meal here and there and the rations from the Agency. It would be hard to refuse them something to eat when I am working and we have enough. Is it so difficult for you?"

Juanita held back what she was going to say. She could see that her husband was being pulled two ways. It would be easier for him if she didn't pull her way. "No, it isn't too difficult." She began to search her mind for cheaper ways of feeding their visiting relatives. She would have to think of something or else start a bill at the trader's.

One evening, Juanita came home from the Employee's Club to find that two families had arrived while she was gone: an uncle, Juan Platero and his family, and a clan relative with his wife and two daughters who had been there before. "They arrived at the Agency late and want to stay all night here," Lu explained. Juanita's eyes took quick inventory of the two apple boxes which served as a cupboard. No bacon, a few potatoes, flour, a can of tomatoes, and coffee; was there enough to feed them?

Rosita wasn't asleep yet. Juan Platero's wife was holding her, dangling a single strand of plain shell beads before her eyes.

Juan was Lu's father's own brother and a Medicine Man of some renown in the camps around Crown Point. He was telling Luciano of the families near him who had lost all of their sheep and horses. "Those who didn't lose their horses are killing them for the meat." Juan's dark face grew very grave, and he stroked the slender drooping ends of his mustache as he talked.

The clan relative who was an older, thinner man than Juan, with faded brown eyes and wisps of graying hair escaping from his club knot, told of families farther away from Crown Point that had not been heard of since the heavy snow. Luciano said that he knew of these families; the government was dropping food from airplanes to the people who were snowed in. The women shook their heads and murmured words of sympathy.

When Lorencito and his father-in-law arrived, Juanita's eyes strayed involuntarily to the cupboard. She was certain now that the food would not be enough. Lorencito touched hands with her gravely, as he always did, and introduced his wife's father. This man was short, powerfully built, and very dark-skinned. Juanita touched hands with him.

Soon everyone was sitting on the floor around the stove, as though nearness to the heat would take the chill and bitterness from the talk of the hard winter. Lorencito was leaner, older looking; the turquoise pendants were gone from his ears, and the lines of humor about his eyes were overlaid with other lines. For a moment his face relaxed as he took Rosita from Mrs. Juan Platero's lap and sat her on his knee. He began to talk to her in Navajo. His voice was higher than usual and his words oddly accented; some of the phrases he repeated over and over. Rosita crowed happily as she listened to him and began to kick out with her feet against his knee. The older clan relative leaned down to Rosita and seemed to repeat some of the words which Lorencito was saying. The tone and accents were foreign to the way he usually spoke but somehow not incongruous.

That's baby talk, Juanita thought, if I've ever heard it.

Rosita reached out her hands for Lorencito's ears, and then for his nose. Lorencito moved his head toward her, shaking it a little. The baby grabbed his hair in her fists. Everyone smiled a little as the Medicine Man disentangled his hair from Rosita's fingers.

Juanita put more wood in the stove and filled the coffee pot with water. She began to take the few potatoes from the sack. She'd cook what there was and see how far it would go. Lorencito was talking to Lu. "Ask my sister-in-law if she will cook some of those hot cakes like she cooks you for breakfast."

"Would the rest of your relatives eat them?" Juanita asked.

Lu nodded. "Lorencito says when the Navajos have money and are in Gallup they often buy them at the restaurants."

Juanita put the potatoes back into the sack. She had plenty of flour, baking powder, all of the ingredients for flapjacks. There was even half a can of syrup. Cooking them would be simple. As she stirred up the batter the skillet was heating on top of the stove. What went into flapjacks didn't cost much either.

When Juanita undressed for bed that night after the light was out, some of Lu's relatives on the floor were already breathing in the heavy regular rhythm of sleep. The hoghan was filled with the strong odor of mutton grease and the equally strong odor of stale wood smoke. She opened the window above their bed a little. The night air was clean, sweet, and cold. Luciano stirred restlessly. Juanita settled down beside him. Perhaps she wouldn't have to start a bill at the trader's tomorrow, after all.

A strong, cold wind was blowing. Luciano sat close to the woodstove holding Rosita on his lap. Juanita was ironing. She finished one of Lu's blue shirts and straightened it over the back of a chair. There had been no visiting relatives for over a week. "It still seems strange to get up in the morning and not have to step over a dozen sleeping Navajos," Juanita mused.

"Lonesome?"

"Well, not exactly."

Lu got up, holding Rosita against his hip while he put another chunk of wood into the stove.

The knocking first sounded while Lu was stirring up the fire and shutting the stove door. "Lu, there's someone at the door."

Luciano listened and shook his head. "You must have heard the wind." The knocking sounded again, a few light timid raps. Juanita took the baby while her husband went to the door. "I wonder who it could be, this late."

The young man standing in the doorway was no one she knew. Luciano did not seem to know him very well. Luciano filled the doorway and did not ask the young man to come in. Juanita could hear the stranger's voice, low and insistent. Occasionally his voice rose on the accent of a word, as though fear or excitement affected his speech.

"What does he want, Lu?"

"He wants to spend the night here."

"Don't you know him?"

"Not very well. I've seen him a few times in Gallup."

"It's so cold tonight; why not let him stay. It would be a long walk to the nearest hoghan."

Luciano was still uncertain.

"I don't mind, honestly I don't," Juanita assured him.

The stranger was very slender, and his wrinkled trousers clung to his long thin legs. He wore only a torn leather jacket over his shirt and had no blanket. His moccasins were soaked from walking in the snow. He did not seem at ease with them as he sat down near the fire, glancing furtively about him. Clearing his throat nervously, he spit against the stove. Finally he moved with his back to the empty fireplace so that he faced the windows. Luciano asked him the usual questions: "Where are you from? Where are you going?" The stranger pursed his lips and pointed with them to the north, then mumbled something about seeing the agent in the morning.

Juanita put the ironing board away and set the iron on the mantle to cool. "I think I'll make some coffee. This man seems half frozen." She could hear her husband's low voice and the stranger's occasional brief answers as she settled Rosita in the wicker basket and gave her the last bottle for the night.

The stranger accepted the coffee gratefully and relaxed somewhat as he drank it. He did not refuse a second cup. Luciano spread one of their blankets on the floor by the stove for him, and the young man moved it closer to the fireplace where he sat.

"It's strange that he's traveling in wintertime without a bedroll," Juanita observed after they had gone to bed.

"It's strange too that he wouldn't talk about himself. Most men like to."

No sound came from the pallet by the fireplace. Juanita went to sleep thinking about the peculiar behavior of their visitor.

In the morning when she awakened, their visitor was gone. She questioned Lu, "Didn't you ask him to stay for coffee?"

"I didn't see him. He wasn't here when I got up."

It was certainly nothing to worry about and yet she couldn't refrain from speculation over their strange visitor. She told

Mrs. Skinner about it when her friend stopped at the log hoghan before noontime.

"That rather fits in with all the excitement at the Agency." Mrs. Skinner sat on the edge of the bed and opened the paper bag she was carrying. She held up a Mason jar. "May I stay to lunch? I brought chicken soup."

"Did you make it, Mrs. Skinner?" Juanita set the jar in the apple box cupboard. Finally she asked about the excitement at the Agency.

As Juanita folded the clean diapers and put them away, Mrs. Skinner told her the story as her husband had heard it:

A group of Navajo men from the hoghans near the Agency had brought a young man in whom they accused of practicing witchcraft. Some of the men discovered this young man at a Sing with an effigy of the patient, strands of hair attached to it. These men wanted to kill the young man immediately, for surely he was one of the ma-itso. Older men, some of whom had worked at the Agency, persuaded their friends not to be so hasty. They were too near the Agency; someone would hear of it, and then they'd all be arrested for murder. Why not take him in and let the agent punish him?

Since they arrived so late in the evening, Mr. Stacher said he would keep their prisoner overnight and deal with him the next day. The young man had not broken any laws from the government's viewpoint (witchcraft not being officially recognized), so Mr. Stacher hesitated to put him in jail. Instead, he sent him to the powerhouse to sleep, knowing that he would consider himself safer there than attempting to escape on foot in the snow. But evidently the young man did not feel safe in the powerhouse, for when the men went after him they didn't find him there. Instead he showed up at the Agency walking from the direction of the school.

"Sounds suspiciously like our visitor. Wait until I tell Lu, and I was the one who insisted that he stay with us."

"Luciano probably knows by this time. Everyone is talking about it. Those Navajos who brought the man in are still waiting around the Agency to see what Mr. Stacher intends to do."

Juanita added wood to the fire and emptied the soup into a saucepan. She set bowls and spoons and a box of crackers on the table. She and Mrs. Skinner had discussed *ma-itso* before. Juanita had told her about their warning from the wolf clan while at Lu's mother's. Mrs. Skinner had not been incredulous; she had heard stories of similar happenings around Crown Point. She thought as Juanita did. Such a clan existed and stories of its evil power were not always exaggerated, but only the intended victim's mind could give the wolf clan that power.

The wolf clan was not often in Juanita's thoughts. She and Luciano rarely spoke of it unless some of the relatives gathered about the woodstove in the evening and began the talk of *ma-itso* in lowered voices.

Ma-itso was something which existed in the background—a shadowy something which could never be strong enough to dominate their daily lives.

Luciano came home while Juanita and Mrs. Skinner were eating. When they questioned him, he told how part of the men were asking that their prisoner be released to them.

"What will Mr. Stacher do?" Juanita asked.

"Probably send him to another part of the reservation, and send men with him to be sure he gets away from here."

"That's how he's handled these cases before," Mrs. Skinner volunteered. "It puts an agent on the spot. He can't send the man back to his own community where he will be killed. What proof does the agent have of his guilt? And he can't bring him to trial for being something which isn't supposed to exist."

Juanita buttered a cracker. She could see how an agent wouldn't dare recognize the existence of *ma-itso*. Official recognition would only strengthen the Navajo belief in witchcraft and strengthen the hold which the wolf clan already had on their minds. "But I wonder what Mr. Stacher thinks, unofficially."

"It might be surprising." Luciano pulled a chair to the table and helped himself to the crackers. "He's been among the Navajos since he was a young man. He could probably tell a lot. Some of the Navajo around here say that he has a picture of one of the *ma-itso* before he got out of the wolfskin. They say they've seen it."

"I've heard that, too," Mrs. Skinner affirmed. "And not from the Navajos."

TWELVE
Waano-Gano

The full tragedy of the hard winter was not known until spring. Not until the snow was gone and families from a distance began to come into the Agency was the news carried of the tremendous loss of stock, of the families who had starved, the casualties of a winter that had made it almost impossible to get out for food or wood.

The shadow of the tragedy extended long, dark fingers across the sunny days of spring: a dilapidated wagon drawn up before the agent's office, half-fed, half-clothed children crouching in its bed: the carcass of a horse bleaching among the wildflowers on a hill: the bones of sheep that had gathered for shelter beneath a cedar tree.

Occasional letters from Mrs. Pentz during the winter had kept Juanita and Lu informed of the welfare of his family. The weather in Cañoncito had not been as severe as that in Crown Point.

There was more news of Lu's family and relatives when the government "farmer," who visited the Cañoncito district, came to the Agency. He brought the aluminum identification discs—government tags issued to all Navajos—one for Rosita and one for Juanita. The heavy snow would make good grass this year, he told them, but he feared the Cañoncito Navajos would have a lean year until the ripening of the corn, beans, and melons in their fields.

When the "farmer" left, Juanita examined the aluminum discs in her hand more closely. Each disc was the size of a half-dollar with an eagle on one side and an identification number on the other, and two small holes drilled near the edges. She put them away for safekeeping, but her husband didn't let her forget about them. He often teased her about trading her name for a number when she married him.

Juanita decided when the long-rumored salary cuts were finally put into effect that it would be a lean year at the Agency too. Luciano's salary was cut to $47.50 a month. Now there was even less opportunity to save money for furniture.

With the salary cut came an addition in Lu's duties. He was made responsible for the school's flock of chickens. Lu hated chickens. "I'd rather milk the goats," he grumbled. But he scattered grain to them, filled their water crocks, cleaned the pens, and gathered eggs twice a day. No one around the Agency guessed that it required almost superhuman effort for him to perform these simple tasks.

Luciano had stopped by on his way to the school kitchen with the morning gathering of eggs. "They'll be starting work on the hoghan in a day or two. Mr. Stacher just told me."

As she bathed Rosita and dressed her for the day, washed and hung out diapers, and prepared the feeding formula, Juanita's mind was full of pictures of the remodeled hoghan, pictures which included a couch and low chests, a small drop-leaf table and shaded lamps, furniture suited to the low-roofed, six-sided room. She kept reminding herself that they couldn't buy furniture on Lu's salary and then the thought occurred: what would prevent *her* from getting work?

Once she consciously recognized the idea of getting a job, there was no putting it aside. When she took the rugs out to shake them and hang them on the line to air, she was examining all phases of the idea. It would be necessary to hire someone to care for Rosita during the hours she was away from home, but that shouldn't cost too much if she did the housework and laundry herself. Lu probably wouldn't want her to work and it might not be possible to get work in Crown Point, but the idea was worth trying.

At noon, she told her husband what she had been thinking. He was not at all in favor of her working. But then, she hadn't expected him to be. "You couldn't do the work here and work at the Agency, too, even if there was a job. It would be too hard for you."

"I don't think so. I'd like to try it."

It was Lu's pride speaking when he said, "But it isn't necessary for you to work." He stood by the fireplace gazing down at the hearth. "We're getting along."

"We aren't getting any nearer to some of the things we want."

The visits of relatives during the winter, the drain on his salary, and the wiping out of their savings in order to feed them was on both of their minds, and yet neither one of them spoke of it.

"Lu, the things we want are for both of us," she hesitated a moment, "and for Rosita; it's only fair that I should help in gaining them." Juanita's voice was low, but clear and certain with her belief that she was right. Her very attitude was convincing as she stood against the breakfast table, her hands in the pockets of the red gingham apron, her cheeks flushed, her eyes wide with eagerness to convince him.

"You won't be content until you ask about a job, will you? All right, I'll stay with Rosita while you talk to Mr. Stacher." It was evident Lu thought that there would be no jobs available.

Mr. Stacher was surprised to see Juanita, and more surprised when she told him that she wanted to apply for full- or part-time work. He laid aside the papers outspread on his desk; his sole concern for the moment seemed to be what she had to say. Juanita found his interest disarming. Although she hadn't intended to, she told him the reason behind her wanting a job.

Mr. Stacher smiled. "I must say that I admire you and your husband. You both seem determined to get ahead here on the reservation." He pulled a small desk file toward him.

Juanita filled out the card, listing her experience in general office work, filing, and bookkeeping. "But I wish you'd keep me in mind for any job which doesn't require specific training."

Mr. Stacher placed a call on the Agency phone and then turned to Juanita. "There'll be a job open in a few days helping Mrs. Brown in the kitchen at the Employee's Club. You'll have to see her about the exact duties. The salary is $37.50 a month and meals. It isn't the kind of work you've been doing, and if you'd rather wait until there's a vacancy in the office, I'll put your application on file."

Juanita made the decision instantly. "No, I'll go over and talk to Mrs. Brown now."

The work at the Employee's Club was light—preparing vegetables and salads and helping with the dishes, and Juanita was gone from the hoghan for only a few hours in the morning and again in late afternoon. One of the older school girls took care of Rosita in the morning; Luciano was off duty before Juanita went back to work in the afternoon. But her time had to be strictly budgeted to accomplish the work at the hoghan and at the Club, and leave a few hours free in the evening.

By mid-summer they had saved enough for a substantial down payment on furniture for the remodeled hoghan and arranged to pay the balance on a monthly payment plan. Some of Luciano's objections to Juanita's job were lost in pride of their newly remodeled home, and in a corporate sense of achievement.

They were sitting outside the hoghan one evening watching the brilliant afterglow of sunset when they heard someone singing at the far end of the square. "That isn't a Navajo song but the voice is certainly familiar." Lu looked down toward the agent's office. As the song sounded nearer they could distinguish the figure of a man walking toward them. Juanita was the first to recognize him. "Lu, it's Waano-Gano."

"How did he get to Crown Point?" Luciano rose to greet him.

"Come inside where we can see if it's really you." Juanita opened the screen door and turned on the light.

"Well, I expected to find you two in a hoghan, but not a glorified one."

The large six-sided living room paneled in deep cream wallboard was attractive in the lamplight. The strong colors of the Navajo rugs spread over the mottled dark linoleum were repeated in the curtains, the Chimayo scarves, and the feather dance bustle on the wall. Narrow, four-shelved bookcases stood on either side of the walnut cedar chest. A mahogany gate-legged table occupied the center of the room, with mahogany chairs to match. Rosita's crib was in the space between the low walnut chest of drawers and the maroon upholstered studio-couch.

The three friends all began to talk at once: what was Waano-Gano doing away from Los Angeles? When had he last seen Delilah and her husband, Glympia, Roan Horse, John

Second Plant? Were they still working around Hollywood? How were Juanita and Lu getting along, and the baby? Then they stopped and began to laugh.

Waano-Gano answered first. "I've been visiting relatives in the Cherokee country, the Smokies; stopped at the Chicago Fair on the way here." He was a little shorter, a little younger than Luciano; his hair was black and thick, his eyes dark brown and intense beneath heavy black brows. There was vitality and intensity in his wiry body, and his serious dark face; it pervaded the very timbre of his voice. "Saw some of Standing Bear's relatives at the Fair; they were in the delegation of Sioux from South Dakota." His voice lowered. "The faces of some of those old-timers. A few of them posed for me. I tried to capture something of what was behind those faces and put it on paper. I only half-succeeded." His voice trailed off. It was plain that sketching and painting to Waano-Gano were no less important than breathing. He began to wander about the room looking at the pictures on the wall, the Sioux breast-piece, the bows and quivers of arrows. He asked about the two large pottery bowls on the mantle of the stone fireplace, and the woven basket that hung on either side. He bent to test the tone of the log-shaped drum at the edge of the hearth.

Luciano laid his finger against his lips.

"Oh, the baby—Rosita! Say, I haven't seen her."

Lu smiled and lifted the blanket which shielded the top of the crib.

Waano-Gano gazed at the sleeping Rosita for a moment and then turned to Juanita. "This is going to upset my schedule," he said seriously, "but I'll have to stay over long enough to sketch that baby."

"She's hardly a baby any longer; in two months she'll be a year old." Juanita covered the crib again. "Of course, we're prejudiced, but we think she grows sweeter each day."

Juanita left the men and went into the small compact kitchen. "Are you hungry?" she asked their guest. "We eat dinner early and usually have a sandwich and coffee about this time."

The kitchen was bright with red and white curtains and a blue enamel kerosene stove. Narrow, open shelves held the blue Willowware, and built-in cupboards and drawers held new pots and pans and the wedding gift linen. As Juanita filled the coffee pot she could hear Lu and Waano-Gano talking of their friends in Hollywood.

Hollywood was far away. Pink stucco, palm trees, Wilshire Boulevard to the sea. The Indian chiefs and princesses who looked good in beads and feathers but had never seen a reservation. The young Indians who had left school or jobs in other parts of the country for what promised to be lucrative work in motion pictures, and who hung around White Bird's Store waiting for a call from Central Casting. Hollywood was fabulous, unreal. Had she and Lu ever lived there?

"Do you remember Richard Bay Horse?" That was Waano-Gano's voice. Juanita remembered the lean young Navajo who sometimes came to their apartment. He and two other boys owned a second-hand car between them. When the fellows were working on the same picture, Lu rode to the studio with them. "He was killed on location just before I left. Horse threw him."

"And he was a good rider," Lu observed. "I guess those things just happen."

As she sliced the cheese for sandwiches, Juanita thought of John Nickle, one of the silversmiths at White Bird's, who had cut the silver buttons from his blouse and handed them to her when he learned that she and Lu were getting married. "I want to give you something." John had a wife and little boy with him in Hollywood. It was said that he had another wife and her children at home on the reservation taking care of the sheep.

When Juanita brought the sandwiches and coffee from the kitchen, Waano-Gano was telling Lu how the scenery around Crown Point impressed him. "I've never seen scenery on such a grand scale." He looked up at Juanita. "I can't tell you how right you two were to come here. You have a home and a future here. And you're surrounded by real beauty."

Lu held the cups as she poured coffee. "But he hasn't seen anything, has he? He hasn't seen Cañoncito."

"Cañoncito? Is that where you were when you first came here?"

Lu nodded. "My family and most of my relatives live there." He began to describe the shallow grass-green valley on one side of Des Jin. "Once you see that valley and mesa in late afternoon sunlight, you won't want to leave until you've painted it. And the red sandstone walls around Cottonwood Spring. . . ."

Juanita could not be certain because her husband's face was partly turned from her, but she thought she saw, for an instant, the shadow of nostalgia which had so often darkened her husband's eyes in Hollywood.

The shadow was gone when Lu spoke again, or maybe it had never been. He was smiling.

It was Rosita's first birthday. More than a year had passed since their arrival in Crown Point. A trying year: the long winter in the unrepaired hoghan, feeding relatives when they couldn't afford to, and both of them working to get a little nearer to things they wanted. Juanita stood at the window watching the leaves fall from the trees in the square. They had a home now; they were getting ahead. The year had not been without compensation.

Luciano rummaged in the bottom of one of the kitchen cupboards until he found his kit of silver tools. Whistling softly under his breath, he went outside to build a fire of juniper wood. He was going to make a bracelet for his daughter.

When Rosita was dressed in a new blue print dress, her hair combed so that it fell softly against her shoulders, her mother led her out the door and they sat down against the wall of the hoghan to watch the making of the bracelet. While Lu waited for the fire to burn down, he set out the small pan to hold the glowing coals, the bellows, the bowl-shaped crucible, and the piece of iron rail which he used for an anvil.

"It's been a long time since I've handled silver." In fact, not since they had come to New Mexico, had they had extra money to buy silver. He laid the small bar of metal on his knee and placed the oblong turquoise and the two smaller ones beside it.

Lu's fingers were deft as he put the metal into the crucible among the coals and worked the bellows with sure, even strokes. The soft whistling changed to a gay, wild song.

The sun was warm against the south side of the hoghan. The sky was blue and cloudless. It was not a day for thinking, but for sensing and enjoying the warmth and peace. Yellow leaves dropped slowly from the two large cottonwoods beside the school dining room. All of life and happiness seemed permanent at that moment.

When the silver was melted and poured into three straight iron grooves and cooled, Luciano hammered and shaped the narrow bands of silver on the anvil, drew the three pieces together at each end of the bracelet for soldering, and spread the bands in the center. Then the turquoise stones were set in simple silver mountings: the oblong stone placed in the center across the spread of silver bands, the smaller stones on either side. After the bands and the mountings were soldered, there was much filing and polishing.

Lu looked up. A dark lock of hair had fallen across his forehead. "I like to think that somewhere ahead, times will be better and there will be silversmithing jobs in Albuquerque. Then we can at least go home on weekends to Cañoncito."

So, she hadn't imagined the shadow in Lu's eyes.

But her husband said no more; he was intent upon an exacting bit of filing. Juanita steadied Rosita as she tried to get closer to the rasping sound of the file. At last, Luciano put the bracelet on his daughter's tiny wrist and clamped it. The ends overlapped. "This won't be too small for a long time." Rosita sat down heavily against her mother, her eyes widening as she gazed at the silver and the blue stones.

Juanita touched the bracelet. "Say 'pretty', Rosita."

Luciano sat on his heels before her. "The word is *nah-zhunni*, my daughter."

That winter Juanita often saw the shadow in her husband's eyes—the shadow which meant he was thinking of home, of Cañoncito. It was darkest when relatives visited them, or when there was a letter from Mrs. Pentz with news of his family. Yet he did not speak of his feelings and Juanita hesitated to question him. She knew of no alleviation, at the present time, for his homesickness; perhaps it was deeper than homesickness.

But there was no trace of the shadow today. They were walking toward a mesa where, while hunting with Lorencito, Lu had noticed fresh fox tracks. Good pelts were worth something at the trader's. Juanita carried a coffee pot and blanket bundle which held bread, bacon and eggs. Luciano carried traps and a small frying pan over his shoulder. He laughed as they jangled together.

Once the buildings of Crown Point were behind them, it seemed that the white world stretching before them was their own—each ledged mesa, snow encrusted; each twisting arroyo, the banks powdery soft and white; each clump of evergreens, branches outstretched and laden with billowy clouds of snow.

Their life in Crown Point was pleasant to Juanita, satisfying, perhaps more varied than life in Cañoncito. There were visits with friends they'd made at the Agency: Laura Taggart, Margy Box, Grace and Theron, and the Skinners. There were employee dances where Juanita wore the little-used black taffeta dress and waltzed with Lu, immaculate in newly-pressed blue serge. There were squaw dances and one-night Sings where they wore their warmest clothes and sat up most of the night, Rosita sleeping peacefully, wrapped in Juanita's Pendleton. There were trips to Gallup in the Skinner's Ford—shopping and dinner in town and a movie. There were visits to Lorencito's and to Il-tha-bah's. Il-tha-bah had a new son, Keetso. And there were walks like this out into the open country, or horseback rides to distant mesas where they seemed to be able to separate themselves from everything else. What they said to each other on days like this seemed to have more meaning than what they said at other times.

When they came to the mesa where Luciano had seen fox signs, he went about setting the traps. "Four red fox skins would just about pick up that old-style concho belt I saw at the trader's."

"Don't count your foxes before you catch them," Juanita teased him.

With the traps set, they walked on a little farther, their boots crunching the snow. Luciano began to gather dead wood, knocking the snow from it. When his arms were full, they headed for the sheltered side of a mesa.

"Hungry?"

"Starved!" Juanita unwrapped the food and spread the folded blanket for them to sit on. Luciano broke some resinous branches from a nearby piñon and soon they had a blazing fire. She scooped snow into the coffee pot, set it at the edge of the fire, and began to slice the bacon.

"I'm not just talking about the concho belt—we may never have a chance at one like it again. Families don't often part with those things."

"How did the trader get this one?"

"During the hard winter. The owner didn't have the money to redeem it, borrowed as much as he could on it, and let it go."

"What's going to happen to these Navajos? Will the government try to help them?" Juanita had heard enough from their relatives to know that some families had no means of subsistence left. "Things were bad enough before the hard winter."

"I've heard it's even worse in other parts of the reservation."

"We are lucky to have what we have now, aren't we?" Juanita arranged the slices of bacon in the skillet, and added coffee to the melted snow water.

"Yes, and yet we've worked for it doing work we don't particularly like . . ." Luciano seemed deep in thought for a moment.

Perhaps I'll never know, Juanita reflected, what it's meant to Lu to work this past year-and-a-half cutting hair and mending shoes and inspecting little boy's ears, when his mind is full of songs he hasn't time to sing, and his fingers are sick for the feel of silver.

"I've realized this is no time to think of where I want to be, or the kind of work I like to do. I realize it all over again each time some of our relatives visit us. A job is important—any kind of job." Lu looked sideways at her. "But I think I'll have a new job soon—a better one."

Then he told her about the vacancy at the power plant, a job which paid almost a hundred dollars a month and provided a house on the north side of the road. "I'm going to ask Mr. Stacher to let me try it. I know I can take care of those engines."

The coffee was boiling. Juanita broke the eggs into the bacon grease. "If you make more money, we can save more money, and we'll be closer to the time when you can look for a job near Cañoncito."

Luciano gazed into the fire and then beyond it. "I can't explain the way I feel about Cañoncito. There isn't really so much difference between there and here. There's certainly more security in Crown Point. More opportunity too; I think Mr. Stacher likes us and wants to help us. Yet Cañoncito is different. And that difference seems important."

Juanita watched the shadow as it began to deepen in her husband's eyes. In that moment she began to understand. The mesas and canyons around Crown Point were little different from the mesas and canyons of Cañoncito. A canyon was a canyon, but if it was the place where a man was born, it brought back memories—memories of a little boy herding sheep where the chamise bushes were gray-green with new leaves, picking cactus apples in late summer when the earth hummed with the voices of a thousand singing insects, and riding the bare back of a shaggy pony when his legs were scarcely long enough to hold him on. Then it was more than just a canyon.

A mesa was just a mesa, but if the crumbling rock house perched on the edge was built by the little boy's grandfather, and the peach trees below, sheltered from the wind, had been planted by that grandfather, and if the boy had filled his eyes with the sight of those trees in blossom in the springtime and filled his mouth with the small ripe fruit in late summer—then it was more than just a mesa.

Juanita touched her husband gently with one hand. "Someday we'll live there. We'll have a home in Cañoncito."

THIRTEEN
Wolf Tracks

Living on the north side of the road had many advantages. The white stucco house was larger, more modern than the log hoghan. There was a fenced yard where Rosita could play and a garage where Luciano could set up a forge for silversmithing. Luciano's working hours were definite, from four in the afternoon until midnight; the rest of the time was his own. There were no more chickens to take care of.

Spring and summer passed. One pleasant, uneventful day gave place to another. Juanita and Lu breakfasted late. Sitting at the table in the long kitchen, they lingered over a second cup of coffee, listening to Rosita's chatter from the highchair, watching the wagons on the road which passed the Agency office. Sometimes they recognized the teams and the occupants of a wagon. "Better put on a big pot of beans," Lu would say, "we'll have visitors sometime today."

After breakfast Juanita washed and put away the dishes, left Rosita with Lu, and hurried to the Employee's Club to help with the noon meal. Sometimes she found her husband and daughter both in the garage when she came home, Lu working at the forge, Rosita sitting on the workbench as close as she could get, round-eyed with interest. Rosita slept in the afternoon while Juanita prepared Lu's lunch and got him off to work. Often she was still asleep when the school girl came to take care of her, and Juanita went back to the Club for the dinner hour and the dishes afterward.

It was in the evening when Juanita, at last, had time for her housework, laundry, sewing, and mending. Many nights she was still working when Lu came home at midnight. They would have coffee and sandwiches, or bacon and eggs before going to bed.

Just before Rosita's second birthday, Juanita quit work at the Club. She had planned to work another month or two until the new bedroom and dining room furniture were entirely paid for. But in making her plans she hadn't considered that she might not be as well in her last few months with this baby as she had been before Rosita's birth. Lu encouraged her to quit. Wasn't he making enough now to support a family—a wife and daughter and a new son? This baby would certainly be a boy.

Having all day, every day, to do housework seemed strange to Juanita. There was time to make new dresses for Rosita, house dresses for herself, and make-over curtains for the kitchen. Laura Taggart helped her. There was also time to read and rest in the afternoon, and more time to spend with Lu.

Breakfast had lasted through a third cup of coffee this morning. Juanita was tracing the design of the oilcloth with her finger as she told Lu of the good report she'd heard of Dr. Pousma at Rehoboth. "The hospital here has been crowded for months. Perhaps it would be wiser to go to Rehoboth this time."

They heard the creaking of wagon wheels and the clop-clop of horses' hooves before they looked up to see a covered wagon pulling off the road opposite their kitchen dooryard. Three women got down from the wagon bed, adjusting their Pendletons across their shoulders, reaching back into the wagon for bundles tied in flour-sacking. As the team and wagon continued on down the road, the women walked to the kitchen door. Juanita recognized the smallest one, although her wizened face was almost hidden by the fold of her Pendleton, as old Seraphina. She spoke to her and was rewarded with a stub-toothed grin. The two other women were Luciano's aunts by clan relation. Juanita had met one of them in the cook shelter at her first Sing.

When the women were seated and had let the blankets slip from their shoulders, and Rosita had been lifted from her highchair and placed on old Seraphina's lap, Luciano asked for news of his family and of Cañoncito. His mother was well. Yee-ke-nes-bah had married and brought home a husband. A proper amount of time elapsed with polite questions and answers. Had there been much summer rain? Was the grass good? Was there much wild hay in Apache Wash this year?

One of the aunts carefully folded her skirt into pleats against her knee as she talked. They had brought their younger children to the Crown Point school. They would be going back to Cañoncito in a few days with the family that had brought them in the wagon. Luciano interpreted part of what she was saying to Juanita then added, "Things must be really tough. Those long-haired families would never send their children to school if they could feed them at home."

Juanita shook her head in sympathy. "Are you sure Shimah and her family are all right?"

"They say so."

Seraphina watched with bright eyes and listened carefully as Luciano told the news of families around Crown Point. It was as though she wanted to remember each small detail to carry home in her shrewd old head and repeat around the fire in her relatives' hoghans. She began to chuckle in her thin, high voice. "Tomas Mexicana—you remember him—got drunk this summer and tied his wife by the hair to his saddle. Drug her around a bit."

The other women smiled. "She doesn't order him to do things so often now as she used to."

"And Minnie Pablo is going to have a baby," old Seraphina added and chuckled. "She won't tell who the father is."

Juanita cleared the table, pausing when Lu repeated parts of the conversation. She set the stew for their lunch near the back of the stove to simmer, peeled potatoes, and added an extra can of tomatoes to it. She sensed when the talk turned from gossip about Cañoncito families to something more serious. She noticed the lowering of voices, and heard one significant word: *ma-itso*.

The *ma-itso* had become very bold in Cañoncito since the hard winter. Sheep and horses that had survived the deep snow were now being stolen right out of their corrals. There was no doubt that the *ma-itso* was responsible. Mixed in with the tracks of the stolen animals were always the tracks of a very large wolf.

After Luciano had gone to work, Juanita and his relatives conversed sketchily with gestures and scattered Navajo words. Rosita did most of the entertaining. She brought out her toys to show them and enthusiastically patted the ones they praised, listening gravely when the relatives talked to her in Navajo.

Mrs. Skinner stopped in for a moment. "Gonna be home tonight?"

"Of course."

"Just wanted to know. Might be over."

One of the aunts offered to make fried bread for supper. Juanita wrapped three flat, round pieces in a napkin and took them to Luciano with his evening meal.

The power plant was near—across the road and then across the flat stretch of ground behind the Employee's Club. The interior of the plant was dim except for the naked light of two electric globes. The big generators loomed black and shiny. Luciano checked the gauges and then sat down on the workbench where Juanita was spreading his supper.

"How are you feeling?" he asked, wiping his hands again on the rag in his pocket.

"A little weary."

"Relatives too much for you?"

"Not really. It's the waiting more than anything. I felt this way last time in the last month or so."

Juanita sat opposite Lu on the workbench while he ate. Every evening she brought his supper to him at this time, and usually Rosita came along to tell her daddy "goodnight" before being put to bed.

"We'll have to do something about our relatives," Luciano commented. "Our house is too convenient for all those who come to the Agency. We've had more visitors than ever since we moved to the north side of the road."

"We probably look more prosperous now." Juanita broke a piece from Lu's fried bread.

"They don't realize that their visits are hard on us. Stopping with relatives when traveling has been going on for generations. If we were passing through country where some of them lived, we'd be welcome."

"But what can we do?" asked Juanita. "As you once said, we can't just tell them not to come here."

"I don't know. But we should do something."

When Lu had finished eating, Juanita gathered up the dishes and went back to the house. Seraphina and the two aunts were taking off their moccasins and spreading out their Pendletons on the living room floor. Old Seraphina made a gesture. Did Juanita have any extra blankets?

The lights were out and the relatives were settled under the borrowed blankets when Mrs. Skinner opened the door, knocking as she came in. Juanita called, "I'm putting Rosita to bed; come on back here, Mrs. Skinner." There were whispers and giggles, and when Juanita came in, she found a living room full of women. "Surprise!" they greeted her.

The two aunts were sitting up, blinking in the light. They'd moved their blankets against the wall and were trying to smooth their hair and push their feet into their moccasins. Seraphina continued to lie huddled in her Pendleton with her head half-covered, feigning sleep. Her appearance proclaimed that she had gone to bed and she would stay there. But curiosity overcame her when the women set a ribbon-trimmed bassinet in the center of the floor. Seraphina sat up beside Lu's aunts and stared wide-eyed at the bassinet piled high with tissue-wrapped boxes.

It seemed to Juanita that almost all the women connected with the Agency were there: matrons and teachers and nurses, Mrs. Brown, Grace, Mrs. Purns, Mrs. Hager, Laura Taggart, Margy.

Juanita sat down weakly on the studio couch. "I'd forgotten things like this happened."

"Just because we're stuck up here on a mesa doesn't mean that we don't know the proper things to do at the proper times," Mrs. Skinner told her. "Now you just concentrate on opening packages." Most of the women had found chairs; others took cushions and sat on the floor. Mrs. Skinner pushed the bassinet in front of Juanita.

As she opened the first package, Juanita noticed that Lu's relatives were watching with interest. She held out the soft blanket with appliqued animals for them to see. They took it, fingering it gently, murmuring *nah-zhun, nah-zhun.* Seraphina turned the blanket over and over in her gnarled hands before placing it in the outstretched hand of the woman next to her. The gifts went around the circle, and there were "ohs" and "ahs" at each dainty dress, each frilly bonnet, and even practical things like undershirts and stockings and diapers. The card on the bassinet said "Skinner."

"Where did you find such a fancy basket?" Juanita teased her.

"Find it!" Mrs Skinner made a noise in her throat. "Why, I practically created it from the ground up. Haven't you noticed me lately with my white enamel decorated fingers?"

Grace and Mrs. Purns came out from the kitchen with ice cream and cake.

"Ice cream in the middle of winter! I simply won't believe it." Juanita took dishes from the tray for Lu's relatives.

"We had half a dozen school boys fighting to turn the freezer when we told them they could lick the dasher."

Juanita watched as old Seraphina dipped into the ice cream experimentally, laid her spoon down and looked about her with excitement in her eyes. She directed a quick, sly grin at Juanita and tried again, this time devoting herself to the ice cream until the plate was clean. I wonder what the old lady thinks about all this fuss over a baby that isn't even here yet, Juanita thought.

"Grace, did you save any ice cream for the father?" Mrs. Skinner called into the kitchen.

"Yes, and we'd better take it to him before it melts."

Juanita could picture Lu's face when he was served pink and white refreshments from the shower. To tease Mrs. Skinner, he'd probably spread the paper napkin—with fat cherubs and pink rosebuds—over his coveralls.

The women had washed the plates, brushed up the cake crumbs, helped Juanita fold the tissue paper and ribbon, and placed the gifts and cards together in the bassinet. The last ones were now getting into their coats and leaving.

"We didn't intend to stay long," Mrs. Skinner explained. "Just long enough to see you open the things. You need your rest and most of the gals have to go to work in the morning."

Lu's relatives spread out their blankets once more and settled down to sleep. But long after she'd gone to bed, Juanita could hear the excited tones of their muffled voices; now and then old Seraphina's thin, high voice piped up above the others.

When Juanita came home from Rehoboth Hospital, the earlier wild ride down the rutted canyon road seemed like a dream. Awakening in the middle of the night, her body already encircled with the pains of birth . . . Mrs. Skinner, frightened, calling Dr. Pousma, who started out to meet them and somehow missed them on the way . . . Lu's face deathly calm as he tried to drive fast over the canyon road while avoiding the rough places . . . the glaring light of the operating room . . . the head nurse working alone. But all of that was part of the dream and the only real thing was her small, delicate daughter, Tonita.

Rosita spent much of her time in her rocker, waiting patiently to hold her baby sister. But most of the time Tonita slept in the white bassinet where Rosita could only look at her.

Luciano hired one of the school girls to do the laundry and help Juanita with the housework, but even with the extra rest, Juanita's strength did not return. She kept thinking, tomorrow I will feel better. Tomorrow this weakness will leave me. Refusing to give in to the weakness, Juanita got up each morning before her husband awakened, fed the baby, dressed Rosita, and put water on for coffee. One morning she had just called Lu to breakfast when she heard the timid knocking at the kitchen door.

"Shimah!" Juanita exclaimed when she opened the door, "How did you get here?" Happiness surged through her as she held her mother-in-law's hand. She had forgotten how small Lu's mother was, even when bundled from head to skirt in a blanket, and how very soft her voice was. It had been over two years since she'd last seen her at Correo.

Shimah moved near the stove and held out her work-gnarled hands to it. Juanita could see the snow caught along the ruffle of her skirt, caked on her moccasins. She must have walked into the Agency from some relatives' camp.

Luciano came into the kitchen, buttoning his shirt; water glistened on his hair. Rosita tagged behind him. He took both of his mother's hands and they stood looking at each other, smiling slowly. The tenderness in their faces made Juanita's eyes sting with tears.

Then Shimah saw Rosita. "Ee-yah!" she exclaimed softly. "Is this my granddaughter?" She held her hands out shyly toward the little girl.

"That's your grandmother—*ne-nilly*," Juanita told her daughter.

Rosita held back for a moment, clutching her father's trouser leg. Then finally, as though lured by her grandmother's soft, coaxing words, she started toward her. Shimah's face shone. She patted Rosita's hands and touched her sturdy arms and legs, exclaiming again and again over her. And where was the new baby? Luciano brought the sleeping Tonita from the bassinet and laid her in his mother's lap. Tonita's dark hair clung in soft tendrils about her face; she looked much like Rosita had as a baby, only smaller and more delicate.

"She's so little," Shimah said to Luciano. Tonita began to pucker her mouth and lift the dark lashes from her cheeks, slowly. "And she has gray eyes."

"Tell Shimah she must name this granddaughter too, as she did Rosita." Juanita poured the coffee and set a plate of bacon on the table. Her mother-in-law was deep in thought while Juanita turned the flapjacks in the skillet.

"My mother's sister's name was Ne-nes-bah; she was a good woman and that is a pretty name," Shimah said at last.

"Ne-nes-bah," Juanita repeated.

"She-turns-around," Luciano interpreted for her.

Shimah held Tonita on her lap while she ate breakfast. She jiggled her knees gently and talked in soft murmurs to the baby.

"It's too bad we are so far from Cañoncito, when your mother enjoys her grandchildren like this," Juanita told her husband.

"Now that she's here, perhaps she'll stay with us for a while." Luciano turned to his mother.

"Yes, my son," she answered, "I came to visit you."

Shimah seemed to enjoy staying with them. She watched the children tirelessly and gently but firmly convinced her daughter-in-law to sleep every afternoon. Every day she prepared a medicine tea from the dried leaves and stems of an herb she carried in her flour-sack bundle. The tea was bitter but Juanita drank it. Shimah had told Luciano that this medicine was good for renewing strength. When all the herb was gone from her bundle, Shimah walked several miles to a relative's camp to replenish her supply.

The combination of Shimah's strength and gentleness never failed to amaze Juanita. There were other qualities too: Her mother-in-law's patience when she began to teach her to make fried bread—a pinch of baking powder, a pinch of salt, so much flour, and so much water (you could tell by the feel of the dough as you worked it), and the grease should be hot in the skillet, and if you pierced the center of the dough before frying it the bread would not pop. Her mother-in-law's strength when she butchered the sheep that Juan Platero brought over—managing the animal by herself, skinning and disemboweling it. There was much laughter in the kitchen that day when Juanita attempted to cut up the carcass. She struggled and struggled, turning the freshly-killed sheep on the table; but finally Shimah showed her the right place to cut so the ribs would fall away easily from the backbone.

Besides learning more about Navajo cooking, Juanita was learning more about the language in the time spent with her mother-in-law than she had since coming to the reservation. When she and Lu were first married, Juanita intended to study the language seriously and be able to speak it, but several things thwarted her intentions, including the language itself, with its clicked Ts and explosive Ks. When she learned words and phrases, there were still the idioms of expression and the grammar, which were not easily mastered. Even Lu, who spoke both Navajo and English fluently, could not always supply the necessary rules for Juanita to use in sentence structure. The time spent with Shimah was a good opportunity to improve her pronunciation and add to her vocabulary.

Shimah was a patient teacher. She repeated words over and over until Juanita got the right inflection. By gesture Shimah was often able to convey the difference in the use of certain words. At the cookstove she held her hand to the fire to indicate that it was hot *si d'oh*, and then pointing outside and moving her hand above her head to indicate the heat of weather, she said *d'es d'dhui*.

Juanita thoroughly enjoyed the time spent with her mother-in-law, and dreaded the day when Shimah would decide that she was needed in Cañoncito and could stay with them no longer. Juanita was feeling better, stronger; the weak feeling seized her less often and not so suddenly as before.

But the drop-in relative problem worsened while Shimah stayed with them. True, the very distant clan relations did not come so often nor stay through as many meals, but relatives around Crown Point came often to visit with Shimah, some of them old people who did not often travel the distance to Cañoncito.

There were always visitors at the house before the Yei-be-tchai to be given near Marianna Lake. Families came from great distances to this winter ceremony, and for many, the closest way was through Crown Point. Most of these relatives were strangers to Juanita, "longhairs" who seldom came to the Agency. Shimah seemed pleased to have these "longhairs" gathered about the table in the middle of the day, talking with her son. She helped Juanita cook for them.

Juanita stood beside the stove, turning the fried bread, holding each golden crusted round above the skillet while the grease dripped off before adding it to the stack on the plate. Shimah was busy kneading dough, pinching off pieces to pat into round balls that would later be stretched and flattened before going into the skillet.

There were two families of relatives at the table. A clan brother of Shimah's, his wife and two children, and an old uncle of Shimah's with his son, daughter-in-law, and three grandchildren. The two smallest children crawled about on the floor, chewing fried bread, and getting underfoot until one of the women caught up her own with soft clucking noises and held it for a while on her lap. She then became interested in the conversation and the child slipped unnoticed down her full skirt and was crawling about on the floor again.

The relatives ate slowly, scooping up the fat pinto beans from the dark juice with their fried bread. The old uncle sipped his coffee noisily, setting down his cup to be filled again. He asked Luciano about relatives near Crown Point and Luciano answered respectfully and at length, leaning slightly forward, his dark face serious.

The women smiled at Juanita, sometimes addressing questions to her. But mostly they talked to Shimah, and there was much to talk about—the upcoming ceremony, whose family was giving it, and the families they'd stopped with on the way to Crown Point.

Juanita set the second pot of beans on the table, another plate of fried bread at each end, and then began to fill the coffee cups again. It was good that both the baby and Rosita slept at this time of day. She was tired. There had been this many relatives and sometimes more around noon the last few days. Even though she prepared the simplest and cheapest meals she could for them, she knew her money for supplies would never last through the month.

The uncle, whose long gray hair was held in a club knot by a faded piece of red cloth, was telling Luciano how the people of his section had been living for two years on the harvest from the small fields and jack rabbits and prairie dogs they had killed.

Shimah's clan brother spoke. "There aren't enough jack rabbits left for one good rabbit chase."

The full-skirted women laughed and nodded.

Juanita looked from one strong, dark face to the next. There was no self-pity there, no note of complaint in their voices as they spoke of the effects of the hard winter. She knew that she could never say anything inhospitable to keep them, or any other relatives who would come after them, from stopping at their house.

A wagon pulled into the back yard. Il-tha-bah and her husband did not get down from the seat. Shimah giggled a little and gestured that her son-in-law was out there. She remained at the stove while Juanita threw a coat about her shoulders and went with Lu out to the wagon. Lu's sister was thinner than when Juanita had last seen her. Occasionally Il-tha-bah coughed raspingly into the corner of the towel she wore about her shoulders beneath the Pendleton. They couldn't stop to visit; they were on their way to the Yei-be-tchai. Bijo stuck her dark head through the opening in the canvas top of the wagon and smiled shyly at Juanita.

Il-tha-bah tucked the blanket more securely about the baby on her knee and assured her brother and his wife they would stop by on the way home, as she wanted to get some cough syrup at the hospital.

"We brought you something." Il-tha-bah's husband got down and went to the back of the wagon. He returned with the full carcass of a sheep and lifted it on to Lu's shoulder. "There should be lots of mutton, even deer meat, where we're going."

Shimah was pleased with the mutton. "My son-in-law is a good man," she murmured.

Lu and the male relatives went into the living room; the two women and their children had settled themselves on Pendletons and were leaning back against the kitchen wall. Shimah began to sharpen the butcher knife as Juanita cleared the table of the odd assortment of plates and china and tin cups; the Willowware was seldom adequate when there were visitors. They laid the sheep carcass upon the oilcloth. The women relatives watched Shimah slice the mutton into thin strips. These strips of meat were hung and stretched from the rafters of the garage. The ribs were cut into sections and hung from the rafters too. Shimah gathered up all the thin strips of meat left from the table, and put them into the kettle on the back of the stove for stew.

Juanita tried not to notice the anticipation in the dark eyes of the two women and their round-eyed children as they watched Shimah get out potatoes and onions and ground red chili to be added later to the stew.

When Il-tha-bah and her family came back through Crown Point, they stopped to see Juanita and Luciano. Il-tha-bah's husband remained discreetly beside the wagon until his mother-in-law had disappeared into the kitchen.

Seated in the front room, Il-tha-bah held Keetso in her lap. There was little she and Juanita could say to each other without Luciano. Lu was asking his brother-in-law about the Yei-be-tchai. Il-tha-bah's husband answered, "There seemed to be more families there than last year. We saw Miguelito Secatero from Cañoncito." Rosita had already brought out her toys and she and Bijo were playing together on the floor.

Il-tha-bah stared with unconcealed interest at the pictures and decorations on the walls. She bent to examine the weave of the Navajo rug at her feet. It was a type of weave known as *yish-bish*. Who made it? Juanita shrugged her shoulders. She didn't know. Lu had bought it at a trader's several miles from Crown Point.

Bijo came to stand beside her mother. Juanita remembered how when she first went to Cañoncito, Il-tha-bah used to bury Bijo's moccasins in damp sand each night so they could be stretched and worked to fit her daughter's growing feet. The little girl had grown since then; she was almost old enough for school. Luciano told his sister this.

Il-tha-bah shook her head. The Agency boarding school was too far from her hoghan; she did not want to be separated from her daughter.

As she watched Il-tha-bah, Juanita noticed a wild, strong look about her face which sharpened her features and set her apart from Lu's other brothers and sisters. After a while Il-tha-bah lifted little Keetso against her shoulder and went into the kitchen where Shimah was waiting. The soft accents of Il-tha-bah's voice, punctuated by an occasional perturbed "Ee-yah" from her mother, drifted into the living room.

When Il-tha-bah and her family had gone, Shimah seemed preoccupied as she helped Juanita with a late lunch before Luciano went to work. While they were eating Shimah asked, "Is the doctor at the Agency hospital always right?"

"What makes you ask that, Shimah?" Luciano set his coffee cup down and waited.

His mother tilted her head to one side and pulled thoughtfully at the silver circle in her ear. She then told them how Il-tha-bah had stopped at the Agency hospital and asked for some syrup to ease her coughing. One of the nurses had examined her and sent her to the doctor, who had sent for an interpreter. He told both Il-tha-bah and her husband that she was seriously ill and should go right away to the government hospital in Albuquerque.

"Tuberculosis," Juanita said aloud.

Shimah's dark eyes misted over as she explained what the doctor had said. Only at the hospital could Il-tha-bah's sickness be cured. And if she didn't go right away, her coughing would get worse and no one would be able to help her. But Il-tha-bah didn't believe the doctor. She wasn't going far away to the hospital in Albuquerque. There was nothing wrong with her that the Medicine Man couldn't cure. Shimah turned her saddened face to her son and repeated the question. "Is the doctor at the Agency hospital always right?"

Shimah, Luciano, and Juanita were having breakfast in the kitchen. The baby was fretful as Juanita held her on her lap. Rosita sat at the end of the table in her highchair, pleasantly engrossed in pushing the remainder of her oatmeal around in the bowl.

Luciano had just finished telling his mother that he would borrow the Skinner's Ford and drive her to Il-tha-bah's on Sunday. Perhaps his sister could at least be persuaded to go to the hospital in Albuquerque for another examination. Rosita looked up from her oatmeal and pointed the dripping spoon toward the west window which looked out on the arroyo. "I see big dog down there."

Juanita paid little attention to her except to rescue the dripping spoon and wipe her daughter's hand. Rosita was at the age where she tried strange things to gain an audience.

"When, sweetheart?" Lu asked her.

"Not now," Rosita assured him, her eyes widening. "Yesterday."

Juanita saw the concern in her husband's eyes. "Don't take her too seriously, Lu. She's been talking like that lately; she seems to have big dogs on her mind." Swinging the baby to her hip, Juanita got up to pour more coffee. Several things could have impressed themselves upon her daughter's young mind: the fox which Lu caught and took to the trader as a last payment on the concho belt, the strange, large dogs that followed the wagons on the way to the Yei-be-tchai, or possibly the school girl who had helped with the work might have tried to make Rosita mind by telling her that big dogs would get her.

Lu was still questioning Rosita. Where had she seen the dog? How big was it? His daughter continued to stretch her chubby arm toward the arroyo.

"We'd better not let Rosita play outside too late in the evening after this."

Juanita lifted her eyebrows in question.

"Somehow she must have seen the same thing I've seen a few nights coming home from work."

"You didn't mention seeing anything."

"Well, I wasn't sure. These moonlit nights sometimes play tricks on your eyes."

Shimah leaned closer at the change of tone in her son's voice. As he talked, Lu repeated some of the words in Navajo. Coming home from the power plant these last few nights he had seen dark figures like dogs or coyotes sitting on their haunches on the other side of the arroyo. "Only they seemed even larger than coyotes," he added.

Shimah began to talk excitedly. She had intended to wait until after breakfast to have Lu inspect them, but this morning she'd found wolf tracks around the house.

"Probably some animal attracted by the meat hanging in the garage," Juanita observed.

Lu pushed his chair back from the table and started outside. Shimah followed him to point out the place where she had seen the tracks.

Juanita put the baby into her bassinet, cleaned Rosita's hands and face, and helped her from the highchair, then began to clear the table. The tracks could just be those of an animal after the meat in the garage. There was no use getting upset over a thing as natural as that.

When Lu came back in he got his shotgun from the closet and began cleaning it. "Those are wolf tracks," he told her.

While Juanita and Shimah washed and dried the breakfast dishes, Luciano brought tools and some pieces of lumber from the garage and built a rack for the shotgun beside the kitchen door—a rack which held the shotgun handy and yet was too high for Rosita to reach.

"When I'm gone at night, don't be afraid to use it on anything four-legged you see prowling around here," he told Juanita.

The next few nights Shimah listened intently for noises outside, and each morning she inspected the ground around the house for tracks. But there was nothing.

Sunday evening after they returned from Il-tha-bah's, Shimah started supper while Juanita washed that day's diapers and took them out to the clothesline.

As the clothesline was beside the garage, one end of it faced the wide arroyo which cut behind the house and wound around to border the north side of Crown Point. Juanita was scarcely aware of her surroundings, she was so preoccupied with thoughts of Il-tha-bah and how resolutely she had resisted any suggestion that she go to the hospital. Already relatives were arriving to prepare for a Sing to be held over her.

Juanita had hung up two diapers when she became suddenly aware of something across the arroyo. She looked around carefully, but nothing seemed unusual. In the dim light she could see the sharp banks of the arroyo, the clumps of juniper in dark patches on the other side. Then gradually, two of the dark juniper patches began to take on the indistinct forms of dogs sitting on their haunches.

Juanita smiled to herself. This must be what Lu had seen, the queer-shaped juniper bushes. They looked surprisingly like coyotes, only larger. She even thought now that she could see the large pointed ears. The likeness startled her for a moment. She pulled her eyes away and resolutely began hanging up more diapers.

Suddenly Juanita saw movement. One dark figure detached itself from the other and moved farther down the arroyo. A third form appeared almost directly across from her on the opposite bank. Juanita stood absolutely still. There was no sound except the flapping of the clothes on the line.

When Juanita reached the kitchen door, she called to her husband to bring the shotgun. "Those figures that you saw are out there again." This couldn't be her voice, tight and choked.

Two of the dark forms were loping off down the arroyo when Luciano reached the bank, but the third sat directly across from him like a very large coyote on its haunches. Luciano raised his gun and fired directly at it. The animal gathered itself into a ball and plunged down the bank of the arroyo, and across the wide, sandy bed.

"Lu! Watch out! It's coming for you," Juanita screamed.

He raised the gun to fire again, but the figure turned sharply and ran down the arroyo. Luciano jumped down the bank and fired after the fleeing animal, but it was soon out of sight around the bend.

Luciano was lighting matches and examining the sand. "Those are wolf tracks all right, and big ones."

Juanita shivered.

Her husband laughed softly. "It's cold out here; come on in the house."

"I will in a minute. Wait until I hang out the rest of these diapers."

FOURTEEN
A Visit from Nadine and Michel

Spring was slow in coming to Crown Point. There were warm days and then a sudden flurry of snow. This was one of the warm days, and Luciano could put off preparing for a garden no longer. He had borrowed a hand plow and was plowing up the ground enclosed by the front yard fence. The freshly turned earth was brown and mellow and fragrant. Juanita thought there was no odor as pleasant as the odor of fresh-plowed ground.

"I wish we had more land fenced in. These spring days make me want to plant lots of things besides corn," Lu said as he leaned against the plow handles. "Beans and squash and watermelon."

"Wait until we start our home in Cañoncito. You'll have a hundred and sixty acres under fence," Juanita answered from the shelter of the back doorway, while keeping a steadying hand on the baby. Toni was making fascinated reaching motions at a long-legged, black bug crawling along the step. Juanita and her mother-in-law had just finished cleaning house readying it for Nadine and Michel, who were expected sometime today or tomorrow. This was hardly the vacation season, but Nadine had written that for the first time since their marriage, she and Michel had managed to get a vacation together. So, vacation season or not, they were driving to Crown Point.

Rosita was following Lu in the furrows made by the plow, chattering endlessly, trying to keep up with her father and at the same time keep out of the way. The cuffs of her blue-striped coveralls were turned up, and there was a long dirt smudge across her forehead.

Juanita smiled as she listened to her husband patiently try to answer all of their daughter's questions: "Going to plant corn

here, Daddy? Where you going to plant watermelon?" Rosita
had been like this all winter, following Lu like a small
shadow, sitting beside the forge while he worked, trying to
match her voice with his when he sang, trying to match her
steps with his when they walked down the road to the
trader's. Often when Shimah saw them together, she would
hold her hand to her mouth, and her eyes would shine. "She
is like her father."

Rosita was the first to notice the long gray car as it pulled off
the road. She began to jump up and down with excitement,
but when the car door opened and Nadine and Michel got out,
Rosita ran to her mother and hid shyly behind her. Lu left
the plow at the end of the furrow and began brushing his
hands against his Levis. There was the confusion of greetings
and questions and laughter as they all went inside the house.

Shimah had washed her hair and put her good skirt on over
the everyday one in preparation for the visitors. She came
from the kitchen, the full yellow skirt swinging at each step,
her dark hair smooth and shining in the fan-shaped loops of
the club knot. Shyly she offered her hand to Nadine and then
to Michel.

Juanita was truly proud as she said, "This is my
mother-in-law."

Shimah sat politely smiling, even though she could not
understand talk which flowed about her.

The children seemed to captivate Michel. He talked to first
one and then the other. He had a gentle and reassuring way
about him; in no time the baby was smiling at him, and
Rosita was his friend. Michel was of above average height
and decidedly husky. His voice was deep and muted. There
was a Nordic blondness to his hair and skin, and his blue
eyes were alight with humor.

Before Luciano left for work, Juanita went into the kitchen to
prepare a late lunch and Shimah offered to make fried bread
for the visitors.

Nadine stood in the doorway watching Juanita slice meat
from the roast and dish up the potato salad she'd prepared
the night before. "It's much different here on the reservation
than I expected it to be—not quite so primitive." Nadine was
small and delicate, her skin very fair, her hair a soft, wavy

brown. "But even so, don't you ever get homesick for California? Aren't there things you miss?" Her words reflected the gentleness and understanding that had first attracted Juanita to her.

"I'd like to visit California sometime. I think Lu would too, but I doubt if either of us would want to live there again." She laughed softly. "About the only thing I really miss is silk hose. I have only one pair for special occasions." Juanita held out a leg clad in tan lisle stocking. "Lu won't let me go bare-legged. He says our relatives wouldn't think me modest. Silk hose wouldn't last out here anyway. There are too many things to snag them on."

Nadine began to put the plates and silverware on the table. "Poor Nita. Now I'll know what to send you at Christmas."

Laughter and banter passed across the table at lunch time. Nadine told how Michel devoted himself to his new hobby, photography. "He keeps us broke buying film, and has turned our back porch into a dark room."

"Just when I'm getting good, she starts making all this fuss," Michel protested.

Shimah put more fried bread before them, and Luciano told her of the visitors' compliments on her bread-making. Embarrassed she hid her face in her hands.

Michel was telling Juanita he'd like to get some pictures of hoghans, corrals, and perhaps a Navajo shepherd with his sheep. "Do you think the families living around here would object?"

Juanita turned to Luciano. "Ask Shimah if she knows of any family around here who would let Michel take some pictures."

Shimah was quiet for a long time, one hand to her mouth as she thought. "The country where your sister lives is very beautiful. She wouldn't object to your friend taking pictures. Ask him if he would drive us all down there; I would like to go."

On Sunday they drove to Thoreau and then south along a wagon trail through wooded country. Il-tha-bah's hoghan was built in a clearing among tall cedar trees, the log framework blending with the tree trunks. Smoke rose lazily from the earth-packed dome and drifted away becoming lost among green cedar branches. A new brush shelter had been put up beside the hoghan. Luciano explained to Nadine and Michel that Sings for his sister had been going on for several weeks.

Juanita was not surprised when Michel asked, "But why don't you persuade your sister to go to a hospital?" She thought of how often Lu had talked with Il-tha-bah's husband and the relatives who came to help with the Sing about his sister's sickness. It was hard for him to tell them that the "coughing sickness" his sister had could best be cured in the big hospital at Albuquerque. They listened to him and were not unfriendly, but it was Il-tha-bah who refused to go. Something in that wild, strong spirit of hers refused to leave this place among the cedars. For a long time now, Lu had spoken no more about it. He came and brought food to help with the Sing and drove home silently each time, knowing that she was no better and perhaps a little worse.

Shimah got out of the car and padded across the packed earth of the clearing to the hoghan while Juanita, Nadine and the children followed and entered the shelter. Several male relatives came over to ask Lu about driving them to the trader's at Thoreau. Michel assured Lu he wouldn't mind driving there and back again. The back seat of the car and the extra place in front were soon filled. The men who couldn't possibly squeeze inside stood smiling amiably as the gray car left.

It was pleasant sitting in the brush shelter. The fresh-cut cedar boughs were pungent and spicy, and the smoke from the cook fire mingled with the smell of the stew. Juanita explained to Nadine that she usually stayed out here with the children; she didn't like to take them into the crowded hoghan where there was sickness.

Women relatives came up to touch hands with Juanita and gravely touched hands with Nadine when Juanita introduced her as her friend. They lingered for a moment trying to coax a smile from Toni or a shy soft answer from Rosita.

Nadine moved her legs more comfortably to one side of her as she sat upon the sheep pelts. "Do you ever get accustomed to sitting this way?" She watched the strong, dark faces of the women around the cook-fire, the half-naked babies playing on the ground outside the shelter, the old men gathered beside the hoghan, and heard faintly the monotonous chant coming from within the hoghan. She said pensively, "It's another world, isn't it?"

Juanita nodded.

"It still doesn't seem possible that your life has changed so much, and you have changed so little." Nadine touched Tonita's knitted boots. "It's been such a few years since you lived in California and were scarcely aware that a place like this existed."

"I know," Juanita answered. But it was an answer without meaning. She'd never really thought before of the vast difference between her life with Lu, and the life she'd lived before she met him. Perhaps she'd been too busy just living this life and looking ahead to the things they wanted, there wasn't time to look backward.

It was a long way back to her high school days in Texas. Beaus and school plays, dances, horseback rides, and swimming parties at Lake Wichita were the important things in her small town existence. Even then, when she borrowed Paul Varney's horse and rode along Red River the day seemed too short. She would have liked to ride across the land toward the far line of the horizon, but the tightly fenced farmlands barred her way.

The restlessness had begun when school was over and she took the job as clerk in the town bank. She became increasingly aware of the narrowness and smugness of the small town life about her. "Career girl" was a new and frowned upon phrase; most girls got married or stayed home with their folks and taught school or clerked in one of the main street stores.

One by one, Juanita's girlfriends had married and started life according to the accepted pattern. New brides followed in the footsteps of the mothers. They either lived with the folks or, if the couple could afford it, moved into one of the new box-like houses on the south side of town. The Economy Market carried the best line of meat and groceries, and Persinger's was the place to buy drygoods. The bridge club met on Wednesday afternoon; Saturday night was the dance at the Elk's Club. Occasionally a few of the young matrons went to Wichita Falls for the day, attending a matinee and coming home with the latest in hats or frocks and perhaps some yardage for new curtains. Such a trip was the subject of conversation for a week.

Juanita had not known exactly what she wanted, but she was sure that what she saw around her wasn't it. When a bookkeeping position opened at the bank, Juanita asked for the job. It paid more money, and if she saved enough, perhaps her parents would not object to a trip to California to visit her mother's sister, Ina.

What was it about being young which made everything seem possible? Juanita put the baby on the sheep pelt beside her so that she could manage the bowl of stew passed to her. She tilted the glass jar of spoons toward Nadine. Nadine was absorbed in watching one of the older women make paper bread.

Did that enviable state of mind belong exclusively to youth and must part of it be forfeited with each year of growing older?

One thing about the trip to California stood out clearly now—the stopover in Albuquerque for breakfast. She had breakfasted hurriedly and gone to stand on the arched porch of the Alvarado for her first glimpse of the city. Curio shops and souvenir stores lined First Street; Central Avenue stretched to the west, its modern store fronts glaring in the morning sun. Along Central came a spring-wagon piled with hay; dark-haired children rode atop the load. On the driver's seat a long-haired man in a white shirt trimmed with lace managed the horses. A plump, dark-eyed woman whose head was covered with a red shawl rode beside him.

How picturesque, Juanita thought. This was her first glimpse of southwestern Indians.

There was much to see in Los Angeles, and for once the restlessness had abated. When summer was almost over, and she should have been thinking about returning to Texas, Juanita was instead watching the want-ad columns in the papers and going to employment agencies for interviews. Her first job was across the city from where Aunt Ina lived. After a few weeks, Juanita rented a small apartment to be closer to her work. The girl who lived in the apartment above and who so often played the piano in the evenings was Nadine.

Juanita's thoughts were interrupted by the return of the gray car bouncing along the wagon road outside. It stopped on the edge of the clearing, and Michel and Luciano got out and came to the brush shelter.

"I got some good character shots of those men," Michel told Nadine.

"They could hardly refuse after the ride," Luciano laughed. "After Mitch gets some shots of the hoghan, we'd better start home. It would be better to drive the canyon road in daylight."

Juanita asked Nadine to watch the children. "I should go in to see Il-tha-bah before we leave."

She waited until there was a break in the singing and people began coming out of the hoghan to go inside. Luciano followed her.

The hoghan was dim except for a small fire. Il-tha-bah lay on a pallet against the back wall, resting. She smiled faintly and held out her hand to Juanita. Luciano's sister was thinner and her strong fine features appeared gaunt and sharp in the shadows. Pale yellow sand, the remains of the sandpainting, was scattered on the floor to the west of the smoke hole. A tall, thin Medicine Man sat beside a square of print cloth on which lay feather-decorated rattles and several seashells half full of medicinal tea. As he rested, he stroked with slender fingers the fringe on his long medicine pouch.

Luciano bent over to better hear his mother's words as she talked to him from her place beside Il-tha-bah. "She says that we should go home without her. She will be needed here."

"But how can she stay without meeting Il-tha-bah's husband face to face?" Juanita asked as they left the hoghan.

"There is a ceremony with tobacco that takes care of that."

Mrs. Skinner wanted to help Juanita entertain her guests and so invited them to her house for lunch. "This would have been a dinner party," Mrs. Skinner explained as they arrived, "but I would have had to serve you at the power house."

Luciano's mouth lengthened into a smile as Mrs. Skinner gestured to him, but he did not answer.

Mrs. Skinner's house was furnished simply; bright colors gave the rooms a homey cheerful appearance. Juanita carried Toni across the hall to the bedroom. "She usually sleeps at this time every day. We'll see if she does this afternoon."

The dining room table was laid with a gay print cloth and glass dishes. The centerpiece was a bowl of early daffodils from the Agency garden.

Nadine and Michel were immediately at ease with Mrs. Skinner. Conversation was spontaneous as the meal began: depression talk, Agency gossip, Nadine and Michel's trip.

"Is this your first time out here?" Mrs. Skinner asked.

"No," Nadine touched her napkin to her lips, "Nita and I came as far as the Grand Canyon once." Then she told of how the two of them had saved for a whole year and spent their savings in two weeks, paying ten dollars a day for their room at the Phantom Ranch. "Nita was so fascinated by the scenery, I began to worry about getting her back to work."

Mrs. Skinner removed the consommé cups and brought the salad and meat pie from the sideboard. She was silent for a moment and then said, "I'm going to ask a personal question, which isn't polite, but a woman can't deny a healthy curiosity indefinitely. How did you four so vastly different people meet?"

Michel was the first to speak. "I assure you, Mrs. Skinner, that it was in an atmosphere in which anything might have happened. Isn't that right, Lu?"

"Yes, and Skinner might have enjoyed some of those Sunday evenings. Much more exciting than an Agency dance." Luciano tucked the napkin more securely under Rosita's chin.

"Nadine and I met when I first came to California from Texas," Juanita began. "The rest takes quite a lot of explanation." Already her mind had slipped back to review the links of the chain. "I was transferred to a bank in Huntington Park. One of the accounts on my set of books was Chief Standing Bear. One day he invited me to an

Anglo-Indian meeting in the court where he lived. I took Nadine. And I guess that was the beginning."

Nadine tried to describe the mixed group at that first meeting: artists, writers, missionaries, schoolteachers, and Women's Club members among the non-Indians; musicians, artists, dancers, motion picture extras, and curio store clerks among the Indians. "It was the first experience for either of us in an organization of that kind. After one meeting, we attended others. The organization was new and sincere about its aim: the betterment of relations between races, and more tolerance through understanding. The young people in the group were likable and friendly. First thing we knew, we were active members."

"Chief Standing Bear and his niece, Sunflower, were the guiding hands behind it all." Nadine told briefly of Standing Bear's efforts to gain understanding and justice for all Indians by writing of his own people, the Sioux, and by lecturing and sponsoring programs of authentic Indian music and dancing. "When he began training a group of girls to do the old Sioux dances, he asked Nita to come and practice with them. She learned the dances easily and naturally. Soon she was one of the most accomplished of the group."

Mrs. Skinner looked at Juanita in amazement. "Why don't you tell people these things? So that's where all the Sioux trappings on your wall come from."

Juanita laughed. "Then we moved to the court in order to be closer to Standing Bear when there were programs. Alfred Wolf's Indian orchestra began holding rehearsals in our apartment. How I kept a job during those years I don't know." Juanita remembered the increasing number of programs for clubs, schools, and churches. The group also increased its activity in soliciting funds and clothing to be sent to the reservation, organizing an Indian employment service, and campaigning for authenticity of Indian material in publications and films.

Those were busy years, and somewhere in that time she had ceased to regard Indians as a race apart and thought of them only as individuals. Perhaps the young people, White Flower, Delilah Wolf, Roan Horse, Waano-Gano, and all the rest, who sometimes gathered in the evening at their apartment, were responsible for the change in her point of view. When they got together the conversation might be about anything from the latest find in La Brea tar pits to the current picture at Grauman's Chinese theater. These young people were her companions on trips with Standing Bear to Horseshoe Ranch and during barbecues at Yorba's. They were all equally interested in horseback riding, art exhibits, archery meets, and gatherings at White Bird's Store.

Luciano touched her hand. "I thought I heard the baby cry. Hadn't you better see if she's awake?"

Nadine was telling of the celebrities: Hernando Villa, Frank Tenny Johnson, Lee Shippey, Lushanya, and Bill Hart, who occasionally came to the meetings.

Juanita closed the bedroom door. Toni had not been awake long. She changed the baby's diaper, straightened out her clothes to make her more comfortable, and then lay down beside her to lull her back to sleep. As she lay beside her daughter the memories of her California days continued to flood her thoughts.

The gatherings on Sunday night had been the most fun: All of the apartments in the court ablaze with light: Sunflower's, her mother's, Standing Bear's, their own. People arriving and walking down the long drive to the patio behind the court. Flood lights cross-lighting the center of the patio, benches grouped in the shadows, climber roses nodding from the trellis along the white stucco wall. No particular program planned, it was just a general get-together.

The Stones showed some of their latest camera studies: sand dunes, a Joshua tree on the Mojave, and the waterlily buds at Westlake Park. An archaeologist who had recently returned from the interior of Mexico spoke of the ruins being uncovered there.

Sunflower, her long braids dark against her white buckskin dress, was busy guiding late arrivers to empty benches and making them acquainted with the people around them. The last group that Sunflower seated was Aunt Ina with some of Juanita's friends who had come to see just what these Sunday evenings were like. So many times Juanita had left early from a Sunday afternoon bridge game or begged off from a theater party, giving these Sunday evenings as the reason. Juanita could see Aunt Ina, impeccable in a white linen suit and a tiny white hat, looking all about her. The two men in white flannels lit cigarettes and turned their heads toward the sound of the dancers' leg bells which came from Standing Bear's apartment.

Standing Bear walked to the center of the patio, asking for attention with a roll of the beater on his hand drum. "White Flower and Juanita will now do the Corn Dance." Standing Bear was handsome in an eagle feather headdress, a bone breastpiece over his white shirt, beaded arm bands, red leggings drawn on over dark trousers, and beaded moccasins.

In a low, resonant voice he began the Corn Song. His voice gained volume and the beats fell heavier on the drum. White Flower and Juanita danced their way through the crowd to the inside of the circle. They were dressed in eagle feather headdresses, elaborately feathered dance bustles with two trails of feathers to the ground, bells from hips to ankles, and otter skins about their ankles and about their necks to hold the bone breast pieces secure. They advanced side by side, rattles in one hand, eagle wings in the other, moving with the slow stately rhythm of the song. The last measure of the Corn Song called for fast and intricate stepping. The bells clamored full-voiced; feathers flashed in the lights, and then the dance ended abruptly with three short stamps.

The Indian orchestra assembled next and played popular selections as well as various tribal songs, which Alfred Wolf had orchestrated. Four Iroquois boys sang, Lone Star played the trumpet. Waano-Gano stood against the stucco wall with Frank Tenny Johnson expounding an idea for an oil painting. John Second Plant, holding a double-headed drum in the curve of his arm, played and sang while the Pueblo boys, knee bells jingling, performed the ceremonial Buffalo Dance. White Bird, regal looking in a black and white blanket coat, talked with Standing Bear about the Indian boys and girls getting better outfits to appear for picture calls.

When more of Standing Bear's dancers entered the circle for the Victory Dance with lances and shields, the Pueblo boys stood watching. As the dancers finished, the Pueblos moved into the circle with small hoops, vying with each other their slender, sinuous bodies moved in rhythm to the drum.

That's all the Sunday evenings were: singing and dancing, listening and watching, exchanging ideas, and meeting new people interested in joining the organization, or in a program for their club, church, or school.

The serving of coffee broke up the challenge dancing and the young people laughed and joked together as they sat down on benches among the watchers to enjoy the refreshments. Juanita sat with her aunt and friends, asking how they liked the program, laughing as they examined her headdress and dance trappings.

Thinking back, nothing in her life before the years in Standing Bear's organization had prepared her for life with Lu. She had always had a love of horses and open country. But there in Standing Bear's court her restlessness had crystallized into a boundless energy expended while attending various lectures and programs, in winning support for the Indian organization, and in studying to increase her own knowledge of Indian people.

During those years she became certain of what she wanted from life—a chance to live, not just exist. A full, useful life with someone who loved life as she did. Luciano had been that person and the life he offered her was really two lives, a life in between the Indian world and her own upbringing.

When Juanita returned to the dining room, Michel was telling how he had first met Juanita at his club, and how she had invited him to one of the Sunday evenings where he met Nadine.

"But Luciano," Mrs. Skinner asked, "where does he come into this?"

Lu smiled. "That's very simple; while I was in Hollywood working in pictures, I met Delilah, a girl I'd known in school. She kept saying, 'There's someone in Huntington Park I want you to meet.' One night when we had finished at the studio she took me out there. That's all there was to it." He shrugged his shoulders and laughed softly.

That, Juanita thought, and the weeks he came to the court and talk with the other Indian men, to sit in Standing Bear's apartment, or to sit in our apartment listening to Nadine play the piano. All she had ever got was an occasional dark, sidelong glance. During the months after he first asked for a date, they had spent enough time together on horseback rides, at dances and shows, and at the archery range to know that they felt the same way about so many things: a love of open country, an aversion to the complication of city life, and a belief that people should get married when they fell in love.

It was as though Luciano knew what she was thinking. They exchanged a long glance across the table.

New pale green grass spread across the pastureland beside the highway. Cholla cactus raised their arms to the sky. Juniper, dull green and tipped with the yellow-green of new growth, dotted the early spring landscape. They were taking a sack of flour to the Sing and some oranges for Il-tha-bah. When they turned onto the wagon trail which led through the cedars, the Skinner's Ford bucked and bounced as always. Juanita held Toni firmly against her and put one hand upon Rosita to keep her in the seat. The air was invigorating. Juanita was feeling quite well except for a slight cold.

Luciano whistled softly under his breath, a long low whistle, when they pulled into the clearing. Then Juanita, too, saw the green and orange spring-wagon. Of course, there were many other green and orange wagons in the Navajo country besides Wounded Head's, she told herself, but it would indeed be a coincidence to find another one pulled by a pair of sleek, plump sorrels. So Juanita was not surprised when she carried Toni and led Rosita into the cook-shelter to find Wounded Head's wife sitting among the women around the fire.

Juan Platero's wife arose to pull the scattered sheep pelts together and make a place for her relative and the children. Then she took Toni from her mother's arms and held her while Juanita shook hands with each of the women before settling herself on the pelts. Wounded Head's wife was most cordial and turned to better see the children. She smiled and raised her eyebrows in approval when Rosita whispered "Yes" in Navajo to her questions.

This woman seems so harmless, Juanita told herself, she seems as quiet and colorless as a field mouse. But Juanita could not relax and breathe deeply of the fresh clean scent of cedar as she usually did or enjoy the sweetened hot coffee which Mrs. Juan Platero handed her. Her eyes returned again and again to the blouse that Wounded Head's wife was wearing. The small silver buttons that decorated the points of the collar, the larger silver buttons in a row down the placket, held a peculiar fascination.

This meeting could be nothing but accidental. Wounded Head and his family probably came through the Agency for the Yei-be-tchai and then stayed on, visiting relatives, as so many other families had. No doubt they heard of Il-tha-bah's illness in one of the camps and drove over to the Sing. It was probably as easily explained as that. Sinister motives could not be behind every move this family made.

Yet when Wounded Head and his son came to the shelter to eat, Juanita could not control the clammy feeling that wrapped around her body and possessed her. Unconsciously she gathered Toni a little closer to her and looked about until she saw Rosita in one corner of the shelter with Bijo. Wounded Head nodded to her; his son followed with a ghost of a nod. Then they sat down against the wall of cedar boughs, crossing their slender legs and reaching out their long hands for the bowls of stew passed to them.

As always, the expressionless face of Wounded Head challenged Juanita. She found herself thinking of it as a mask—an expressionless mask—to hide his real thoughts and feelings. The dainty, almost effeminate way he handled his food was peculiar. Was each mannerism studied to hide his real desire to wolf down what he ate? Wounded Head and his son did not ask her simple, polite questions in Navajo as the other men often did, and neither did they pause for a moment to speak to the children. The two men only sat and stared at her with cold indifference in their eyes.

When Luciano came after her, Juanita had never been more ready to leave a place. Driving home they discussed their mutual surprise at seeing Wounded Head's family.

"Il-tha-bah's father-in-law was talking to some of the men outside the hoghan. He said that Wounded Head is getting very bold to stay so long around this part of the country. He used to live near here. Il-tha-bah's father-in-law also said he'd never heard of Wounded Head fighting Mexicans. He believes that scar is from an old arrow wound when he was nearly caught on a wolf hunt."

"Shimah must have been upset with Wounded Head's family here."

"She was, yet she could do nothing but be polite to them."

The road was still winding among the cedar trees when Juanita was seized with the first spasm of coughing. She coughed so hard and seemed to be so near choking that Luciano pulled the car off the road and stopped. He took Tonita from her lap. "Perhaps if you get out and straighten up your body it will help."

Juanita stood outside the car until the coughing passed.

"Walk around a bit and breathe deeply," Luciano suggested.

"My cold must be getting worse. Do you have a handkerchief?"

Her husband laid the baby on the seat beside him, telling Rosita to watch her and not let her roll off. He began to rummage in his pockets. "I've got a clean one somewhere." He got out of the car and searched through his pockets again. "Here it is." He unfolded the handkerchief and handed it to her.

Juanita walked among the trees, trying to fight down the strangling sensation in her throat. Weeds brushed against her legs and drooping branches of the cedar trees touched her on the head and shoulders. When the coughing came again, Juanita leaned weakly against the rough trunk of a tree, struggling to get her breath. She tried to clear her throat, but a scratchy feeling remained. Luciano began to pound her on the back. The scratchy substance was in her mouth. She spit into the handkerchief.

Luciano's eyes narrowed and his lips closed into a thin, hard line when she held out the handkerchief. Flecks of blood dotted the white cloth, and there among the mucus were three thin wedges of wood. The texture of wood was unmistakable, even though each wedge was no wider than one-eighth of an inch.

Rosita had climbed out of the car and was clinging to Juanita's skirt. "What is it, Mama? What is it?" she asked.

Luciano spoke to her gently and told her to get back into the car. When he turned to Juanita, his face seemed drawn, older.

"It's one thing when the *ma-itso* gets after me, but it's another when they start working on you."

Juanita's eyes widened. "But Lu, this needn't be *ma-itso*."

The sun rays were slanting from the west through the trees, and a wind had risen to rustle the weeds and grass, to scrape one tree branch against another.

"Were any of Wounded Head's family near you when you were eating?"

Juanita shook her head. "I had only coffee and a small bowl of stew. Mrs. Juan Platero passed those to me."

"One way they work is to make pieces of wood or glass or turquoise beads lodge in your body; then they don't have to be near you when it happens."

Juanita remembered hearing the old grandfather tell of how members of the Wolf Clan sometimes sang over an effigy of their intended victim until a turquoise bead lying nearby rose from the ground and lodged in the effigy. At the same time another bead pierced the real body of the victim and afterward the person died. That story could have been embellished by the imaginations of a superstitious people. But there was nothing impossible about a member of the clan dropping foreign particles into food when there was an opportunity. Yet, did Wounded Head's wife have the opportunity and wouldn't those pieces of wood have been noticeable in the stew?

"This is certainly *ma-itso*," Luciano murmured. "What else could it be?"

Juanita sat down on the running board of the car. She was exhausted from coughing; her eyes were moist. She put one hand to the dark coil of her hair, placing the pins more securely. "I don't know," she said slowly.

Her husband stood beside her, looking down at her gravely; his arms hung limply at his sides. "I was selfish to bring you out here just because I was lonely for this country and my people. I let you talk me into it because I wanted to come home so badly. I knew then that it was no place for you. And now you're exposed to a danger from which I can't protect you."

Juanita got into the car. She touched her husband's arm as he slid under the steering wheel. "You mustn't think that way, Lu."

They rode home silently except when Juanita tried to answer Rosita's questions and quiet her. Luciano was silent all through the evening meal. Finally he pushed his chair back from the table, not looking at Juanita when he spoke.

"It isn't too late to go back to California. I could get a job there. You'd be safe from things like this."

Juanita answered him gently. She'd recovered from the coughing and had time to think things over. "Let's not be foolish, Lu; this is where we want to be. We came to New Mexico because we thought there was a better chance for happiness here; and I still think there is. As for *ma-itso*, I'm no more afraid now than I ever was." She tilted her chin at a determined angle. "If they were working on me, they didn't succeed, did they?"

Juanita knew when she saw her mother-in-law at the door, holding Bijo by the hand and carrying little Keetso against her shoulder, that Il-tha-bah was dead. She called Lu from his forge in the garage. The spring-wagon in which Shimah had arrived was disappearing down the road; the driver had left Shimah's small blanket bundle on the doorstep.

Luciano picked up the bundle and held the door while his mother took the children into the living room. After Shimah had unwrapped Keetso and laid him on the couch beside her, she sat back smoothing her skirt with her hands. She looked thinner and more tired than Juanita had ever seen her.

Shimah began to cry softly, shaking her head slowly as she told them of the different Sings and singers they'd had for her daughter. Luciano sat down beside her. She leaned toward him, sobbing against his shoulder. Nothing she could do, nothing the Medicine Man could do, had helped Il-tha-bah.

Luciano held his mother gently, his long brown fingers clasping her frail shoulders. His eyes were dark and troubled. He had known it might end like this, and nothing he could have done or said would have stopped it. His eyes filled with tears. Juanita turned her face away.

Rosita was bewildered by her grandmother's grief and by the subdued manner of her playmate; Bijo had always played with her before. She brought out one after another of her toys—the set of blocks, the red wagon. She offered her teddy bear to Bijo. But Bijo only shook her head and moved closer to her grandmother, twisting her fingers in the full long skirt.

"Have you eaten today?" Juanita asked her mother-in-law.

She hadn't. The man with whom they rode started early and there was no time to cook anything. Juanita went into the kitchen. Hot coffee would be most important. Perhaps Shimah and Bijo would eat scrambled eggs and toast if she fixed it. She warmed milk with a little Karo syrup for Keetso.

Seated at the table, sipping her coffee slowly, Shimah asked her son if there would be someone at the Agency driving toward Albuquerque.

"But won't you stay with us for a while and rest?"

Shimah shook her head. "I've been away too long already." She was anxious to get back to Cañoncito. The children would stay there with her until Il-tha-bah's husband was able to care for one or both of them. Luciano was certain there would be a car or truck going from the Agency toward Albuquerque in the next few days. Perhaps for a little money he could get the driver to make the extra trip to Cañoncito.

The morning that Shimah was leaving, Juanita stood in the doorway holding the baby and trying to keep Rosita back out of the wind. Shimah first put her bundle into the truck, then Bijo, straightening her skirts as she got in herself and arranging her Pendleton over her head before taking baby Keetso from Luciano. As the truck started, Shimah raised one hand sadly toward Juanita and the children.

Luciano stood beside the road until the truck was out of sight. There was no way of knowing when they'd see Shimah again.

FIFTEEN
The Wheeler-Howard Bill

Summer haze veiled the mesas. Small winds moved the white clouds lazily and rustled through the seed-tipped grass. The corn plants stood close together, leaves touching—broad leaves of deep and vibrant green. Luciano knelt, pulling weeds and working the earth into mounds at the base of the corn stalks. The squash plants were beginning to vine and send forth delicate green tendrils. Juanita stopped long enough from weeding to dislodge the tendrils along the walk and direct the squash vines back among the corn.

As Lu stood up to rest his shoulders, he turned his head toward the sound of a motor. "Here comes the mail truck; I'll run down and see if we have any letters."

When he came back from the post office he was holding up a long white, envelope for Juanita to see. "We're going to have visitors."

"Who and when?" Juanita stood up, dusted her hands together, and wiped perspiration from her forehead with the back of one hand.

"Standing Bear and Sunflower are stopping on their way from the Sioux country. They should be here sometime this week."

"The carpenters got through with us just in time, didn't they?"

The spring program of paint and repair at the Agency had included their house. With the remodeling, the problem of visiting relatives was solved. Remembering the rock houses near Shimah's hoghan where relatives often stayed, Juanita and Lu had drawn simple plans which shut off the long room, which was the kitchen, from the rest of the house. The dining room was divided into a small, compact kitchen and a dinette.

This new arrangement simplified housekeeping for Juanita and made it easier to look after Rosita and Toni.

The long room was still equipped with stove and sink, along with long table and benches. Some folding cots from the commissary had been added. On Mondays it was the laundry room, but at all times it was at the disposal of relatives who came to Crown Point. It gave them a place to cook and sleep, with ample space and shelter. Juanita might bring in some canned tomatoes or a can of fruit to add to a meal the relatives had prepared. But no longer were relatives a problem—whole families to be cooked for whether or not she and Lu could spare the supplies; whole families staying several days, sleeping on the living room floor. Relatives had been their greatest problem—not the immediate family, but distant relatives. There were so many of them, and some were always coming to the Agency.

The newly remodeled three rooms were clean and bright with paint. Pictures, bows and arrows, and the feather dance bustle had been replaced on the wall and Navajo rugs re-spread on the floor. The blue chimayo draped across the gate-legged table matched the deep blue and cream curtains at the windows. Over the bookcases hung two round, shallow medicine baskets which Lorencito had given them.

When Standing Bear and his niece arrived, the old chief did not sit down at first but walked about the room. As always, the dignity and erectness of his body seemed to give him added height. His dark hair was close-clipped and shot through with gray. His wise, dark eyes had a patient, tired expression. Yet there was no hint that his years were approaching seventy-five. The handsomeness and vigor of his youth were still strongly marked upon his face and body.

He turned to Juanita and Lu. "Everything looks good. Both of you look good. You did right coming here."

Standing Bear picked up Tonita from the studio couch. "It's been a long time since I held a baby." He sat down, resting her in the crook of his arm and drew a large gold watch from his pocket to show her. Rosita edged from her father's side to better look at the old chief. Soon she was standing by his chair, her hands in the pockets of her starched print dress, her eyes round and serious.

Sunflower laughed softly. "It will be worth hearing what Chief tells when we get home, especially when he talks with the ones who predicted a quick retreat from the reservation for you." Sunflower was small and dark, her voice and gestures reflected with the same calm that lay deep in her eyes and across her face.

"Sometimes it was discouraging when we first came here," Juanita said.

Standing Bear looked at Luciano. "I know about that. When I came back from school I tried to live on the reservation; after the Buffalo Bill Show I tried again. It wasn't easy."

Juanita had often heard the chief tell of how it was necessary to ask the agent's permission for everything and how he had finally gone to Washington and demanded his citizenship papers so that he would be free to come and go as he pleased. The policy of the government toward the Indians had changed since then. But men and women like Standing Bear and Sunflower were working for more drastic changes.

Knowing Standing Bear's appreciation of old things, Luciano brought the conch belt to show him. The chief fingered the heavy hand-tooled conches. "It took someone a long time to make this." He handed it to Sunflower.

Luciano told him of the hard winter and of the still desperate condition of many Navajo families. "How did you find the Sioux?"

"My people have been poor for a long time; now they are poorer." Sadness altered Standing Bear's face.

"So many of the old people are dying," his niece continued, "bad water, lack of food, and their spirit is broken. We know, we talked to some of them for the last time."

Luciano told of the recent beef rationing—how the government had bought up surplus stock from the ranches, butchered the animals, and distributed the meat from the Agency commissary. For a few days Crown Point had been full of Navajos. Old women, young women, and even small children carried away meat wrapped in flour sacks. Men and women rode on horseback with quarters of beef behind the saddles. The country around the Agency had been dotted with their camps—brush shelters and makeshift tents beside covered wagons, where whole families were busy cutting meat and hanging the strips in the sun so that it could be packed away for the journey home.

"Rations help at a time like this," Standing Bear nodded. "But rations don't solve the problem. The problem will never be solved until the government helps the Indian to help himself."

The discussion continued, becoming more general when Sunflower told of the Indian legislation before Congress: a bill which was supposed to restore land, religious liberty, and civil rights to the Indians. The conversation became personal again when Standing Bear asked Lu about the job he'd held at the school.

Juanita went into the kitchen to prepare lunch. Sunflower followed her. "Don't go to any trouble for us, Juanita, because we can't stay."

"Can't stay! You mean after four years you aren't going to spend a few days with us?"

Sunflower smiled and shook her head. "You know how Chief is when he makes up his mind about anything. We've enough material for another book and several articles. He wants to get started on them. Lately, he's been worrying about getting old and not being able to accomplish all he wants to."

When their visitors had gone, Luciano came into the kitchen where Juanita was washing dishes.

"Standing Bear hasn't changed, has he?"

Juanita shook her head.

"Some of the things he said started me thinking. Of course, I could never write or lecture, but if an old man like Standing Bear can do all he does, surely there's something that one Navajo can do to help his people."

The middle of summer, news came about a big meeting. All the Navajos around Crown Point were invited. There was to be a big barbecue and then some men from the government would talk.

People began arriving at the Agency before the day of the meeting. It seemed to Juanita that Crown Point had never been so full of high-wheeled spring-wagons and white-topped covered wagons. Black-eyed women in full, swinging skirts; babies riding securely in the folds of bright Pendletons; tall old men with their long hair tied back with yarn; short old men with graying wisps of mustaches; laughing young men with broad hats tilted, and faded silk handkerchiefs knotted about their throats. They came in trucks, in cars and on horseback. Men brought their whole families, and soon the open country around the Agency was dotted with their camps. The cook-fires at these camps lit the night like a thousand twinkling stars.

Much preparation had been made to feed these people. Loaves of bread and trays of cookies were baked at the school bakery. Potatoes and stewed vegetables were prepared in the school kitchen. A distributing point for the food was set up on the north side of the road, where the arroyo curved; the barbecue pits were here, and mutton and beef and goat were roasting slowly. All afternoon, men and women and children came to get paper plates heaped with food, steaming cups of coffee, and large, round sugar cookies. In the evening they gathered in the school auditorium to hear the speeches.

After that day there was a strange new phrase introduced into the talk around the campfires at Chapter meetings and at the other public meetings held at the Agency. The phrase "Wheeler-Howard" stood out, oddly accented from the even flow of Navajo words. No one knew for certain what this "Wheeler-Howard" bill was about. It was new; it meant great changes and greater prosperity for the Navajos and all Indians. The government men said so.

These men read long sentences from a paper and the interpreters tried to change the long sentences into Navajo. But no one was quite sure what the paper said. Some of the words might mean one thing and they might mean another. For many of the terms there were no words or combinations of words in Navajo. So Juanita and Lu were not surprised when their relatives began to stop them and ask, "What is this Wheeler-Howard paper? Do you understand it?"

Lorencito and father-in-law sat on one side of the long table drinking coffee. Juanita put a pot of fresh coffee in the center of the table and set out cups and spoons for Juan Platero, his wife, and some of their family who had just arrived.

Luciano turned to Juanita. "Lorencito says he talked to one of the men who interpreted at the big meeting. The interpreter wasn't even sure what the paper said in English."

Juanita was not surprised. She and Lu been there and heard the speakers read directly from the Wheeler-Howard bill. They had obtained a copy of the bill. Each provision was stated in legal phrases. They had studied the bill over and over and there were still certain passages not clear to them.

"What do they mean about the land?" Juan Platero asked.

Luciano explained how in the past on many reservations small parcels of land had been allotted to the Indians, and the rest declared surplus and thrown open to white settlers, so the amount of Indian land had been decreasing, while in most cases the Indian population had increased. Now the government wanted to add more land to the reservations where it was needed by restoring the surplus land or using other land to take its place.

Mrs. Juan Platero and her relatives nodded over this. More land to graze sheep meant more sheep.

Luciano had difficulty explaining the soil conservation program. It took many words to convey some of the English words: stock reduction to stop overgrazing; government measures to improve the breed of sheep and horses; the development of a better water supply by improving springs, building dams and reservoirs, drilling wells, and undertaking irrigation projects—all this so the Navajo would have more water for larger fields.

Lorencito's father-in-law rolled a cigarette and lit it, squinting his eyes as he watched Luciano through the smoke. "That paper said something about jobs for us and pay from the government."

The way Juanita understood it, most of these jobs would be created by the development of the water supply and the improvement of roads on the reservation, as well as by the building of more day schools. She used the blade of the kitchen knife to open another can of cream. The relatives were still drinking coffee as they discussed what had been explained to them.

Luciano had explained only the parts of the bill which would most affect the Navajos. There were many other provisions in the new plan about self-government, incorporation for business purposes, civil liberties, social services, and increased control of tribes over themselves and their own resources. Eventually government supervision would no longer be necessary. But the provisions about jobs and land and water seemed to be the immediate need of the Navajo families Juanita and Lu knew.

Lorencito smiled a little and pulled at his ear when his father-in-law began to talk again. What did Luciano think of these changes? Were they just so many promises like those the government had made before?

Luciano did not answer quickly. He told his relatives first that he did not like to advise them because they were much older than he; they knew more about conditions in the Navajo country than he did. What the government promised now seemed to be a way for the Navajos to help themselves. This Wheeler-Howard bill did not affect a community unless the people of that community voted for it.

Finally, Lu decided, "If the paper says all that I believe it says, I'm going to vote for it."

The community day school program was separate from the Wheeler-Howard bill. Some day schools had already been built; the new administration would build more. The theory of the day school program appealed to both Juanita and Luciano. Children could go to school without being separated for months, sometimes years at a time, from their families. They could learn the new without losing the old.

When the people of Cañoncito asked for a day school, Mr. Stacher sent Luciano with the superintendent of the Crown Point school to make a survey of the number of school-age children.

It was while he was gone that the idea came to Juanita. "Why not?" she asked herself. Surely there will be jobs connected with a day school that Lu and I can hold. She didn't want to think of it too much, to plan on it. After the long hours and varied responsibilities of an assistant disciplinarian's job, Lu might not want to be connected with a school again. Yet the thoughts would not leave her mind. We could have jobs, we could earn a living, and still be where we want to be—in Cañoncito.

On the day when Lu was to return home, Juanita was scarcely aware of doing her housework. She dressed the girls and gave them their breakfast, thinking: Shimah could see her granddaughters every day then. As her thoughts continued she brought the rugs and blankets in from the morning airing on the clothesline. In a year or so we could save enough money to build a home on Lu's land. She began to fold the sheets and towels which were washed the day before and sprinkle down their clothes for ironing: We could have our own horses, Lu could plant as large a field as he wanted to in springtime, and perhaps, connected with a school, we could at last be of some help to Lu's people.

The house was in order, and Rosita had been changed from coveralls to a print dress for the afternoon. Juanita had not quite finished at the ironing board in the long room when Lu came home. Rosita ran out to meet him; he lifted her to his shoulder as he walked to the door. Juanita knew when she saw him that he was not the same. He kissed her lightly, and asked what had happened while he was gone from the Agency. Rosita wanted to know if he had seen Bijo. He smiled as he answered her but his dark eyes remained sober—staring at far off things.

Juanita didn't question him. He's still seeing Walking Around Mountain, blue with distance, and the cottonwoods around the spring; he's still seeing Des Jin, mysterious and brooding, all rose and purple in the evening.

Luciano finally spoke of his trip home. He straddled a kitchen chair, resting his elbows on the back of it. "I'd forgotten how red the earth is around my grandfather's hoghan."

Juanita waited, seeming to fix her attention on the buttons of the shirt she was ironing.

"He didn't know me this time until I talked to him."

Juanita rested the iron on end. "He didn't know you?"

"He's gone blind. Someone has to lead him."

"Can't anything be done?"

"Perhaps if I were home he'd let me take him to the doctor in Albuquerque."

Blind. . .and she'd looked forward to the day when the old grandfather would see Rosita and Toni. She'd pictured him holding them at arm's length and searching their long brown eyes, their straight black hair, their sturdy bodies for resemblance to his grandson. "Mr. Stacher might let you have a few days off to take him in to Albuquerque."

"It would take more than a few days. Old people like my grandfather can't be hurried. I'd first have to convince him to go with me."

Juanita hung the shirt on a hanger, buttoning the three top buttons. She smoothed the collar down and hooked the hanger over the small line stretched across the end of the room. She was so anxious to tell Lu what she'd been thinking. She was even prepared for his probable observation that there was the small matter of getting the jobs first. She'd thought of that when the idea of jobs in the new day school had first occurred to her. But getting the jobs seemed far from impossible when she could see so clearly what going home to Cañoncito would mean. "So many things would be better if we lived there instead of here," she began.

Lu ran his fingers through Toni's hair as she leaned against him. His eyes were still shadowed with the faraway look, as though he hadn't heard what his wife was saying.

"I thought a little bit about this before I went on that trip, and I've been thinking all the time I was away. Why can't I get a job in that new day school?"

They went to see Mr. Stacher. He told them that the government was establishing offices in Gallup. A woman who had been successfully connected with other education projects would interview applicants for positions in the day schools.

"We'd better dress up for this," Luciano told her as they got ready for the trip to Gallup. He polished his black shoes and brushed the dark suit. As he set his Stetson on at a conservative angle he asked, "What did Skinner say when you offered to trade our girls for her Ford today?"

"She just laughed and handed me the car keys." Juanita slipped the dark red jersey blouse carefully over her head and tucked it into the belt of the black pleated skirt. "Will you get my coat while you're near the closet, Lu?" A dash of powder on her nose, and lipstick toned down a little more—"I'm ready. Are you?"

They didn't talk much on the way to Gallup. The interview ahead meant so much. And they'd talked already, over and over, about the things they'd do when they returned to Cañoncito. They smiled at each other sideways as they entered the building and then appeared serious and composed when they took their places in the line in the hallway.

They stood in the hallway a long while, going over in their minds all the answers to possible questions they might be asked, looking at the people who came out of the office and the ones who waited to go in, but not looking at each other. They stood long enough to get a nervous, clammy feeling, and then the couple ahead of them went into the office and they were next outside the propped-open door.

The sound of voices carried out into the hall plainly—the sharp business-like tones of a woman's questions, the soft, hesitant answers. Then that couple came out and Juanita and Luciano went in.

The woman behind the long table was absorbed in a picture spread out on the table. From the flat look of the figures, Juanita guessed it to be the work of an Indian artist. She looked around her. The office was bare of all furniture except for the table, a chair behind it, and a make-shift stand to hold a bulletin board. It was evident that the office had been opened in a hurry and was only temporary.

The woman looked up suddenly. "Names?" She was small and stout and bristling with efficiency.

"Occupational experience."

Juanita heard Lu's stilted answers and her own. She was conscious of the open door.

"Education."

Their answers seemed inadequate, once spoken. Juanita felt a desire to interrupt the routine questions and tell the woman at the table that they'd successfully held jobs at the Agency although they'd had no previous experience. They could certainly adapt themselves to this job, but there was no opportunity to break through the formality of the interview.

"You'll be notified if your applications are accepted."

They were obviously dismissed. The woman was again absorbed in the picture on the table. Luciano took a step forward. Juanita looked down at the Stetson in his hand that he'd placed so confidently on his head a few hours before. She couldn't look at his face and see the disappointment she knew was in his eyes.

"Our applications are only for the day school at Cañoncito. That's my home, my people live there." He started to say more.

The woman made a notation on their papers. "We'd rather not place Indian assistants in their own community. It might make it difficult for them to remain impartial." She rapped the edges of a stack of papers on the table top and smiled impersonally. "But you'll get notifications if you're appointed."

Juanita and Lu turned toward the open door. They felt helpless. They walked down the hallway, and out to the street. And that was all.

Then came the waiting—weeks of it with no word. Mr. Stacher received no word either. He was sympathetic. He'd like to see them get jobs in Cañoncito. He'd sent good recommendations for both of them, but hiring the day school personnel was out of his hands.

And each day the Cañoncito day school came nearer to completion.

"There's another way," Juanita told her husband. "It's often said that the way to be heard is to go straight to the boss."

Somehow it was easier to write to Commissioner Collier than they had thought. They listed the information they'd given at the interview and then wrote other things about adapting themselves to new jobs at the Agency, wanting to work where Lu's home was, and wanting to help Lu's people.

The waiting this time wasn't so long. Mr. Stacher sent for them. "Your appointments to the Cañoncito day school came today and with them a letter from John Collier."

Luciano shifted his weight from one foot to the other. "We wrote to him . . . after we waited so long and didn't hear anything."

"Can't see that it hurt," Mr. Stacher chuckled. "Until the teacher is appointed to the school this September, Luciano, you'll have to take full charge."

SIXTEEN
Cañoncito Day School

Cañoncito in the early spring . . . the first pale green of grass on distant slopes, on rolling flat land . . . snow not yet melted from the north banks of the arroyos . . . sleek brown hawks riding the wind . . . the yellow-green new growth of juniper . . . Blue Clay Gap sharply outlined in the western stretch of mesas . . . the orange wing-flash of flickers.

Each morning flung its challenge to ride out horseback, to race along sandy stream beds, to explore the canyons—a challenge that Juanita and Luciano could not accept. There was much work to getting settled at the day school.

Luciano took great pride in his responsibility. The long, low building of native stone, nestled in the shelter of the low mesas that adjoined his mother's pastureland, was almost finished. Before the workman had completed the finish work inside the building, he and Hoskey, the Navajo assistant, were cleaning and leveling off the school grounds. Government officials came at all hours to inspect the building and leave instructions. The first equipment and supplies began to arrive.

One of the men of the community, Frank Woods, a tall, young Navajo with long legs, narrow hips, and a good-looking face, rode to the school to talk with Luciano.

"I think this day school is a good thing. I want to send my children here," he told him. "And I want to do some work around this place to help you."

Luciano explained that he did not have the authority to hire any more help.

"You mean pay me?" Frank settled back in the saddle. "I didn't come for that kind of work. This school is a good thing. I want to help without pay."

After that there were Luciano, Frank, and Hoskey working around the school. The windows had to be scraped and washed and the rooms cleaned as the workmen finished. There was water to be hauled from the spring, wood to be brought from the mesas and chopped into lengths for the stoves. Sometimes while the three young men worked, the building resounded with their high, clear voices blended in song.

Shimah came over from the hoghan to help her daughter-in-law, because Juanita was very busy watching the two girls and attempting to achieve some order out of their furniture and belongings piled into the three-room apartment which adjoined the day school. Shimah wandered down the long hall which connected the kitchen and the living room murmuring *"nah-zhun, nah-zhun."* She peeked into the bedroom, which opened off the center of the hall, and into the bathroom beside the bedroom. For a long time she stood admiring the gleaming white toilet, washbowl, and shower stall. The living quarters had been well planned with plenty of deep-silled windows, thick, smooth plastered walls, and ceilings supported with rough-hewn vigas.

When the kitchen cupboards above and below the sink had been lined with paper, Shimah handed dishes, cooking utensils, and supplies to Juanita from the packing boxes.

"You know Juan Chavez," Shimah stated rather than questioned.

Juanita nodded.

"He had to separate from one of his wives. The two women couldn't get along."

"Which wife left?"

"The one he took last. Juan added many sheep to her flock."

"They had a little boy, didn't they?"

"Yes. He will stay sometimes with his father, sometimes with his mother." Shimah made a dividing motion with her hands. Then she held the chair steady while Juanita stepped up to hang blue and white gingham curtains at the windows.

With all of the furniture in it, the kitchen still looked spacious. The woodstove and large water tank occupied one wall. The breakfast table and chairs were against the opposite wall. Juanita searched through the box of linens until she found a blue cloth to spread on the table. Shimah helped Juanita shove the furniture around in the long, narrow bedroom. This would be the girls' room; they were getting old enough to have a room of their own. With the low dresser against one wall and the bed beneath the window, the alcove was left for doll furniture and toys.

That night Luciano pretended to grumble because his daughters had deprived him of a bedroom. But after a few nights of lying on the studio couch in the living room while the fire burned lower and lower on the grate, he gave up grumbling and said, "There's nothing like an open fire, is there?"

The fireplace was made of rough stone; they'd spread a Navajo rug in front of it. Here was where they sat almost every evening.

One evening when Juanita was trying to get the last of the wall decorations hung in the living room, Luciano decided that he didn't quite like the furniture arrangement. He moved the bookcases from one wall to another until they satisfied him best on each side of a deep-silled window.

"Lu, if you aren't careful you'll wake the girls," Juanita cautioned him.

He began to experiment with the leaves of the gate-leg table until the chimayo draped over it gave just the right effect. He took Juanita's Pendleton down from the closet shelf and spread it across the studio couch. Then he sat back on the cedar chest and shook his head provokingly as Juanita hung pictures on the wall.

"Here," she turned and handed him the woven plaques. "You try some of your ideas."

When Lu had finished in the living room, he saved the bows and arrows and some of the pictures for the walls of the long hallway.

"We certainly have accumulated a lot since we've been married."

"I guess two children and two good jobs are accomplishments," he teased.

"We have almost everything we planned on having when we came here."

"Everything except some good horses and a house upon our own land. Of course this place will do for a while." He gestured about him.

"But for the first time, everything we want is within reach."

Luciano returned the chair to the kitchen. Juanita could hear him opening cupboard doors. Finally he called, "Is there anything to eat?"

"There's bread and butter and jam."

With a slice of bread smeared with jam held solemnly in one hand, Luciano knelt before the fireplace to spread the coals and add another chunk of wood. "Suppose we'd listened to all the people who said we couldn't make it here. We'd still be in Hollywood."

"Probably." Juanita sat down on the rug beside her husband. "But we aren't."

They sat silently, looking into the fire. Lu finished his slice of bread, took the poker, and rolled the chunk of wood farther back on the grate.

After a while, he turned to face her, looking at her a long time before he spoke. "Have these years out here been too hard for you?"

Juanita's mind skimmed lightly over the short rations of that first winter, the months at Mrs. Pentz's, the deluge of relatives at Crown Point, her illness after Tonita's birth. She shook her head slowly. "No harder than they've been for you." She drew her knees up, linking her fingers over them. "I've often thought of this but never said it. It couldn't have been easy for you to bring a strange wife among your people."

Luciano's eyelids closed half way, lazily, his lips lengthened into a smile. "It wasn't."

Juanita and Luciano were riding to Juan Chavez's. Now that Lupe, Luciano's younger sister, was taking care of the girls, Juanita had more time with her husband. When Lupe had come home on vacation from Santa Fe school, it was the first time she and Juanita had met, but they became friends almost at once. Lupe was pretty and gay. She wore her hair in a long bob, the ends turned under; her eyes were like Luciano's, large and dark and oftentimes alight with mischief. She seemed always to have time to play games with Rosita and Toni.

Juanita soon discovered that Lupe's affection for her older brother amounted to a sort of hero worship. With Lu's encouragement she had stayed in school at Santa Fe; she wanted to graduate and then study to be a nurse or teacher. "But when I first went to Santa Fe, I didn't like it," she told Juanita. "I wouldn't stay until they sent Luciano from the school in Albuquerque for a year. After that I was all right."

It was difficult for Lupe to live at the hoghan; there was no way to wash or iron her clothes. "Juanita, ask my brother to let me stay here with you," she had suggested. "If you asked it would be better, and I'll be lots of help this summer. I'll take care of the girls for you."

Juanita and Luciano tied their horses to Juan Chavez's corral fence and walked to the brush shelter where the family sat. The shelter was built to one side of the hoghan, with the opening on the north. Almost even with the cedar post beside the opening was a circular fire pit with three or four blackened automobile hubs among the ashes on which to set pots and pans.

After gravely shaking hands, Juan Chavez and his wife made a place for their guests on the sheep pelts inside the shelter. Mrs. Chavez was a tall woman; her face and figure were angular, suggesting endurance and strength. This was the wife who had won out. Juanita couldn't help thinking of what her mother-in-law had told her.

Mrs. Chavez rose quietly and went into the hoghan. When she returned, she carried an oblong white melon, which she split into sections and offered to her guests. Juanita leaned far forward as she bit into the ripe white center. The melon tasted cool and sweet. She looked around her in the shelter. The beginning of a rug was on the loom, a pleasing

combination of deep red and old gold yarn. It evidently was a
double weave from the number of healds in the warp. A bag
of wool and a spindle lay where they'd last been used, beside
the sheep pelts in front of the loom. In one corner, the
children were dividing the remaining sections of the melon.
There were two boys, perhaps three, of school age.

The school-age children were the purpose of this visit. For
several days, Luciano and Frank and Hoskey had been riding
or walking to the scattered hoghans in the area to talk with
the families about the school and to enroll as many children
as each family would send. It was sometimes impossible to
enroll all the children of school age from one family. Luciano
had told Juanita of some of the excuses the families gave: this
boy was needed to herd the sheep, that boy must stay home
to bring in the horses and take them to water, this girl was
becoming a good weaver.

But Luciano and his host were not talking about the school
yet. Lu was inquiring what the other man had planted in his
fields. Juan Chavez had a reputation in the community for
being industrious. He planted large fields and had a row of
good peach trees. As he answered Luciano, his voice was low
and quiet, his slender face was smiling and friendly, his
almost-black eyes were bright with humor. Then he pointed
with his lips to a large cloud of dust in the distance. "That's
the Lagunas coming home with their sheep. Somewhere north
of here they have a lambing place. They take the flocks up in
early spring, but can't bring them back until the lambs are
old enough to travel that distance. We always let them cross
our land; it's shorter."

While the family watched the flock of sheep, the cloud of dust
moving nearer, Luciano asked Juan Chavez if he'd thought
about sending his children to the new school. Mrs. Chavez
reached for the spindle and the bag of wool, raising her right
knee slightly as she spun the spindle against her thigh. Juan
rubbed his fingers against his chin. The two older boys had
been going to boarding school; with one wife gone, he'd
thought about keeping one of the boys home from school this
year to help around the place. The youngest boy was too
small and so were the two girls. "What about this school?
There's more I'd like to know about it."

Luciano told him that there would be a school bus to pick up
the children at the hoghans each morning. They would learn

to speak and write English, and they would learn how to figure with money and numbers. At noon they would get a hot lunch in the dining room. The older boys would be taught silversmithing, carpentry, and new things about farming and raising sheep. The older girls would be taught sewing, cooking, washing, and ironing and mending. The school bus would bring them home in the afternoon. They would be home on Saturday and Sunday. Children could go to school and still be of some help around the hoghan.

As Luciano talked, the smallest boy edged closer to Juan Chavez's wife. He must be the one who stayed here even though his mother had moved away.

"He wants to know if he can go to that school you tell about."

"He may be too little. How old is he?"

"About five years."

"We could try him out and see how he keeps up with the older ones."

Mrs. Chavez spoke briefly to the little boy. He nodded as she talked and ran back with the other children.

"We want the parents to come to the school, too," Luciano told the Chavezes. "There'll be sewing machines for the women to use, and tools in the shop when the men want to make something or to repair a plow or a wagon."

Juan Chavez sat quietly while Luciano spoke, but when Juanita and her husband rose to leave, he said, "You can write down the two older boys, and the little one."

Halfway to the horses, the smallest boy came running after Juanita and Luciano. Mrs. Chavez called him back, and he began to cry.

"You said I could go. You told them I could go to that school." He dug his fists hard against his eyes.

Luciano bent down, sitting against his heels, and pulled the little boy to him. "No school today, little brother. You wait here. When it's the day for going to school, I'll ride over and tell you."

The time was near when Luciano would open the day school for the summer trial term. Preparations for the opening continued each day. The two classrooms were put into order and stands were made for temporary blackboards. Chalk and erasers, books, and pencils and paper were stacked in the classroom cupboards. The sewing machines were uncrated and set beneath the windows of the large dining room. The long oak tables and benches were wiped off with a damp cloth and moved toward the sides of the room, leaving a wide aisle down the center.

When the kerosene refrigerator arrived, it took Lu and Hoskey and the man on the truck to unload it and set it up. Lu stood by with the instruction paper in his hand, with deep wrinkles across his forehead as the man explained how to start and keep the refrigerator working.

The supply closet in the hall outside the dining room was stacked high with bolts of material for school dresses and toweling, boxes of thread, bar soap and soap powder, and bottles of disinfectant. Juanita spent many hours at the sewing machine, hemming bath towels and tea towels and making aprons of heavy blue and white striped material to wear in the kitchen. Sometimes her sister-in-law Yee-ke-nes-bah came to help her. Yee-ke-nes-bah, who had been no older than Lupe when Juanita first saw her, was quite a settled lady now with a husband and her own flock of sheep. She was expecting her first baby in two months or so; perhaps that accounted for the new poise she had acquired and the placid look on her face and in her eyes.

Juanita was glad for companionship on the afternoons when Luciano went down to his mother's pastureland to cultivate the corn he'd planted. Together, Juanita and her sister-in-law arranged the big kettles, bread pans, and heavy iron skillets in the cupboards. Yee-ke-nes-bah marveled at the size of the cans of vegetables and fruit they stacked on the pantry shelves, at the number of sacks of flour and sugar it took to fill the bins, and at the size of the sacks of rice, beans, and potatoes. The government was supplying plenty of food for the anticipated enrollment of forty children.

The cement floor had been mopped and shower curtains hung in the boys' lavatory; Luciano was setting up the hand washing machine in the laundry room adjoining the girls' lavatory. Rows of combs and toothbrushes hung in cases awaiting name tags. Everything was ready for the opening of school. When an Agency truck stopped in front of the building and the driver brought in the heavy square bundle, Juanita wondered what new addition to their supplies this might be. She cut the cord and spread the heavy wrapping paper open on one of the long tables in the dining room. Then she began to laugh. There were stacks of forms and inventory lists which the school housekeeper must fill out. Ruled pads for itemizing the menus for each day, number of cans of food used, fresh supplies, amount of yards of material used and for what purpose, the number of adults each week using the facilities. Every item, every action, must be accounted for.

Luciano came from the laundry room to investigate the cause of Juanita's sudden merriment. Still laughing, she leaned back against the table holding up one of the forms for him to see. "And I've been thinking all this time that my bookkeeping might get rusty."

It was Sunday, and Lu brought the horses down from his mother's. The buckskin had fattened with early summer grass and not enough work. An old horse that Lu called Pete stood sleepily in the sun, flicking his tail across his brown rump when too many flies settled there.

"Don't let Pete fool you," Luciano told her. "He's a good horse and fast, but you have to let him know you mean business."

Rosita and Toni stood at the corner of the day school with Lupe and watched them ride away. Pete ambled behind the buckskin. Juanita watched Lu for a moment, the relaxed easy set of his shoulders, the unconcerned thrust of his boot tips into the stirrups. . .a young man in a blue shirt, Levis, and an old Stetson. . .a young man happy and at home on a horse. Pete stopped to nibble grass. Juanita broke a branch from a juniper and rapped him smartly along the flank. Pete broke into a trot until he was even with the buckskin, then dropped behind again. Luciano began to laugh. "You aren't being firm enough with him. Assert yourself."

Juanita dug her heels into his ribs and twirled her reins alongside his head; the horse quickened his pace to a trot and changed easily into a long bounding lope. As Pete passed the buckskin, Luciano reached out with the reins and stung him on the rump. The two horses were off across the open stretch of country.

"Shall we ride around Arrowhead Mesa?" Lu wheeled the buckskin sharply to the left. Pete wheeled at almost the same moment.

"There's something I've wanted to tell you," Lu began as they galloped side-by-side down the canyon. He pulled up suddenly on the buckskin. Pete planted all four feet and stopped too. Juanita slide back off his neck and settled herself again in the saddle.

"Doesn't Pete have what it takes when he gets going?" Lu's eyes were sparkling with merriment.

"Is that what you stopped to tell me?"

"No. I bought Pete from George Abeyta. He's the best horse for a rabbit chase in the country. A rabbit can't lose him, and when he stops, he stops on a dime."

Juanita rubbed her hip bone where she'd grazed the saddle horn. "I believe you."

They rode around Arrowhead Mesa.

"Let's ride on farther to Des Jin," Juanita suggested.

"The thunderheads are beginning to pile up. We might get caught in a shower."

"What's a little rain?" Juanita urged Pete ahead. "Anyway, these summer thunderstorms are beautiful."

The trail up the high mesa was steep and narrow. Several times they dismounted and walked the horses. Once on top, they could see all of Cañoncito. Each little canyon was outlined below them, winding between broken floors of tableland, opening out into rolling pasture, ending abruptly against high-ledged mesas. Even the paths of the arroyos could be traced. The low stone day school blended against rock of the same color. No hoghans could be seen, but patches of vivid green corn were clearly visible.

That distant rolling sound was thunder. Juanita watched fascinated as, far to their left, low flashes of light against dark clouds heralded a thunderstorm. Long dark cloud fingers reached toward the earth. Rain came like very thin gray veils slowly enveloping each mesa, each canyon. Juanita stood leaning against Luciano, lost in the beauty of the storm.

Lu shook her shoulder gently. "Look over this way. There's another storm coming and this will be on us."

One look at the black clouds massing behind them and Juanita picked up her horse's reins and lost no time in gaining the saddle. They were halfway down the side of Des Jin when the storm broke above them. Rain beat heavily on the trail and beat against their shoulders; wind and rain whipped their wet clothes against their bodies. The trail was slick with water.

"We'd better lead the horses down."

They dismounted on the narrow trail, walking cautiously over slippery rock in boots that squished water. They continued the descent from the mesa top; there was no place along the trail for shelter. The rain beat against Juanita's face; her clothes were heavy with it. The leather reins were slippery in her hand.

"This place ahead is a bad one," Lu called back. "Every man and horse for himself."

Juanita watched him lead the buckskin across the narrow shelf, which sloped dangerously to one side. He and the horse were almost lost from sight behind the wall of water that sprayed over the trail from the overhanging rocks. She paid out the reins until only the ends remained in her hand. Edging sideways along the narrow place until the reins were taut once more, she urged Pete to follow, pulling gently on him. Each time a hoof slipped, scraping upon the rock, she held her breath.

The remainder of the way was easier. At the bottom of the mesa, they mounted the horses and rode down the canyon, against the rain, across flat land, and past the ruins of Joe Platero's old trading post.

"The storm seems to be going our way," Luciano shouted at her.

214 The Winds Erase Your Footprints

When they came to the arroyo at the edge of the day school grounds, it was full from bank to bank with muddy, rushing water.

Luciano and Juanita rode along the arroyo until they came to a place where it began to widen. "Still think thunderstorms are beautiful?" he teased her.

Juanita nodded her head emphatically and urged her horse into the water.

SEVENTEEN
Celebration and Rodeo

The opening of the Cañoncito Day School was to be a day for feasting and celebration. There would be a rodeo, races, a chicken pull, plenty of mutton and coffee and bread, and that night a squaw dance. Word of the festival carried a long way.

When the day came, Cañoncito was the gathering place for scores of Pueblos, Spanish people, and visiting Navajos. Camps sprang up along the range of low hills. There were tents and lean-to brush shelters; here and there a Navajo family camped apart with its flock of sheep grazing beside the wagon. Strips of canvas and old blankets were stretched from the sides of cars and trucks to wind-gnarled cedars. Horses wandered and hobbled among the camps. The new road winding in front of the day school had been overhung by occasional clouds of dust since early morning. The school grounds were dark with the parked cars of numerous government officials and employees.

When Juanita opened the school kitchen that morning and laid the fire in the big woodstove, she was certain that she could manage the noon meal alone which was to be served to government officials and employees in the school dining room. After all, as housekeeper she'd soon be cooking for larger numbers every morning with very little help.

First thing, she issued the government supplies to the Cañoncito women who would be cooking for the visiting Indians. She issued flour, lard, coffee, sugar, salt, dried fruit, potatoes—everything for the feast but the meat; the people of the community had agreed to butcher their own sheep.

The fire in the big woodstove was making the kitchen uncomfortably warm, so Juanita opened more windows and the back door, and loosened the sash of the red-checked apron tied around her. But before she'd finished peeling potatoes and onions for the mutton stew, her thin blue dress was clinging to her back, and wisps of her dark hair curled damply at her temples.

Lupe came in with the girls, looking cool in a short-sleeved white pique dress; her dark hair was turned under where it fell about her shoulders, and was held back with a blue ribbon. "We've had showers and breakfast and straightened up the kitchen. Would it be all right to go out on the rodeo ground to watch the races?"

The girls were fresh and sweet in their starched print dresses. Juanita nodded, and wiping her hands on the dish cloth, she smoothed the dark bangs on their foreheads. "Don't let them stay out in the hot sun too long."

"May we eat with *shi-nelly*?" Rosita asked.

"I expect so."

Visitors began coming into the kitchen. There were Navajos, Pueblos, and government employees. They were ready to inspect the cupboards, the array of pots and pans, and to ask questions about the new school. Several times Mr. Stacher brought in groups of officials, and Juanita paused from kneading dough for the fried bread to acknowledge introductions. She opened the cupboards, the drawers, and the door to the large, amply-stocked pantry.

Lu appeared often at the kitchen door with old schoolmates and friends from Crown Point. His eyes were bright with the excitement of the celebration and his pride in the new school. When he came in with some Pueblo men with whom he'd gone to school, Juanita asked, "Do you know how many people will be eating in the dining room?"

"More than we expected. People in government cars are still arriving."

Juanita drew back the tea towel from the pan of dough. "I wonder if I've prepared enough."

"I doubt it. Why don't you ask Alice Watson to help you?"

She should have thought of that before. Alice was jolly and good help; she'd taken care of the girls a few times before Lupe came. Having been to school, she spoke English and could interpret for some of the Navajo families who came through the kitchen. Juanita crossed the grounds from the back of the school to the scattering of brush shelters where the women were cooking. The shelters were topped with new green brush; thin streamers of smoke spiraled upward from the juniper fires beside them.

Decidero Platero's wife and her daughter were lifting a washtub of potatoes and boiled mutton from the fire. Old Seraphina sat almost in the ashes of one of the fires, as she was slapping bread dough in her hands and laying the flattened pieces on a sheet of iron to bake. Juanita smiled to her and she spread her wrinkle-puckered mouth into a grin.

Some of the visiting Navajos and Pueblos had already begun to drift toward the shelters for coffee, bread, and a bowl of stew.

In one of the shelters, Frank Woods' mother and two other women were washing and drying dishes. Frank's mother stopped to empty the greasy water from the blackened kettle she was using for a dish pan. Several camp dogs were hanging around the shelter, waiting to pounce upon any scraps which would be thrown out. The women made shooing motions at them and muttered "coo-jhee," but the nondescript dogs ran only a little way, and then stopped to watch and wait.

Alice was stirring a kettle of dried apricots and raisins. "Sure, I'll come to help you," she told Juanita. She handed the long-handled spoon to a younger woman who was sitting in the shade, nursing her baby.

Laughter came from the school playground where the children were competing in games and foot races. A shout arose from the rodeo grounds beyond the school. Alice paused in the kitchen doorway to listen. "I'll bet somebody got the chicken." Alice was short and plump; she wore a full pink gingham dress rather than the heavy skirts and velveteen blouse of the other women. Her thick black hair was combed back into a club knot.

Juanita wished she could see the excitement. Even a chicken pull without a real chicken was exciting. Men were racing their ponies toward the place where a small sack of sand was half buried in the ground; they were getting into tangles, and spilling from the saddle as they leaned far over to snatch the sack. When someone was successful in pulling the sack from the ground, the race was only half over. One had to get it back to the starting line without any of the men wrestling it from him. What it must have been like in the days the old grandfather talked about: riding for a real chicken that dodged its head excitedly and squawked, and then racing back with it, trying to keep the other riders from pulling it apart.

Alice was mixing more dough; Juanita put lard in the skillet to heat. She took cups and saucers from the cupboard and silverware from the drawer to set the long tables in the dining room. The big coffee pots were on the stove, and the huge kettle of stew was bubbling. She stopped for a minute to fan her flushed face with her apron.

Luciano came in through the kitchen. "Tired?"

"No, not really; it's just the confusion and the excitement."

"The government couldn't have used a better way to sell this day school idea. Already the Navajos from other sections are asking about day schools. It keeps me busy having to explain everything to them."

The noon meal went smoothly. Juanita ladled the stew into bowls in the kitchen, and Alice carried them into the dining room. Two older girls who had been to boarding school helped pour the coffee and carry the hot, thick bread to the tables.

After lunch, with that much help, it didn't take long to clear the tables, wash the dishes, and restore the kitchen and dining room to order. Juanita went to look for Lupe and the girls on the school grounds.

Rosita and Toni didn't want to take a nap; there was too much going on outside. Regardless Juanita finally got them settled in the darkened bedroom. If they slept now, they could stay up late enough tonight to see part of the squaw dance.

By late afternoon, the noise of the celebration subsided. People gathered around scattered campfires for coffee and an evening meal. Sheep *baaed* from the hillside where they were being driven into temporary corrals for the night.

But with the arrival of the Indian school bands in busses (one from Albuquerque and one from Santa Fe) people drifted back to the school grounds and the celebration began anew. Indian dancers from the Santa Fe School entertained with tribal dances. The bands played marches and popular songs, so enthusiastically the chain of rock-ledged hills gave back an echo.

Then a torch flared near the great pile of logs at the far edge of the school ground. For two days, men had hauled wood and stacked it into one long pile in the shelter of a low mesa. One small yellow flame ate hungrily into the dry wood. The torch moved; another yellow flame and then another appeared from the pile of logs.

Navajos began to move slowly toward the fire. Some of the older ones spread their blankets upon the ground, settling themselves in to watch. Men pulled wagons to points of vantage so that the old people and children could see the fire-lit circle. Government employees drove their cars closer and sat on the fenders and bumpers. As the Navajo men gathered nearer the fire, the women and their daughters kept to the shadows. Visitors began to wander over to join the loosely formed circle of Pueblos, some Spanish people, a few government officials. The campfires on the hillside were like slumberous, half-closed eyes.

The first squaw dance song started softly, and a little uncertainly, as a few young men grouped themselves about an older man with a drum. But the song grew louder as other men joined the swaying group. More figures gathered in the shadows, and more young men joined the singers. As the fire burned brighter, the drum sounded louder and the voices rose. They swelled for a moment into one great voice. There was stealthy movement in the shadows; young girls, a few at a time, walked into the cleared space, and walked with short gliding steps up and down before the young men. Brightly colored skirts swung in small arcs to the measured rhythm of the walking. Dark velvet blouses made rich backgrounds for the display of white shell, turquoise, and heavy silver. Young faces, with their chins tilted high, were impassive, but brown eyes were appraising, purposeful, and dancing with merriment.

One by one, young men were dragged from the group of singers, and from the watching circle—young men who made a great show of not wanting to be chosen, who pulled away only to be snatched back by persistent hands on their shirts or blankets. Triumphantly, the girls led their partners forth, holding or linking arms, and turning slowly in a circle.

Juanita and Luciano watched from a wagon bed. Rosita and Toni knelt wide-eyed between them.

"I see Lupe out there," Rosita whispered.

Lupe was wearing a dark blue silk skirt, and a dark blue velvet blouse. The blue looked almost black in the firelight. Her long hair was caught up into the double fan shape, and her eyes were narrowed into mischievous slits of laughter. She was dancing with one of the visiting Navajos.

"Yes, and I see a concho belt and a couple of necklaces that look familiar," Luciano observed.

The singers finished one song and a voice led off into another one. Juanita swayed her shoulders slightly to the rhythm. "I loaned them to her. It's fair to catch a man in borrowed finery, isn't it?"

"For the loan of so much jewelry, we should at least share in what she collects from her partners."

Juanita laughed. "I'll tell her in the morning that you expect a fifty-fifty split."

A pause came in the singing, and each girl held fast to her partner until he paid the price she asked. Then she released him, and promptly began surveying the men for another partner.

They're like sleek young animals after prey, Juanita thought. Some of the girls were not yet experienced in this fascinating role of huntress, and they stood together giggling before finally getting up the courage to tug at some boy's blanket.

The singers started another song with a faster rhythm for the "skip dance." The girls were getting adventuresome. They singled out some of the government men, and amid laughter and shouts of encouragement from the older Navajos, they dragged them into the clear space. The government men were good-natured and they feigned reluctance to dance, as the Navajo men had, but finally linked arms and followed the other couples, moving with short, skipping steps in a revolving circle.

A pair of young boys (the smaller one looked like Lu's little brother Wudy) linked arms and followed the last couple in the circle. Giggling and stumbling over each other, they mimicked the dancers. Old people smiled indulgently, and the children in the group of watchers laughed with glee. This encouraged the young clowns, and they became more vigorous in their mimicry.

When the pause in the singing came, it was a long pause; the government officials dug deeply into their pockets while the young Navajo men laughed aloud to see them pay much larger forfeits than they themselves had paid for release.

Most of the young girls had left their families now and were pursuing partners. The visitors had joined the fun. There was much joking and laughter. The fire flamed higher, lighting the figures in the circle and casting shadows against the low mesa. Luciano stirred restlessly in the wagon, jingling the change in his pockets.

Juanita smiled. Toni had gone to sleep while leaning against her. "Why don't you dance? If they let married women dance, I'd be out there too."

Luciano tilted the Stetson rakishly and vaulted over the side of the wagon. Juanita watched him as he joined the swaying group of singers and lifted his voice with theirs.

The summer trial term was to begin the next day, but the feast and celebration had left the building and school grounds in need of a thorough cleaning. There were papers to be gathered and burned, remnants of campfires to be removed, and parts of the grounds to be leveled again. So summer school began the following week.

Many parents came the first few days with their children, as Luciano had invited them to come. They stood in the hallway or sat on benches in the dining room, silently watching the routine of the new school. Occasionally one of them encouraged a small child who was shy or frightened.

The first day was taken up entirely by outfitting the children with government-issued clothes: underwear, shoes, and stockings; overalls and blue shirts for the boys, with heavy corduroys for winter; the girls would have to wear their own dresses until their mothers could make school dresses for them from the brightly colored bolts in the closet. Combs and toothbrushes were labeled. Labels were printed with ink and attached to the new clothes.

The second day, Juanita and Luciano were more able to follow the planned schedule. The children went first to the washrooms for showers and changing into school clothes. The noise of the showers was frightening to the smaller children. Hoskey, the Navajo assistant, and Lu supervised the boys as they bathed, and helped them with their clothing.

Juanita asked the mothers to help the girls as she divided her time between the washrooms and the kitchen. She had just begun the preparations for the noon meal when cries of protest and much laughter summoned her back to the showers. Mrs. Decidero Platero thought that the stiff-bristled brush at the wash bowl was for scrubbing her small daughter. After the ritual of combing their hair and brushing their teeth, the children were lined up in the hall outside the dining room and then marched into one of the classrooms.

Some of the mothers and older sisters came into the kitchen and wanted to help with the preparation of the noon meal. Juanita was making a stew from canned mutton—mutton killed as part of the new stock-reduction program, then canned and issued to the day schools. Two of the women cleaned carrots, potatoes, and onions for the stew. The older girls who had been away to school got down the heavy white dishes from the cupboard and counted out the silverware from the drawer. Their mothers watched with interest as they set the dishes in patterns upon the tables.

At recess the children were lined up again and marched outdoors. Juanita looked out once to see Lu, Frank, and Hoskey very seriously playing games with them. The smallest Chavez boy was hopping around like a cricket because he was so excited about going to school. When she saw Wudy acting very grave and grown-up in coveralls too long for him and turned up at the cuffs, with his hair plastered down with water, Juanita smiled. Shimah had probably told him before he left the hoghan that just because the teacher was his big brother, he mustn't cut up as he did at home.

The women were a great deal of help, bringing in coal for the stove and filling the water buckets from the barrels. At times

Juanita found it difficult to make herself understood, and one of the older girls would interpret for her, such as one time she told the mothers not to drink the water from the taps above the sink. It was gypsum water, and was only good for washing and cleaning.

For the noon meal, the children marched in a fairly orderly fashion into the dining room. Luciano seated the small children between the older boys and girls who had been to boarding school, instructing the older ones to help the younger ones at the table and to show them about knives and forks. Frank sat at the head of one table, and Lu and Hoskey sat at the others. Juanita brought in the serving bowls of stew, stacks of fried bread, and large red apples for dessert. She waited for a chance to speak to Lu, to ask how the class was going. "Does the system seem to be successful?"

Lu, Frank, and Hoskey had decided on the system among themselves. Juanita had contributed magazines and some of the girls' old picture books. For several evenings they had all sat on the living room floor cutting out pictures and mounting them on wrapping paper and cardboard. The three men agreed that when they were little boys in school, it was easiest to learn English by associating a word with a picture of the object.

Lu smiled. "It's a little early to tell, but it seems to be working."

Shimah had come over from the hoghan to help Juanita in the kitchen, but with Alice Watson and Mrs. Chavez already helping, there was little for her to do. While the older women washed and dried the dishes, Juanita brought the basket of dampened clothes from the laundry room and set up the ironing board in the kitchen doorway. She added wood to the fire, and set the three sadirons.[3]

Shimah was smiling as Mrs. Chavez told her how Juan's youngest boy talked all the time about going to "Washeengtone's" school. She sloshed soapy water around in the dish pan, lifted the heavy white plates one by one, and placed them in the pan of rinse water. She continued to smile, just a little smile to herself. It brought her happiness to be

3 A sadiron is a solid flat iron used to iron cloths, heated on the stove.

thinking about the new school and her son at home working there.

Juanita unrolled one of the boys' blue shirts and fitted the wooden handle to a sadiron. The smallest Chavez boy had begun talking about "Washeengtone's" school after a lecture that Luciano gave to the class. After a week of summer school the strangeness was wearing off; most of the children were becoming less shy. They wanted to play and scuffle in the halls, whisper in class, and look out the windows instead of at the blackboard. They snickered and wiggled about in their seats. That was when Luciano gave them a lecture in Navajo—a lecture they all understood. The playground was for playing, the classroom was for studying, and that was the way it would be. He looked very stern when he talked to them, and the mischievous faces sobered; he wasn't just talking.

Washington had built the school for them. It was a place to learn something. Their parents were sending them here to learn something, not to play all day. That was all Lu said, but he didn't have to give the lecture twice. Alice Watson told Juanita about it. Her daughter Sally came home very impressed. Lu made no mention of it, but lately he'd begun to affectionately call little Chavez "Washeengtone."

Shimah went to the pantry for a piece of steel wool to use on the bottom of a kettle. Juanita folded the shirt she had finished and laid it on the end of the nearest dining table. Two of the young married women of the community were settling themselves at the sewing machines. They nodded shyly to Juanita and began to unroll the material they'd brought to work on.

The sewing machines were the most popular equipment at the new school. Juanita set the iron back on the stove and took another one. Even after the mothers had finished their daughters' school dresses, the machines were always busy. Someone was making a velveteen blouse, or someone else was putting the bottom ruffle on a wide, bright skirt. One afternoon Lu had come into the kitchen followed by two rather embarrassed young men. Would Juanita help them? They wanted to make new shirts.

"Can't their wives sew for them?" Juanita asked.

The young men laughed self-consciously and tried to tuck the folded yellow material farther under their arms. They didn't have wives.

"They must have mothers or sisters."

"It seems that all the women in the family are too busy," Lu told her. "And these fellows want new shirts for the next squaw dance."

With the help of Alice Watson, the shirts were cut. The young men stitched the seams. The cuffs and collars were hard to manage, but finally the shirts were finished. After that, it was not unusual for some of the men to come in to sew new binding on a hat brim or to repair a ripped shirt.

Shimah was wiping out the dishpan, putting it on a hook, and shaking out the dishrag before hanging it up to dry. Then she pushed the bench against the kitchen wall and sat down, rubbing her hands against her skirt. Watching her, Juanita got the feeling that Shimah was not resting, but waiting. Waiting, perhaps, until the other women left to tell her something. Juanita folded another shirt and carried it to the dining table. When she came back Alice Watson had taken a hot iron from the stove and was unrolling one of the school dresses. "I'll iron awhile."

Mrs. Chavez put the rest of the dishes away and sat down on the bench with Shimah. Quite often, when the work was done, the mothers waited until class was dismissed to ride home in the school truck.

"Don't these full skirts take a lot of ironing?" Alice asked as she reached for a hotter iron.

"Yes, and I can't wash many of them at a time in the washer. That Navajo style is prettier than plain short dresses, but it makes a lot more work." Juanita put more wood in the stove, then went to stand in the doorway.

Some of the day school ideas had been all right in theory but impractical when tried, like the Navajo-style dresses for the little girls, and the very good lumber the government had sent for the boys to make seats and desks for the classrooms. It might have worked in some schools, but in Cañoncito too few of the boys were old enough. Luciano refused to turn untrained boys loose with the inadequate shop tools on good lumber. "Those little fellows would be hacking each other's legs as well as the legs of the desks." He argued long and hard enough that regulation desks and chairs were finally installed.

But so much achieved at the day school was even more than they had hoped for. It was becoming a community center, which was as it should be.

The enrollment increased during the summer term, and more and more of the older Navajos were making use of the school facilities. They brought their small children and bathed them in the wash bowls in the lavatory. They brought their clothes and washed and ironed them, and used the showers for bathing and for washing their hair. Nowhere before in all their lives had there been such an abundance of water.

Sometimes the women brought pans of biscuits to bake in the oven. The men came in with letters they wanted Lu to read and answer for them. Almost every week now, the people squaw danced for one or two nights on the school grounds. There was a feeling that the day school belonged to the whole community.

Class was dismissed, and the children filed into the washrooms to change from school clothes into their everyday clothes. Juanita stood in the dining room, checking the bundles of school clothes as the children put them away in a long row of curtained cupboards.

Mrs. Juan Chavez, tall, strong, and serene, walked through the dining room and smiled goodbye to Juanita. Alice Watson finished the dress she was ironing, and then she left with Sally. Juanita took an iron from the stove; at least she could finish the shirts this afternoon. She was thinking: of all the families who came to the day school, only one family was missing—Wounded Head's. When Lupe came in with the girls, Juanita related her thoughts to her mother-in-law. "I haven't even seen their wagon go past the school grounds."

Shimah pursed her lips and looked down at the toes of her moccasins. "They know all about things here at the school." She lowered her voice. "They just don't come here in the daytime." Then she told Juanita about the wolf tracks she'd discovered that morning and had followed in a circle around the school. In one place the tracks seemed to stop as though someone had stood outside the west window of the living room. Lupe's eyes were wide and disturbed. "We should have a dog; it would warn us when something is outside."

Luciano brought Bob home one morning on his return from a Sing at Alice Watson's. Bob was a full-grown mixture of collie and shepherd. The shepherd traits were most apparent. The children were delighted with him; they patted his rough coat and rode his back. Bob seemed gentle and easy-going with them. But when someone came to the door of the apartment, Bob's deep-throated growls were not amiable. At night Bob slept on a mat outside the door.

The children begged to take Bob to the rodeo.

"There'll be strange dogs, and he'll be sure to get into fights," Luciano told them.

"I'll take him on a rope," Lupe offered.

It was Saturday. The rodeo would be held in the shallow valley between the low mesas and the chain of low hills. Juanita and Lu had been looking forward to the event. The Agency had requested that someone always be at the day school, so a hurried trip to Correo for their own groceries, and the yeast, fresh eggs, butter, and meat for the school kitchen was as far away as they got from Cañoncito. The squaw dances on the school grounds, an occasional horseback ride, and the rodeos that summer were their only recreation.

Luciano left after breakfast to go with some of the men to round up horses. After putting the apartment in order, Lupe and Juanita got into Levis and shirts. They dressed the girls in clean coveralls, and walked to the rodeo grounds. Bob gamboled along beside them, almost pulling the rope from Lupe's hand.

People were beginning to arrive leisurely, a few at a time, in wagons, old Fords, walking, or on horseback. The women were setting up camps on the slope of the opposite hills. The curved white top of an occasional covered wagon flashed in the sun. An old man passed them on horseback; his straggly gray hair was caught into a club knot. He wore a faded purple shirt, and his arm was hooked securely around a fat green watermelon.

"There goes old Juarito," Juanita said. But the straightness of the rider's back, the powerfully built chest and shoulders belied the word *old*. "I wonder if he's going to ride today."

"He probably will," Lupe answered. "He always does. Has my brother ever told you how all the old men here claim that Juarito as a young man could outrun a fast horse in a race of fifty yards?"

The corral and chutes were almost obscured by the men on horseback who were gathering around the fence of rough, twisted cedar posts. Some wore Levis and Western boots, and battered Stetsons tipped rakishly over one eye; others wore shin-high moccasins and silver-ornamented velveteen shirts, their long hair held in place by bands of faded silk. The horses had on fancy saddles, mended saddles, or even no saddles at all. Keen anticipation showed in the eyes of all the riders, while the lines of their bodies appeared easy and relaxed.

There was a scattering of whoops, and the men on horses parted to spread out across the dusty rodeo grounds. A rocking, bucking bronc came out of the chutes. The rider held on with one hand gripping the surcingle girded about the horse's belly, and the other hand beating the air with his hat.

"That's Arturo Chavez; he'll try to ride anything," Lupe observed. Then glancing up the slope of the hill, "There's Shimah's camp. Shall we go up and sit with her?"

They passed a wagon where a small, shaggy dog slept beside the huge hind wheel. Bob growled. Lupe pulled up on the rope.

Shimah and the old grandfather and grandmother sat in the shade of a blanket tied to a scrubby cedar and stretched across to the side of the wagon. Little Keetso was sitting under the wagon absorbed in the antics of a long-legged black beetle.

"Where's Bijo?" Juanita asked.

Shimah pointed with her lips. She and Wudy were down near the corral.

The grandfather gave a surprised grunt at the sound of Juanita's voice, and reached out a trembling, heavily veined hand. Juanita took it and spoke to him, then called Rosita and Toni, who came to stand in front of him. The grandfather touched their shoulders clumsily to see how tall they were growing and smiled, murmuring to himself. Then he took up the piece of buckskin he'd been softening with his hands and began to work it once more back and forth between his knuckles.

Juanita sat down, leaning against the wagon wheel. Two cloth-swathed water bottles hung from the wagon; to one side of the camp were a few pans and a blackened coffee pot beside the gray remains of the cook-fire.

"*Ee-yah,*" the grandmother exclaimed. Juanita saw that the rider coming from the chute was Luciano. His shoulders were loose and relaxed; his fingers held to the rope looped around the horse's belly, and his knees clamped tightly against the horse's ribs. The jolts of the rearing and bucking snapped at his body less and less, until it seemed he had ridden the horse to a standstill. As he was riding back to the chute between some of the men, the horse reared and began to buck again; the riders scattered, and this time Lu went tumbling into the dirt, rolling himself safely from the flying hooves. He got up, grinning.

The young men who were cutting horses from the corral into the chute began to laugh. "We picked a wild one for you that time, school boy."

The riderless bronc went charging down the valley, eluding the circling men. Women grabbed their children from the ground and climbed to the safety of the wagons. There were shouts and dirt and confusion until a few riders separated from the group of men, and, ropes ready, rode far down the valley after the runaway bronc.

The grandmother turned from watching. "When is this meeting that everyone is talking about?"

"I think she means the Chapter meeting when they are to vote on the Wheeler-Howard bill," Lupe explained.

"That's the next Chapter meeting on Friday," Juanita answered.

Already Luciano had received the ballots which were to be marked "X" in favor of the bill and "O" against it. The instructions had been repeated that government employees must not speak about the bill, except to explain its provisions. They were under no circumstances to attempt to influence members of the community regarding which way to vote.

Relatives had come to Luciano here in Cañoncito just as they had come to him in Crown Point, because much of the bill was beyond their understanding. Luciano and George Abeyta, who was interpreter at Chapter meetings, patiently explained the provisions of the bill at the Chapter House. Luciano explained the same provisions again when relatives came to the school or to their apartment. It was difficult to explain and at the same time not advise, especially here in his own community, among his own people.

Juanita saw the bright flash of skirts as children played along the edges of the low mesas. Down the valley was a camp beside a weathered green and orange wagon; that might be Wounded Head's family. Along the slope of the hill came a little boy driving a herd of goats toward the corral.

One of the men carried a goat out on the rodeo grounds and held it as it struggled and bleated between his knees. A rider separated himself from the other horsemen, while loosening his rope from the saddle, and stationed himself slightly behind the man with the goat. When the animal was released, it went running and bleating across the rodeo grounds with the rider after it, his rope swinging. But the goat could turn shorter and faster than the horse, and after dodging frantically to one side and then another, it ran in among the camps before the rider could throw a loop. The women shooed the goat along with their brightly colored skirts.

Rider after rider tried his luck at goat-roping. A few succeeded, and those who didn't rode back to try again. The people in the surrounding camps began to laugh as Arturo Chavez, mounted on a burro, rode about the rodeo grounds, getting in the riders' way, and making unsuccessful attempts to rope the dodging bleating goats. A very fat woman on the high seat of the wagon next to Shimah's camp wiped her eyes on the edge of her full skirt and began to laugh even harder. The small, green-striped parasol which she held over her head jiggled with each fresh outburst of mirth. The old grandfather questioned the cause of the laughter. When the grandmother explained, he laughed softly to himself. Then he leaned toward Juanita. "What does my son think of this Wheeler-Howard bill?"

Shimah rose to get a watermelon from under the seat of the wagon. Juanita looked down the valley as she tried to put words together in her mind. For the first time she noticed the too-pretty young man who wore beaded bands about his hair to Chapter meetings. He was sitting at the edge of a camp, farther along the hill. His purple silk shirt was new, and he wore a bright pink kerchief about his neck. He seemed quite alone, but he was laughing with everyone else at Arturo.

What should she say to Lu's grandfather? She couldn't tell him that they weren't supposed to discuss the bill. Interpreted into Navajo, it might sound short and harsh. "We're both going to vote for it, grandfather."

The young men were lining up their horses at one end of the valley for a race.

"It's going to be a skirt race." Lupe indicated the piles of women's clothing at the other end of the track. The idea of such a race was that each man borrow a skirt and Pendleton. When the race started, each man rode as fast as he could to his own bundle, dismounted, got into the skirt, put the Pendleton over his head and about his shoulders, remounted his horse, and raced back to the starting point.

Arturo had gotten a horsetail and made himself a woman's club knot, which was tied fast to the back of his head with a wide red band. The other racers were so distracted by his appearance that they hardly heard the shout of the starter.

The rodeo was almost over. A few people were breaking camp. Juarito stopped as he rode by to speak to the old grandfather. Juan Chavez got down from his horse and came to touch hands with him. Several men from other camps joined the group—Decidero Platero, Antonio Shorte, and Cadito Secatero all came forward.

"Are you coming to the meeting?" Decidero asked.

The old grandfather nodded.

"It's hard to decide about that paper. I don't like what it says about killing off the animals to save the land. Killing sheep means fewer sheep, so how can that make things better?"

The riders were struggling into the full, bundlesome skirts. Some of the horses, unused to women's skirts, shied. Clutching the Pendletons about their heads, the racers started back.

"Look at Arturo," Shimah laughed.

He'd fallen off and was rolling over and over on the ground, trying to disentangle himself from skirt and Pendleton.

The group around the old grandfather was having an involved discussion about the new bill, just as every group did when the subject was mentioned. The grandmother was speaking, chirpingly.

Juanita called Rosita to her side. "We'll soon be going."

Lupe untied Bob's rope from the wagon wheel.

"What do you think of this bill?" Juan Chavez asked the grandfather.

The old man pursed his lips, and set his sightless eyes upon the men. "I've thought about it a long time. I'm going to vote for the bill. And my son, Luciano, he's going to vote that way too."

EIGHTEEN
A Birth and a Marriage

The summer trial term was over; the day school was closed. Juanita and Luciano had a few weeks to themselves before school started again in September.

There was time for all day trips on horseback; they rode the trail through Blue Clay Gap and along the mesas which rimmed the Pueblo country. They rode into the country beyond Des Jin that always looked so blue and mysterious in the distance. They followed narrow canyons between mesas that loomed endlessly behind one another. There was time to spend whole days at Shimah's hoghan, the girls playing with Wudy, Bijo, and little Keetso. Luciano spent time at the corral, or in the cornfield with his brothers. There was also time for trips to Albuquerque, including a visit with Mr. Palm at the White Eagle, shopping, browsing in leather shops looking at the saddles, and dinner at a cafe with a movie afterward.

Luciano wanted to take his grandfather to Albuquerque while he had this time, and yet he could say no more than he already had said to his relative. Then one day the grandfather walked over from his hoghan, holding to Joe Chavez' shoulder, tapping the ground before him with his twisted walking stick. "Eh, my son," he said to Luciano, "when you go to that doctor I will go with you. I can come back no more blind than I am."

Luciano arranged for an appointment at the hospital on a day when Dr. Richards would be there. Dr. Richards was no longer the house doctor; through his work with trachoma in the Indian Service and further research, he had specialized in eye diseases and now spent only occasional days at the Indian hospital.

Luciano and Juanita took the grandfather into Albuquerque in the school truck. He sat very upright between them, resting his hands on his walking stick. His pants and shirt had been washed but not pressed, and he wore a faded purple handkerchief about his neck. Wisps of gray hair strayed from under his wide-brimmed hat. As Luciano talked to him, he nodded his head in an almost continuous motion. Rough pieces of turquoise bobbed on bits of string which held them to the pierced lobes of his ears. Juanita sat quietly, listening to the soft flow of Navajo between her husband and his grandfather. She could understand only part of what they were saying.

Goldenrod and wild sunflowers grew rank along the highway. The summer sun had streaked the grass pasture land with yellow and brown.

She hoped the old man's eyes could be successfully treated, for Luciano's sake as well as his grandfather's. It seemed to hurt her husband each time he saw his grandfather faltering along with the stick, and leaning on little Joe's shoulder. The day in the Chapter House when the Cañoncito Navajos had voted to come under the provisions of the Wheeler-Howard bill was disheartening. The grandfather who had talked so much in favor of the new plan had needed to ask someone to hold the paper for him and guide his hand while he made a scrawling, uncertain "X".

And yet, Juanita didn't often think of the old man as blind. Perhaps it was because he was always busy shelling corn, softening buckskin, and rubbing dye into moccasins. Shimah said that he'd even gone piñon-picking with them and sat all day, each day, picking pebbles and twigs from the piñon nuts that the rest of the family gathered.

When they arrived at the hospital, Luciano parked the truck in the circular driveway and guided the old man up the steps. As they sat on the wicker couch in the waiting room, he was telling his grandfather that it might be too late for treatments, and that it might even take an operation to restore his sight. But he shouldn't worry because the doctor was a good doctor. He knew all about eyes.

The old man nodded, but did not answer.

They were summoned into a large room at the front of the hospital, and then they waited until Dr. Richards finished writing at his desk. The doctor looked up and smiled at them, and asked Juanita about her family. She told him that they had two girls now. Juanita leaned on the edge of the examination table after Dr. Richards had guided the old man to a chair. Luciano stood beside his grandfather. The doctor's back was turned toward Juanita as he lifted the old man's eyelids, and examined the eyeballs with the aid of a small powerful light. She saw the doctor shake his head, and saw the hope die in her husband's eyes.

"Nothing can be done," the doctor told him.

"Not even an operation?"

One or two years ago, an operation might have saved this man's sight, but the growths are too advanced now."

He explained about the cataracts which had grown slowly until now they completely covered the pupils of the old man's eyes.

The grandfather sat straight in the chair, staring ahead. Luciano repeated the doctor's words to him. His face did not change; he only nodded.

Luciano guided his grandfather down the steps of the hospital and along the drive to the truck. They started back to Cañoncito in silence. Across the bridge which spanned the Rio Grande, the purple volcano cones were visible in the distance; they were almost to the Rio Puerco.

Juanita could think of no words to break the silence which would offer sympathy to Luciano's grandfather or comfort to her husband.

She knew how bitter Luciano's thoughts must be. They had come to New Mexico to be near his people. And yet a year or two ago, when Lu might have helped his grandfather, they had been in Crown Point, unaware that he was gradually going blind.

Juanita did not need to speak to Luciano; the old man seemed to sense the younger man's despondency. He groped with an uncertain hand for Luciano's knee. "Don't feel bad about this. The darkness is no longer strange, and there is still much I can do to be useful."

Juanita, Lupe, and the two girls were walking toward the hoghan one afternoon. Wudy, Bijo, and Keetso met them at the barbed wire gate into the pasture.

"We're going to pick cactus apples."

Rosita and Toni wanted to go.

"Don't go too far away," Juanita told Wudy as the five youngsters started along the arroyo. Bijo and Wudy were taller, and their dark hair was untidy in the wind, Bijo's long skirt was torn in several places around the ruffle, Rosita, the next largest in size, was dressed in a sun-faded playsuit. Toni and Keetso were smaller, and had to skip to keep up with the group. Bob dashed exuberantly beside them.

Juanita and Lupe found the brush shelter empty; all of the regular activities had been suspended. Shimah had left her loom and was tending a small fire beside the shelter. Yee-ke-nes-bah's loom was also abandoned. The shuttle was wrapped with red yarn left between the warp strings, and the batten comb was on the ground. Instead of being out with the sheep, Khee was at the corral saddling one of the horses.

Shimah turned the small branch of cedar which lay close to the fire and tested the needles with her fingers. There was an undertone of excitement in her voice as she gestured with her head toward the hoghan. "Yee-ke-nes-bah's pains started this morning." Shielding her hand with her skirt, she lifted a lardpail of bubbling water from the fire.

Khee rode off across the pasture. Shimah began crumbling the cedar needles into the boiling water. "If Seraphina is not someplace visiting relatives, she will come to help."

While the mixture in the lardpail steeped beside the fire, Shimah went into the hoghan. When she returned with a small sack of powder-fine meal ground from blue corn, Lupe caught Juanita's questioning glance. "That's to make blue corn meal for Yee-ke-nes-bah. Right after the baby is born, she eats some and then eats more for the few days afterward. It gives her back the strength she used in labor."

When Seraphina arrived, she stopped for only a few minutes in the shelter. Then with all of the dignity of one fully aware of her importance, she went inside the hoghan.

Juanita watched as her mother-in-law strained the cedar liquid through a bundle of dried grass. She then stirred the cornmeal into the liquid, and set the pan over the fire. Lupe picked up the batten comb and began to finish out the solid strip of red in Yee-ke-nes-bah's design.

Yee-ke-nes-bah's baby had not yet been born. Juanita called the girls and started home to prepare dinner. After dinner, they spoke of going over to the hoghan but then they decided not to.

"There'll be enough people at Shimah's without us," Luciano told them. "There will be plenty of time to see the new baby in the morning."

It was past midnight when Luciano was awakened by a knock at the door. Allen had walked over. Yee-ke-nes-bah's baby had not yet been born. Shimah wanted Juanita to come and help.

"But what good will I be?" Juanita asked her husband as they were dressing. "Having babies in the hospital doesn't give you any special knowledge about what to do."

"There may be some way you can help." Lu stopped at the bedroom door to make sure that Lupe and the girls were sleeping.

They walked to the hoghan with Allen. As they approached the doorway, they could hear the rhythm of a chant but no drum.

"Jose Manuel Chavez is singing over her," Allen told them.

To Juanita, the scene inside the hoghan was incredible. The lantern cast a dim light from the peg between the ceiling logs. The children had been put to bed against the north wall, but Wudy and Bijo were wide awake leaning on their elbows. Allen and Khee and Yee-ke-nes-bah's husband sat against the wall, occasionally adding their voices to the chant. The grandfather and grandmother were there, and so were Juan Chavez and his wife.

Shimah and Seraphina were at the back of the hoghan with Yee-ke-nes-bah, and the Medicine Man was standing directly in front of her, chanting and holding a few eagle feathers in each hand. How could any woman have a baby with all these people around?

But Yee-ke-nes-bah didn't seem to notice. Fully clothed, she knelt upon the layers of sheep pelts, with her skirts wide about her and her hands straining at the knotted end of a woven belt suspended from the ceiling log above her. Juanita recognized the light blue and red belt as the one her sister-in-law had been wearing tightly around her waist during the preceding months.

Yee-ke-nes-bah was exhausted by the long hours of pain and labor; perspiration stood out in great beads on her forehead and her upper lip. "Ee-yah," she softly moaned over and over in rhythm with the pain.

When Yee-ke-nes-bah rose to her feet and walked to the doorway, Shimah went outside with her to walk around the hoghan. Returning with pain-halted steps, and her hand muffling dry sobs, Yee-ke-nes-bah knelt again on the pelts. Juanita lost count of the times her sister-in-law walked outside and then returned to kneel on the sheep pelts. Shimah and Seraphina kneaded the girl's body, forcing their hands downward each time that she moaned with pain.

Bringing wood from outside, Juanita added it to the small fire in the center of the hoghan. She filled a lardpail with water and set it up on the blackened rocks to heat. Luciano walked outside with Juan Chavez. Yee-ke-nes-bah's husband lit a cigarette. The old grandfather quietly grunted when he smelled the tobacco. His granddaughter's husband passed the cigarette to him and lit another.

Juanita poured cold water from the water bucket on her handkerchief and bathed her sister-in-law's forehead, holding the cool wet cloth to her temples. She felt so helpless in the face of another woman's pain. Khee and Allen left the hoghan, then returned to help with the chanting. The Medicine Man's voice droned on and on monotonously. There were too many people in the hoghan—the place seemed close with their bodies and their breathing. Yee-ke-nes-bah was so tired; she was suffering. Would this never end?

Seraphina was the one who lifted the baby as it dropped to the sheep pelts. Allen handed her his pocket knife to cut the cord. As Seraphina reached for the water bucket, Juanita spoke quickly in protest and indicated the basin of warm water she was preparing. The old lady ignored the protest, and her bright little eyes snapped as if to say, "I've been managing things like this for fifty years." She scooped cold water from the bucket with her hand and dashed it liberally over the baby.

Yee-ke-nes-bah's baby seemed too plump and brown to be newborn; heavy dark hair was plastered wetly against its head. Dashed with cold water, it immediately began to wail. Juanita smiled. Well, after all, Seraphina's treatment could be no more upsetting than a doctor's spank. Shimah turned from settling Yee-ke-nes-bah on a pallet; she spoke gently to her daughter-in-law. Juanita went to the cupboard for the bowl of thin blue corn meal gruel.

The first Juanita knew of her husband's leasing his allotment was when he showed her the restless, unbroken black horse in his mother's corral.

"That's Raven. I got him from Decidero for the use of our land."

Juanita looked at the dainty, slender legs of the black horse, the short powerful body, the arched neck, the restless way he tossed his head, the thick black mane flying, as though standing still was tiresome.

"Not bad?" Lu questioned.

"Not bad at all."

"We won't be able to start building on the allotment this year anyway. Decidero only wants to run his horses there. That one strand of wire should keep them in. I can finish the fence anytime I want to."

Juanita leaned against the rough cedar post of the corral; she was still watching Raven. "We're becoming a substantial Cañoncito family, aren't we? Four horses."

Luciano laughed. "Five, if you count the colt we're breaking for Rosita."

Juanita looked at her husband standing there in the late summer sunshine, his feet in cowboy boots a little apart, his Stetson pushed back on his forehead. He appeared vastly proud of the trading he'd done to get Raven and extremely contented with life in general. She put both hands to the back of her head, and stretched and yawned a little. "What are you thinking?"

Lu's lips lengthened into a smile. "About a rock house. Allen and I have found two or three places where we can get to good building rock with the wagon. Of course, smooth plastered walls would be nicer, but rock will be cheaper. When we're ready to start building, I think Allen and I could put up rock walls without needing to hire help."

Talk of their own home always started her daydreaming. Before they were married she and Lu had drawn a rough plan for their home. It was close to reality now.

They were standing by the corral in the sunshine, watching Raven and not saying much, when George Abeyta rode up. He wore a new, black satin shirt, his hair had been recently trimmed, and he looked very dressed up and handsome.

"I'm getting married today. Want to come to a feast?"

"Where's the feast?" Lu asked.

"You mean what girl am I marrying?" George laughed. "Tomas Pablo's daughter. Her name is Rose."

"I know the one. She's a school girl, isn't she?" And then, "That hoghan is on the way to Cottonwood Spring?"

George nodded and grinned at Juanita. "Now I can trade that red velvet shirt to someone else."

"You've probably worn it out by this time," Lu accused him.

Laughing, George turned his horse to ride away. "No, I've worn it only a few times. But like you, my cousin, I wore it once too often." He spurred his horse lightly. Laughter trailed behind him.

Slowly, rather lazily, Juanita and Lu walked across the pastureland and skirted the cornfield.

"Since George is a relative, we should take food to the feast," Luciano told his wife as they approached the day school.

In the kitchen of their apartment, Juanita tied a string securely around a half sack of flour and took canned plums and peaches from the cupboard. She asked Lupe to fix dinner for the girls in the event she and Lu were late getting home.

"I'd better change from my Levis," she said, taking a red and white candy-striped gingham from the closet.

They walked to Tomas Pablo's, following the day school road part of the way and then cutting across country toward the spring. Luciano was in high spirits. He walked along swinging the sack of canned goods, singing at the top of his voice. When they were within sight of the hoghan, Luciano stopped. "Hold these a minute." He handed her the canned goods.

Juanita shifted the sack of flour to one arm so that she could hold both sacks comfortably.

Luciano grinned and began walking ahead of her to the hoghan. "Now I'll arrive as a Navajo should: the woman carrying the bundles."

The hoghan and rock house faced the smooth hard-packed earth of the compound. To one side stretched Tomas Pablo's field of tall, emerald-green corn. Beyond, the ground seemed to drop to a lower shelf, cut through with an arroyo, and along the arroyo grew large old cottonwoods, green leaves outspread against a background of red sandstone walls.

"What a beautiful spot," Juanita exclaimed.

"Yes, and Tomas Pablo is industrious. My cousin is marrying into a good family."

The women, the bride and her relatives, were outside making bread in the brush shelter. Juanita put the sacks down by the cook-fire and touched hands with the older women. Rose spoke to her in English. Luciano went into the hoghan.

Rose was a pretty girl. Bending over the fire had given her olive face a ruddy glow. Her hair was not yet grown out from a boarding school haircut, but it was pulled back smoothly into a small club knot. The bright skirt and velvet blouse she wore were new. She asked Juanita if she would like to help make the bread. "These ladies," she gestured to her relatives, "say that two schoolgirls can't make bread alone."

Juanita accepted the challenge. She sat down beside Rose at the cook-fire and began to mix and knead more dough while Rose flattened the balls of dough, pulling and slapping them before putting them into the hot grease. The older women looked on for awhile, joking, and then busied themselves opening cans and preparing the rest of the feast.

Rose's mother and another woman remained behind in the shelter while the bride and the rest of the women went to the hoghan for the basket ceremony. There were a few old men seated cross-legged at the back of the hoghan: Lu's grandfather, old Juarito, Ada Sandoval's father. Juanita touched hands with them before seating herself beside Lu.

During the ceremony Juanita noticed these old men watching her and talking among themselves. The grandfather nodded his head and seemed to be agreeing with what they were saying. Tomas Pablo spoke to Lu—quietly for a moment—and as hard as Juanita listened she couldn't catch the meaning of what he said.

There was a hint of merriment in Lu's eyes as he turned to her. "They want you to make the marriage talk."

"Are you trying to tease me?"

"No, I mean it." He smiled at the look of unbelief on her face. "And you'd better do some fast thinking."

"Do I talk before we eat?"

Lu nodded.

Juanita was conscious of the hoghan full of the married couple's relatives. Her mind was in a turmoil. What to say that would be helpful to George and his new wife? How would it sound to these wise old men sitting at the back of the hoghan who had all made many marriage talks? George looked up, grinning at her. The old grandfather sat nodding his head, smiling placidly as he waited. What to say, except the things which had often guided her and Lu? She spoke in English to George and Rose; Luciano interpreted for the older people.

"There'll be misunderstandings when you're married because no two people think alike about everything. But if you talk things over, both listening to the other's side, the disagreements will straighten out. Both of you may have to give in halfway, or one of you all the way, but that's better than to keep on quarreling."

Rose smiled shyly to herself as though quarreling might be for other people but not for them.

"Always discuss things with each other, because whatever one of you does will affect both of you." The day came back vividly—the day she received the money order from Nadine. Nothing had been worth the look on Lu's face when she told him that she'd borrowed the money.

"When your parents need your help, try to help them." She was thinking of Shimah now. "But if other relatives ask too much of you," she was thinking of their relatives in Crown Point, "remember that your own family—your children—should come before them."

"If someone tries to separate you, your relatives or another man or woman, remember that if you love one another and share things, your plans and your thoughts, nothing can ever come between you."

When she gestured that she had said all she wanted to say, the women began to bring in the food: plates of roast mutton, plates of fried bread, bowls of tomatoes, peaches, plums, and pots of coffee. George and Rose smiled and thanked Juanita. Luciano was still interpreting for the older ones. When he had finished, the old men at the back of the hoghan looked at her, nodding their approval. "*Yah t'eh*," they said over and over, "*yah t'eh*."

Small bowls and cups were handed around to the guests. Everyone helped themselves to the food in the center of the floor.

Leaving the hoghan after the feast, as Juanita and Lu walked toward the arroyo, they watched the sun's rays slant through the cottonwoods. At this time of day the sun seemed to bathe the mesas and the sloping pasturelands in pale golden light.

"I wanted to show you the corral." They stood looking down upon the shelf of land below and the large stout enclosure of juniper logs. "See those horses?" Lu indicated two pintos, a sorrel, and a buckskin. "Those were George's." The wheels of the spring-wagon creaked as George drove away from the compound, Rose seated beside him. "Now they're Tomas Pablo's."

NINETEEN
Christmas in Cañoncito

The fall term of the community day school had begun in September. This was November. Juanita found herself busier than she'd ever been before in her life—and happier.

Each day was planned, the time budgeted; it had to be in order for them to accomplish the work to be done. There seemed so few spare moments from six in the morning when she and Lu awakened—he to start the fires in their apartment and in the school building, she to prepare breakfast, see that the girls were dressed, the beds made, the house in order for the day—to the last moment at night after she had washed their socks and underthings and hung them on the line behind the stove to dry, and Lu had put the new police pup Ginger out on the doorstep with Bob. Finally they kicked the carefully tucked-in covers loose from the foot of the couch and talking over the day, their words getting lower and lower, finally trailing off sleepily. There was a strong rhythm to their life now, a multiple purpose, and deep content in being where they wanted to be with a secure future.

Luciano no longer taught classes; the regular teacher had arrived, sent out by the government to be in charge of the school. The Navajos called her White Haired Woman because her very blonde hair was turning gray. Her husband would take the place of the government "farmer," and oversee community projects including fencing, road-building, and improvements to the water supply which the government started. He would also instruct the Navajo men on stock-breeding and new methods of farming. The government built a large stone house on the edge of the school grounds for the teacher and her husband.

Even with the responsibility of the school shifted to the new teacher, and with the help of Hoskey, Juanita and Luciano found that the work connected with the school made long, full days.

Luciano went to pick up the school children as soon as breakfast was over. When Alice Watson came to stay with the girls, Juanita began preparations in the school kitchen for the noon meal. Once the children had arrived, changed into school clothes, and marched into the classroom, Juanita was free to devote all of her time to the work in the kitchen. But whatever Luciano attempted, whether cutting wood or hauling water from the spring, he was on call as interpreter for the children or any of the older Navajos who came to the school. There was the playground to be supervised at recess, the dining room to be supervised at noon. Afternoons, Lu taught small classes in silversmithing and simple carpentry, and Juanita occasional hygiene classes and supervision of a few older girls sent to help her with the washing, ironing, or mending. Laundry and mending for forty children was no small task.

When Lu pulled away from the school grounds in the truck to take the children home, Juanita began cleaning the kitchen and dining room, mopping the floors, and going over the furniture with a damp cloth. Lu and Hoskey later cleaned the classrooms, the halls, and the washrooms.

With the school building closed for the evening, Juanita prepared supper at home, while Lu chopped wood and then brought it in along with coal for both the stove and fireplace.

The time after supper was never long enough for all the things Juanita wanted to do—her sewing, mending, and letter writing. Lu did a little silverwork, read, or had a tussle with Rosita and Toni before getting them off to bed. Often Lorencito came in the evenings to visit with them; he seemed lonely since his wife had died.

Juanita had worked late the night before, sitting by the Coleman lamp, letting hems out of Rosita's and Toni's dresses while Lu and his older brother talked. She was tired and rather sleepy this morning. Potato soup and hot squares of corn bread, with canned peaches for dessert, were on the menu for lunch. Juanita had the thick yellow cornmeal batter ready to pour into the pans. Pah-des-bah and Lena, who had been helping her that morning, sat on a bench in the dining room scuffing their store shoes against the floor as they talked and laughed softly. They waited until it was time to set the tables.

The White Haired Woman passed them as she came to the door of the kitchen. Both girls were suddenly quiet. The White Haired Woman was short and rather timid looking; her eyes were pale blue behind her glasses. "Mrs. Platero, are your housekeeping reports ready to go to the office?"

Juanita set the pans on the stove with a little lard in them and went to the pantry for the list of last week's menus, the number of showers taken, children bathed, etc.

The White Haired Woman stood in the door hesitantly. "I instructed the children today to tell their mothers to come more often to help you."

"But I have plenty of help, sometimes more than I need," Juanita interrupted.

The teacher continued. "I believe the more women here to help you, the better. It will develop community spirit."

Juanita said no more. To defend her policy of asking only two or three women to help each day was useless. No doubt a government bulletin had been issued, and the teacher was carrying out instructions. The teacher's heels clicked across the dining room floor as she returned to her classroom.

Juanita already knew what happened when too many people congregated in the kitchen. She'd found out early in the summer term. Everyone was in everyone else's way. The work took more, instead of less time. There was gossiping and sometimes quarreling.

It would be impossible to tell the teacher that the community spirit was already there, but it was endangered by some of the new rules and restrictions added since the beginning of the fall term. Giving the women rations, material, and food when they came to help at the school was putting them on a work-for-pay basis rather than allowing them to help because it was their school. Forbidding dancing on the school grounds and the bringing of horses and wagons on day school land would do more than anything else to make the people feel the community day school was less theirs and more the government's.

Luciano came in as she was pouring the yellow batter into the flat pans. Seeing the small frown creasing her forehead, he retraced his steps and made another entrance, this time walking with one stiff leg while he made a squeaking noise with his mouth. Lena giggled from the dining room. Juanita looked up, unable to hold back a smile. Lu was imitating a man they'd known in Crown Point, the unfortunate possessor of a wooden leg which squeaked. She sometimes said, "Lu, you should be ashamed, making fun of that poor man." Yet, she always laughed; she couldn't help it. And so Lu often resorted to this method of making her laugh when she was tired or worried.

"The teacher was just here; she wants me to use more women in the kitchen to help."

"Did you tell her it doesn't work?"

"I told her that I have more than enough help already. But she's asked the children to tell their mothers to come in."

"You'll have to be patient and let her see for herself."

"I know, I've done that a few times before rather than seem arbitrary when she makes suggestions which are impractical for this community. She's so nice in other ways."

The White Haired Woman was nice about letting Juanita off early to go with Lu in the school truck when he drove to Albuquerque for supplies. She didn't care how late they stayed. This gave Juanita an opportunity to do her shopping, and in addition it gave her and Luciano an occasional evening in town together. The teacher could make her authority more restrictive in many ways, but she didn't.

Juanita put the cornbread in the oven. "Lena, you and Pah-des-bah may set the tables now."

Luciano stood close to the draining board while Juanita counted out silverware. "I saw one of the Herreras this morning. They're going to build a new trading post just outside the school grounds and close the little one they started down off the road south of here."

"Near the day school will be a good location," Juanita observed as she got the soup ladle from the drawer.

Lunch over, Lena and Pah-des-bah helped with the dishes. Ada Sandoval came in to use the sewing machine. Juanita went into the dining room to help her cut a pattern for a blouse.

"I mustn't be upset by impracticalities," Juanita told herself. "They're inevitable. This is the first year of an experiment in Cañoncito. Things will gradually work out."

Ada Sandoval began to smile, holding her hand to her mouth. Juanita looked out the dining room windows. Lu was walking past on his way to the garage, looking neither right nor left. He walked with the restricted, mincing steps of a Pueblo woman and held one hand above his head, balancing and unbalancing an imaginary jar of water. Anything to make her laugh.

The last two weeks of December were busy exciting weeks. Pictures and stories of Santa Claus were introduced into the classroom. The children worked busily on calendars and bread boards for their mothers. A community Christmas tree was planned, the first one in Cañoncito. Juanita and the older girls made tree decorations: strings of popcorn, stars and bells of colored art paper, and tinfoil-covered cardboard. Luciano went with the farmer and the older school boys to a distant mesa to bring back the tall cedar that would stand on the school grounds between the day school and the Chapter House.

The morning of the Christmas party Juanita worked in the school kitchen with Ada Sandoval and Lena, Alice Watson, and Richard Platero's daughter, Ida, making popcorn balls and doughnuts. All of the huge coffee pots were on the stove full of sweetened black coffee.

The cedar tree stood tall in the pale December sunshine, gaudily decked with the fat white strings of popcorn, glittering stars, and bells. It was also decorated with red tarlatan stockings that were full of candy and toys from the Agency, along with the dolls and tops which the teacher had bought for the children. Stacked beneath the tree were boxes of oranges and sacks of nuts to be distributed, a long wooden packing case from one of the missionary groups, and the gifts which the children had made for their families.

The oranges and candy had been saved to go in the packs of the two Santa Clauses. There was no other way but to have two. Both Richard Platero and Hoskey wanted to be Santa Claus and neither would give in. The teacher had only one Santa Claus suit, but the men seemed to think they could divide it between them.

People began to arrive a few at a time, seating themselves on the chairs and benches in the school yard, getting up to walk about the tree and finger the gifts and decorations. A few wagons came through the cut between the mesas. Some young men rode up on horseback to wait at the edge of the crowd.

When the whole community had gathered—grandfathers and grandmothers huddled in their blankets, beady eyes alert to every detail of the party; school children giggling, scarcely able to stand still in anticipation of the gifts; older brothers and sisters; fathers; mothers holding babies wrapped in their Pendletons—the strains of "Jingle Bells" discorded by two male voices came from the mesa opposite the school grounds. Two partly red-clad apparitions came sliding down the side of the mesa and ran, still singing an occasional word of "Jingle Bells," until they reached the tree. Rosita and Toni grabbed their mother's skirt. Juanita heard Lu's laughter from across the school yard. Some of the old people upset their chairs in an attempt to get back from the tree, and the smaller children began to cry.

Richard and Hoskey looked less like Santa Clauses and more like evil spirits than any two men Juanita had ever seen. Richard wore the top to the Santa Claus suit, Levis, and cowboy boots. His dark, black-mustached face peered from under the white cotton wig and red tasseled cap. Hoskey wore the pants and oilcloth Santa Claus boots, a purple velvet shirt, and the long white beard. He had stuffed wisps of cotton beneath his Stetson.

When the startled crowd finally recognized the two Santa Clauses, and saw that they were handing out gifts from their packs, the group settled down and was quiet. Gifts were distributed from the tree until the children's pockets and hands were full. The older people were making pouches out of their shirts and Pendletons. When the missionary box was opened, there were gifts in it for everyone. Candy for the children, pocket combs in colored cases for the men, and tin measuring cups with colored handles for the women.

Luciano went with Juanita to help bring out the doughnuts and pots of coffee; the older girls would serve them from a table at the side of the school. Old Seraphina followed Lu into the kitchen, padding along behind him, scolding petulantly. She had been slighted when the gifts were given out. She didn't get as much as some of the other women. Just because she was getting old and feeble didn't mean that she didn't like nice things too—there was no reason for her to be slighted.

Lu turned; the high petulant voice died away. "What didn't you get, Grandmother?"

Seraphina's little eyes brightened. "One of those bread boards."

"But you have no children in school."

"Do I have to have children in school? Can I help it if I have no more little ones?"

Juanita kept her face turned as she stacked the doughnuts onto the trays; she didn't want Seraphina to see her laughing.

"But the school children made those for their mothers," Luciano began to explain.

"They are such nice bread boards," old Seraphina said childishly. "I want one of them."

Lu's only argument had been exhausted. "All right, after Christmas I will help one of your grandsons make one for you."

Juanita turned with the trays in her hands and started out the door. Seraphina's claw-like hand darted out for one of the doughnuts. She stuffed the sweet brown delicacy into her mouth. Her eyes twinkled roguishly.

Cleaning up the kitchen and the school grounds after the Christmas party took the rest of the afternoon and went into the evening. Rosita and Toni were tired and no one was very hungry. So, after a light supper, Juanita bathed the girls and put them to bed.

"Does Santa Claus come here tonight?" Rosita asked as she kissed her mother goodnight.

"If you go to sleep soon enough."

"I'm asleep," Toni tightly closed both of her eyes.

Lu brought in the small tree from the garage and set it on the cedar chest. Juanita stood on a chair to be able to reach the top shelf of the hall closet. She handed down the box of tree trimmings and the boxes which had come from California and Texas.

After Lu had opened the box of trimmings, he pushed Juanita gently to the couch. "Now you just sit still and watch an expert."

He draped tinsel about the little tree, hung a few glittering ornaments, and then stepped back to survey the effect.

Juanita pointed,"There's a bare spot over there."

"Shh, I can't do my best work if you talk." He hung a few more ornaments, then stood back and threw tinfoil icicles at the branches. "I've never been able to understand the connection between Santa Claus, presents, a tree, and the story of Christmas, but I think it's fun." Last, he clipped the candle holders to the tips of branches.

Juanita put the candles in the holders and arranged tissue-wrapped boxes and packages under the tree. Lu began examining cards and pinching packages.

"That isn't fair," Juanita scolded him. "I haven't tried to guess what is in mine."

Christmas morning they awakened early. Lu lit the pitch wood and logs stacked in the fireplace. He was just lighting the candles when the girls came pattering down the hallway. "Has Santa Claus been here? Has Santa Claus been here?"

In pajamas and bathrobes, they sat before the tree opening presents. Lu called the names on the cards and stopped to help Toni untie a ribbon and open a box. The soft light of the log fire and the flickerings of candles showed mounds of tissue paper, colored cords, and ribbons covering the floor. There were dolls with real hair for Rosita and Toni from Nadine and Michel, and picture books and crayons from

Waano-Gano. The girls sat wide-eyed, their cheeks flushed with excitement as they opened each package and found a new game or toy. Toni opened her picture book and began to color one of the pages.

Lu touched Juanita's arm. "Last year she was too little to know what Christmas was about."

"Yes, as little as they are, it's evident they're growing up."

Rosita opened a toy weaving set and began to run her fingers through the colored yarn.

"It's going to be fun watching our daughters grow up." Turning again to the tree, Luciano picked up a package and tossed it into Juanita's lap. "I almost forgot this one," he said with elaborate carelessness.

It was a shoe box, and nestled in the tissue were white boudoir slippers, dainty and frothy with a ruff of white fur. Juanita had seen them one evening in Albuquerque when she and Lu were window shopping. They were impractical and much too expensive, but she couldn't help admiring their sleek lines and daintiness. Holding them in her hands, though her shining eyes could see them weeks ahead smudged with coal dust, she said, "Oh, Lu, they're beautiful."

Luciano looked up grinning; he had somehow fitted the new spurs she had bought for him on his house slippers. He pulled up one leg of his pajamas to get a better view of the small neat rowel. "Boy, won't Raven step when I have these on."

After Christmas, they bought new saddles and new Western boots; they'd been saving for them since the opening of the school's fall term. When they rode out on Sunday they were conscious of the elegance of their new equipment. Often Toni stayed with Shimah, and Rosita, Wudy, and Phillip rode a little ways with them. Bob and Ginger running along beside them completed the entourage. Juanita rode Pete and sometimes Lu's buckskin, but very seldom did she ride Raven. And perversely, she found herself liking to ride Raven better than any other horse.

Since she first saw Raven, saucy and spirited, tossing his head restlessly in Shimah's corral, she'd wanted him for her own. Raven had so many impudent mannerisms which endeared him to Juanita: he let his black nose be stroked only when he desired that show of affection; he kept just far enough away from someone with the bridle that there was always the hope, "I'll saddle him without roping him this time"—but no one ever did. He stood quite still until someone put his foot in the stirrup, then moved sideways. He shied at rocks and his own shadow if he was feeling particularly devilish. Sometimes he reared up on his hind legs, or indulged in a bit of bucking before settling down to the tiresome business of following a trail. Raven wasn't mean, just impudent and mischievous. Juanita thought there was no other horse with an easier, more even trot, or a faster, smoother gallop.

She tried to manage some way of getting Raven as her own horse without actually having to ask for him. Juanita knew that Lu would tease her by pretending the horse hadn't been broken long enough to belong to a woman, or by pretending that someone in the community had offered a big price for Raven. She said little things about Raven's daintiness and about him being smaller than most horses which the men in Cañoncito rode, but Lu didn't seem to hear her.

Then one day Lu came riding home on a light bay mare, and leading Raven. From that day Juanita began to be hopeful of acquiring her horse.

Luciano could speak of nothing but the new mare, Lady. He had seen her once and immediately began to bargain for her. Lady's hide shone like copper in the sun, and her mane and tail were a little darker. She was taller and heavier than Raven. Her head and neck were beautiful, and her legs and body perfectly turned and molded. Her power was a steady flame, where Raven's was shooting sparks.

Juanita stayed at the hoghan with the girls on the Sunday that Lu rode out hunting with Allen and Lorencito. The snow was almost gone from the arroyos, and the first gentleness of spring was in the wind. The girls played outside with Wudy and their cousins. Bob and Ginger romped and ran as they did, sometimes knocking Toni or Keetso over in the excitement. There'd be a few tears, a scratch to show to Juanita or Shimah, and then the games outside the hoghan went on as boisterously as before.

When the sun was past the middle of the sky Shimah began to knead dough for bread. Yee-ke-nes-bah laid a small blanket over her baby on the cradle board and helped Juanita peel potatoes. Juanita sent Khee down to the new trading store for canned tomatoes and some long green chilies. Everyone in the family liked roast green chilies. Juanita was just beginning to be able to eat a portion of one if it wasn't too hot.

"How do men always know when a meal is ready," Juanita asked as Lu and his brothers rode up just as the coffee was boiling.

The men hitched their horses to the corral posts, washed their hands in the chipped basin, and came into the hoghan to sit around the fire expectantly. Juanita passed the plates and cups, and set the skillet of fried potatoes on the floor. The children came in for pieces of hot bread and ran out to play again. While the men helped themselves, Juanita and Yee-ke-nes-bah picked the roast green chilies from the ashes, peeled them, and laid them on a plate.

"Did you catch anything?" Shimah asked.

"A few cottontails." Lorencito pointed with his lips. "They're hanging out there in the tree."

Luciano was telling his mother about Lady, what a fast mare she was, how smooth and powerful her gait. "I don't like to ride any of the other horses after her."

Juanita knew she was wrong, speaking out in front of the family. Lu would probably tease her more before them, but it seemed such a good opportunity to get Raven. "If you're going to ride Lady all of the time, someone should ride Raven or he'll get too hard to manage. Why don't you give him to me?" She tried to speak casually. Luciano went on drinking his coffee, but there was a flicker of laughter in his eyes. He turned to Lorencito. "My wife wants me to give her one of my best horses."

Lorencito smiled, scooping up potatoes on his fried bread. "Is she worth a good horse, your wife?" he teased.

Shimah and Yee-ke-nes-bah began to giggle. Juanita waited. She'd said enough, perhaps too much and at the wrong time.

"Lorencito was asking me about Raven. Of course, we haven't arrived at any bargain."

Lorencito nodded, the turquoise swinging from his ears, as he became a party to the duplicity.

Juanita scooped up potatoes on her bread, her fingers steady. She lifted the coffee cup and waited as her husband spoke again.

"Of course, another bidder might get my brother's price up. What would you give for Raven?"

"Most anything," Juanita said evenly. "What do you want?"

Luciano shook his head slowly. "You must want that horse bad. Bad enough to eat a whole green chili for him?" He began to grin.

Juanita set her coffee cup down. "Pass the plate."

Lu started to hand the plate of chilies to her, then drew it back. "No, I'll pick one out for you, a real hot one. I can't let Raven go too easily." He examined all the chilies, his face serious, then he handed one to her. "Here, this one has lots of seeds in it."

Lu's brothers and sister were greatly interested in the bargaining for Raven. There was a little anxiety beside the smile in Shimah's eyes as she watched her daughter-in-law.

Juanita held the long green pepper for a moment before biting into it. "And no bread or water afterwards," Lu added.

The first bite wasn't bad. Not many seeds in the tip. She chewed it and swallowed. Only a few tears blurred her eyes. The second bite was much worse, but the third and last bite left her breathless. Tears were streaming from her eyes. Her mouth and throat seemed afire. She could barely see the figures about her but she could hear their laughter as she gasped and fought for breath and tried to wipe the tears from her face. Shimah handed her a piece of fried bread but Juanita held it firmly in her lap, not lifting it to her burning mouth.

After a long time the worst of the burning sensation was over. She managed to say, "You've all seen my part of the bargain. Now Raven is mine."

Lu was still laughing. "You may eat some bread now," he told her. "I'm glad to know how much you wanted that horse. It would have been disappointing to have a gift not appreciated."

"What do you mean 'gift'? I bargained for Raven."

Lu and Lorencito began to laugh together. "As soon as I bought Lady, I decided to give Raven to you."

Early spring, a promise of new grass on the hillsides, bright yellow sunshine warming the winter-rested earth for the expectancy of life. The red walls of the canyon down which they rode caught the sounds of Raven and Lady's hooves and repeated it over and over. Somewhere among the rocks a mourning dove called its plaintive, heart-tugging "coo-coo cooo coo-coo."

Luciano spoke softly to Lady in Navajo. She flicked an ear at him and slowed her pace. Lu settled back in the saddle. "I wonder how a horse like Lady ever got into this country."

Pulling on Raven to slow his pace to Lady's, Juanita watched the smooth ripple of muscles under the mare's coat of burnished copper. "Probably a wild Navajo mare got mixed up with a blueblood from one of the ranches."

"She's certainly everything a horse should be."

Juanita could see the contentment on her husband's face, the pride in his eyes. They rode along without speaking, listening to the trill of meadowlarks perched on the bare chamise branches and in the tops of junipers, their black-necklaced throats quivering with song.

"I've never felt quite this way about a horse before," Lu seemed to be talking almost to himself. "I think I understand now why the old men want their favorite horses killed over their graves."

Juanita knew of the Navajo custom of destroying a dead person's possessions and killing his horse. Lu had once explained to her that the spirit could then make use of his possessions and ride the horse on his journey to the next world.

"If anything ever happened to me, I know I would want no one else to ride Lady."

The canyon walls were spreading apart now. Juanita and Lu followed the east wall.

Juanita was thinking of Richard Bay Horse. "Lu, what happens when a Navajo dies away from home, as far away as Hollywood?"

"You mean Bay Horse? If his people have any of his things they destroy them. And if he has a horse, it's led out to some far mesa and shot. His possessions and his horse are then of use to his spirit."

They were riding into open land, and ahead was the red mesa with Lu's grandfather's old crumbling rock house on its edge. Unbelievably pale and delicate, like pink mist rising, the blossoms of the peach trees seemed to float against the red rock of the mesa wall.

"Your grandfather's peach trees are in bloom."

"Shall we ride over?"

They rode across the yellowed grass of the flat land, down the steep bank of the arroyo where slender willows lifted bare red branches, and up the bank of the arroyo to the wide shelf of land below the mesa. The peach trees stood in irregular rows, thick gnarled trunks, age-darkened branches spreading wide beneath a heavy veil of delicate pink flowers. A few early butterflies had found the blossoms.

"Did you ever see anything so beautiful?" Juanita asked softly.

They rode the horses between the blossom-laden trees. A petal fell on Raven's neck, and he shook his head, tossing his heavy black mane. A shower of blossoms descended over them. Lu swung from the saddle, looping Lady's reins around a limb of one of the peach trees. Juanita dismounted from Raven, tying him a few steps away. The sun overhead warm against her shoulders, Juanita stretched out in the dry grass beneath one of the big trees. "I could go to sleep, it's so beautiful and peaceful here." Small warm winds ruffled the yellow grass stems around her.

"When I herded sheep I used to lie down on the ground to rest. Sometimes, half-asleep, I couldn't feel where my body ended and the ground began."

Juanita smiled lazily as her husband sat down beside her. She too had experienced that feeling as a child. She told him about it. Luciano stretched out beside her, closing his eyes. Watching his lean brown face, so much seemed unbelievable: the years they'd been married, their children, the work at the day school. Luciano looked no different than the first night she'd seen him. Lying on the warm ground beneath the old grandfather's peach tree, Juanita closed her eyes and the scene recreated itself.

It had been after a Sunday night meeting at Standing Bear's, and Nadine was out someplace with Michel. Juanita had taken down her hair, brushed it, braided it loosely into one thick heavy braid, and changed into a red-corded lounging robe. She'd wait until Nadine was home and her company had left before opening the daybed out into the living room. She sat reading under the soft light of a bridge lamp; the rest of the room was in shadow.

When the knocking sounded at the door, she got up sleepily, flipping the shade of the lamp to light the doorway. Perhaps Nadine had forgotten her key. She opened the door. Standing in the shaft of lamplight was a strange young Navajo. That he was Navajo was unmistakable: the width of the silver concho belt worn loosely about his hips, the number of silver bracelets on his dark wrists, the bright purple shirt, the red silk band binding black, black hair against his proud head, the sharp cut of cheekbones, long mouth stern and unsmiling, large dark eyes regarding her appraisingly.

Juanita found words. "If you're looking for Standing Bear, he lives in the apartment across the drive."

The appraising dark eyes didn't leave her face. The man said quietly, "I wasn't looking for Standing Bear."

Juanita stared at him wordlessly, and he stared back; then his lips lengthened into a slow smile.

Someone laughed from behind him. Another face in the lamplight: Delilah Wolf, still laughing softly. "It's confusing, isn't it, to find a strange young man on your doorstep?"

Juanita was opening the screen door when Delilah introduced them. "Juanita, this is Luciano."

Juanita opened her eyes to find her husband leaning upon one elbow looking at her.

"You smile nicely when you're asleep."

"Perhaps I wasn't asleep."

"Perhaps." He bent his head low over her face, his lips searching for hers.

It was as though she had never been kissed before.

TWENTY
The Wolf Hunt

Wash day was always a busy day, even with some of the women to help. Juanita began to heat the water soon after sun-up. She dipped water carefully from one of the stationary tubs so as not to disturb the water softener and sediment which had settled on the bottom. When the large copper boiler was almost full, Alice Watson helped her lift it to the top of the small woodstove in the laundry room.

"Is Luciano going on the wolf hunt?"

"What wolf hunt?" Juanita began dipping water into the large galvanized tub to be rolled on a dolly to the kitchen and heated on the big cookstove. "I hadn't heard about one."

Alice and Pah-des-bah lapsed into Navajo, then Alice spoke again to Juanita. "Maybe your husband didn't hear about it," she gestured with her head to the open windows over the stationary tubs. "Some of the men are leaving now."

Juanita could see a few men on horseback riding in the direction of Des Jin.

Wolf hunt . . . at this time of year? Juanita and Alice pulled the dolly into the kitchen, and lifted the tub to the stove. "You mean *ma-itso*?" Juanita asked.

Alice shrugged her shoulders. "No one knows for sure. Maybe when the men get back. . . ." Her voice trailed off.

Juanita heard the motor of the school truck. Luciano was leaving to pick up the children. He hadn't heard about the hunt, or if he had, he wasn't going. Somehow Juanita was relieved.

262 The Winds Erase Your Footprints

Rosita and Toni passed the kitchen door, Bob and Ginger, tagging along behind them. "Don't you girls leave the school yard," Juanita cautioned them.

While the water heated for washing, Juanita always prepared the vegetables for a stew and put dried prunes on the back of the stove to simmer. With the noon meal thus simplified, she could give most of her time to the laundry.

She stacked carrots, potatoes, turnips, and onions in the sink. Alice and Pah-des-bah began to clean them.

"What do you know about this wolf hunt?" Juanita finally asked.

"Something has been stealing lambs this spring. The dogs bark but when the men get out to the sheep corral there's nothing around." Alice paused to consult Pah-des-bah.

Now that she thought of it, Ginger and Bob had been restless for a few nights. The dogs had awakened them once, howling, and Luciano had gone outside to look around. "There's nothing out there," he had said upon returning. "Bob must have started baying at the moon and now Ginger's doing it."

Alice began to cut potatoes into chunks; they fell plop, plop, plop into the pan. "Richard Platero heard something around his corral last night and took his rifle with him when he left the hoghan. He saw what he thought at first was a shadow. When it moved, he fired at it. It got away. He couldn't trail it last night so he started out early this morning. The tracks were wolf tracks. When he met Pah-des-bah's husband, they talked about it and decided to get some of the other men to go with them."

Juanita cut the stew meat into small pieces and dropped them into the boiling water of the stew kettle. Coyotes ran near Cañoncito. Early mornings she had heard the weird yelping cries of coyotes from the direction of Apache Wash. They could have been stealing lambs.

Juanita had put soap powder into the washing machine, added hot water, and was pushing and pulling the handle and foot pedal that worked the wooden tumbler when the school girls began coming into the wash room. She hadn't heard the truck when it came back. "Pah-des-bah, will you stand inside the door and see that all the girls brush their teeth and comb their hair?"

Alice was sorting clothes from the big splint hamper. Tea towels and bath towels in one pile; underwear in another; socks, the boys' shirts, and the girls' dresses together. Juanita put the tea towels into the hot soapy water and worked the handle and foot pedal methodically. Luciano came to the back door of the laundry room. "Need any water from the barrels?"

"You might bring in a couple of buckets in case we run short of rinse water."

"Did you hear about the wolf hunt?" she asked as he put the buckets down by the stationary tubs.

He nodded. "I wanted to go along, but with Hoskey gone there's no one to relieve me."

Juanita knew that she was glad that Lu wasn't on the wolf hunt. Suppose it did become a man hunt. She thought of the frightened, hunted look in the eyes of the man who had come to their log hoghan in Crown Point.

Several women came to the day school that morning and congregated in the laundry room. Occasionally, one of the women took Juanita's place at the handle of the machine while she went into the kitchen to be sure there was plenty of water covering the beans she had started earlier.

The laundry room was warm and steamy in spite of the open door and windows. There was the sharp smell of naphtha from the soapy water, and the close, sour smell of dirty clothes. The clothes were soused up and down in the rinse water, wrung through the wringer, and carried out to the clotheslines in one of the splint baskets. But Alice and Pah-des-bah were not too busy to repeat the story of the wolf hunt to each newcomer, and none of the women were too busy to stop and listen. More often than not, the story was greeted with the tense low question, "*ma-itso*?"

The women helped carry out the water when the washing machine was emptied and fresh water was put in. Juanita washed the girls' dresses in warm soapy water, a few at a time. "Be sure to hang them wrong side out," she cautioned Alice, who was pressing the brightly-colored prints into the wringer.

Through the open windows, Juanita could see the men on horseback returning.

A few of the men rode as far as the Chapter House, tied their horses, and walked to the shade at the back of the school where Luciano was working on an extra piece of playground equipment. There was not the usual laughter and banter when the men got together. Juan Chavez' friendly brown eyes were troubled. Decidero's face was unusually grave.

"Where's Lorencito?" Tomas Pablo asked.

This must be quite serious, Juanita thought, if the men are asking for Lorencito. Lorencito had recently been elected Headman.

"Is there no one at my mother's hoghan?"

The men shook their heads.

"He may have ridden to Torreon; he talked of going there."

Alice left the wringer and went to stand by the back door. Juanita stopped washing so the noise of the tumbler would not interrupt. One by one, the women moved nearer the door.

"What are the men saying now?" Juanita asked Alice. They were talking too fast in Navajo for Juanita to even catch the trend of their phrases.

Alice listened for a moment. "They've been following the wolf tracks, and the trail doubled back several times but always went ahead again. Then they lost it on a ledge of rock on one of the mesas." She pointed north with her lips. "One of the men found a spot of blood below the ledge."

Alice paused to listen again, and then the women began to talk in low voices and move away from the doorway as the men separated and went back to their horses.

"The men said that the nearest hoghan was Wounded Head's on that same mesa. They rode up there to ask him if he had seen anything that morning."

Juanita started back to the washing machine, a frown puckering her forehead.

"Wounded Head's wife met them at the door of the hoghan; her son stood beside her. The men could not see past them. She would not let them in. She said her husband was very sick. A horse had kicked him."

Excitement spread through the whole community. Some of the men began to carry rifles across their saddles or old revolvers in their belts. The women who gathered in the day school kitchen or sat outside around the back door talked together in low voices. But no one rode again to Wounded Head's place on the mesa.

"If they think it was Wounded Head that Richard shot, why don't the men go to his hoghan and see if he has a bullet wound?" Juanita asked her husband.

"It isn't as simple as that. Among the men who believe Wounded Head to be one of the *ma-itso*, there are a few who want him killed now, but there are others who are afraid of him. It's one thing to kill one of the *ma-itso* in the wolf skin and it's another to let him get away and give him a chance to work witchcraft against those who are after him. Most of the men want to wait and let the Headman handle it. They say it's a serious thing to accuse a man of witchcraft without more proof than these men have."

Juanita and Lu were just returning home from the day school when Lorencito rode up. Rosita, Toni, and the dogs were almost to the kitchen door. Juanita walked ahead to unlock it. She heard her husband ask:

"Where are you going?"

"Here."

"Where have you been?"

"To Wounded Head's."

It seemed a long time before they were all in the kitchen and she lit the lamp and shoved the dogs back outdoors. Lorencito sat down in a chair beside the kitchen table and pushed his wide-brimmed hat off his forehead. Luciano sat down across from him.

"Well, did Wounded Head's wife let you in?"

Lorencito nodded.

Juanita went outside the kitchen door for the box of kindling, and hurried back in. Her husband was asking if Wounded Head seemed badly injured.

Lorencito pulled thoughtfully at one of the heavy turquoise pendants. "Wounded Head wasn't there. He's dead."

Juanita laid the kindling fire in the stove, poured a little kerosene over it, and lit the match, lowering the lid quickly over the shooting flame.

Lorencito told how he had gone with a few of the older men to the hoghan. Wounded Head's wife was very courteous to them. Her husband had died shortly after being kicked by the horse. She and her son had buried him.

Juanita put water on for coffee, washed potatoes for boiling, and took a package of dried beef from the cupboard. Was it the old grandfather who said members of the *ma-itso* had no fear of the dead?

"Well, that much is over," Luciano shrugged his shoulders.

"No, it isn't over," Lorencito answered. "Many of the men don't believe the story about the horse kicking Wounded Head. They think Richard shot him, and that Wounded Head tried to cover his trail back to the hoghan during the night and held the wound somehow so that blood didn't drip until he began climbing the ledged side of the mesa. They want the body examined for a bullet wound; and they are already talking of having the grave opened. There will be talk about this for a long time, and the men will try to get someone to come from the Agency to examine the body." Lorencito bent forward looking at the toes of his moccasins. "But I don't think we'll ever know for sure about this. Wounded Head's wife and son are the only ones who know where he is buried. They will never tell where the grave is. Even if the men could find it, there isn't one who would dig into it."

"What good would it do," Juanita turned from the stove, "to prove that Wounded Head was one of the *ma-itso*? If he was one, he's dead now and can harm no one again."

There continued to be much talk and speculation in the community. Juanita and Lu sometimes discussed the peculiar coincidence of events surrounding Wounded Head's death. When they were at Shimah's hoghan it was inevitable that their experiences when they first came to Cañoncito and their later experiences in Crown Point should be discussed in connection with the recent wolf hunt.

Juanita could recall the bewilderment she had felt those first few months in Cañoncito, the feeling of something being withheld. She remembered clearly the mixture of belief and unbelief she felt when the meaning of *ma-itso* was explained to her. But she could recall at no time actually being afraid. The strange events in Crown Point had brought excitement and unanswered questions, but not fear. She was still firm in her belief that *ma-itso*, no matter how real or how strong, could never harm them.

And yet she and Lu admitted to themselves that Wounded Head's death had erased a shadow from the background—a shadow which had been on the outermost fringe of their lives and was there no longer. Now when the dogs howled at night, Luciano didn't even get up to scold them.

All thoughts of *ma-itso* were forgotten the day that the White Haired Woman told them their vacations had been okayed. It was bread-baking day. Juanita made thirty-two loaves of bread once a week for the school, besides what she baked for their own use. She had set the dough near the stove to rise early that morning. The pans of scalloped potatoes were all prepared. She could put them in the oven an hour before noon and they'd be ready for the children's lunch. Mrs. Juan Chavez and Gladys Del Garito had grated the cabbage and carrots together for salad and then walked up the road in the direction of the new trading store.

Juanita took the small galvanized tub from the pantry and sifted in whole wheat flour, smoothing it over the bottom of the tub and banking it high around the sides. With the lard and salt within reach, Juanita poured the yeast mixture into the tub and began to work the wholewheat flour into it. Luciano came in from the playground.

"Are you going to make bread for us?"

Juanita nodded, continuing to work the dough.

"Will we have it hot tonight for supper?"

"If you like. I'll wait and put our loaves in last."

"That sounds like the children marching out for recess. I'd better get outside."

The White Haired Woman came through the dining room. "Wait a minute, Mr. Platero, and I can tell you both at once about your vacations. My husband just brought the mail. The office has okayed the month of June. Your salaries will go on as usual."

After the teacher had gone, Juanita and Lu stood looking at each other. Juanita stopped kneading dough, resting her hands on the edge of the tub. "Just the way we wanted it."

"And do you still want to go to California?"

"Of course *you* don't."

Luciano grinned. "Well, it would be fun for a visit."

He returned to the playground and Juanita continued to work the dough until it felt firm, yet light, to her hands. They could stay with Nadine and Michel; Nadine had written she would be expecting them this summer.

She greased the bread pans and set them on the draining board. The girls could see the ocean. The children had no idea what a large body of water was like. They'd only seen the muddy Rio Grande and the thin stream of the Rio Puerco between high banks.

Juanita began to twist off pieces of dough and mold them into loaves. Luciano came in again after recess. He leaned against the door frame. "I've been thinking we should go on the train, really arrive in style. And we'll need new luggage."

"Are you thinking of all those people who said we'd never make it out here?"

"Yes and no. But we want to do this right."

Juanita had filled four pans with bread, eight loaves to a pan. She molded four more loaves into a small pan and set them all back on the draining board, covered with tea towels, to rise again. "We'll visit Aunt Ina. She's never seen the girls."

"And Standing Bear. And Waano-Gano and meet his wife."

"There'll be so many people to see. Do you think even a month will be long enough?"

Juanita slid the pans of potatoes into the oven and began to mix dressing for the salad.

"We'll need some different clothes. Can't wear Levis and gingham dresses out there." Luciano squinted his eyes as though he were looking ahead. "It's only two more weeks until June. We'd better plan to go into Albuquerque to shop this Saturday."

Juanita was taking the last of two large pans from the oven. She rubbed the rounded tops of the loaves with grease. Luciano came to the door. "Have you seen Bob and Ginger? The teacher has some scraps for them."

"I saw them running up the arroyo early this morning, probably going hunting together. They sometimes do."

Juanita added coal to the fire to the oven heat for the last small pan of bread.

It was a half hour later when Luciano came to the door again. He carried the short-handled shovel. Juanita had separated the loaves, left them to cool, and cleaned the large bread pans and put them away. "I'll be finished here soon." She opened the oven door a crack. "Won't take these small loaves much longer."

A certain gravity in her husband's voice caused her to turn and look at him. "You'd better call the girls into the kitchen with you so they won't follow me. I found the dogs up the arroyo. They're both dead."

"Lu, what could have happened?"

"Poison, maybe. No marks on them that I can see."

TWENTY-ONE
A Rabbit Chase

They came back from California after being gone three weeks.
The trader brought them out from Albuquerque. When he
turned his truck around and drove out of the school yard,
Juanita, Luciano, and the two girls stood for a moment just
as they had alighted, the new luggage stacked neatly together
where the trader had lifted it from the back of his truck.

"We're home," Juanita thought, seeing the stone school
building, the low mesas, Des Jin in the distance streaked
with cloud shadows. It was as though she'd seen them only
yesterday and then again as though she were seeing them for
the first time.

There were several horses tied near the Chapter House and
wagons drawn up beside it. "There must be a meeting."
Luciano set their suitcases two at a time on the doorstep.
"Shall we go over?"

As they walked through the open door of the square stone
Chapter House, the words repeated themselves in Juanita's
mind: "We're home." She could see it in her husband's eyes
and in her children's smiles; she knew it in her heart.

Lorencito was speaking to the people assembled. He walked
back and forth, gesturing as he talked. When he saw his
brother and his family, he dropped his hands and walked
toward them, smiling.

Lupe was home from school for the summer. She ran to them
impulsively, taking both her brother's and her sister-in-law's
hands. Shimah was not far behind. It was good to see the
gladness in Shimah's eyes. The old grandfather didn't wait for
Juanita and Lu to come to him either; he started toward the
sound of their voices, tapping along the cement floor with his

stick, and groping with the other hand for little Joe Chavez to guide him.

Three weeks was not a long time to be away, yet they'd missed these people. There was so much in the shy handclasps, the warm smiles, the questions of the different families as Juanita and Lu walked from group to group, which said the people were glad to have them back. Finally they sat down on the bench beside Shimah, Toni leaning against her grandmother, and the meeting continued.

Lorencito was speaking about certain land between Cañoncito and the Rio Puerco which had once been Navajo domain and might be restored by the government to Cañoncito. There were certain provisions which went with the restoration of this land. One by one the men arose to speak for or against these provisions.

As Juanita listened to the low soft voices, she watched the smooth, unhurried gestures and saw the looks of quiet attention on the faces of the listeners, as though they were savoring the argument. These were things she had become accustomed to. Small wonder that the constant noise and hurry of the large city of Los Angeles had been too much for her and her family.

Her mind drifted. For several years their experience with cities had been limited to a few hours spent in Gallup or Albuquerque. They'd forgotten the tremendous noise and confusion common to a very large city. They had not been prepared for the effect a few weeks in such a city would have upon them.

Nadine and Michel's house was on one of the main street car lines. The singing of rails and the harsh clang-clang of the street car bells seemed never-ending. When they went downtown, the surge of people in the shopping districts and the crowds on the sidewalk at Sixth and Spring, at Seventh and Broadway, swept them along. It was the same when they went to dinner at the restaurants, or to see a show at the theater. Their friends planned evenings at the most popular places to give them the things they had missed on the reservation. But the crowds and the confusion smothered their senses until what should have been enjoyment was turned into a nightmare.

The little girls became nervous, restless, and irritable at night. Toni lost her appetite and ate scarcely anything at mealtimes. Rosita talked more and more about her mare and began to worry if she was all right while they were gone.

Juanita looked at Rosita now, standing between her father's knees, her small hands resting on Lu's long brown fingers linked about her middle. A calm had returned to her face and to her eyes, as it had come back to Luciano.

Only when they went to the beach with Nadine and Michel did the children relax and become carefree. The two days at the beach were a small period of quiet and rest in the midst of the clamor and hurry and crowded days of their vacation. Luciano took the girls walking along the sand and showed them the small white shells to hunt and take back to Lorencito for his Medicine work. He told them the long story of the Turquoise Woman who was the wife of the Sun and whose home was on an island out there in the Western Waters.

They had bathed in the waves and in the sun, and built fantastic mounds of wet sand. Nadine and Juanita spent hours in the shade of an umbrella, talking, while Michel and Luciano roamed the dunes with the camera.

Juanita was drawn back to the present. Old Juarito was getting to his feet and beginning to speak, measuring his words slowly as if to better hear and enjoy the sound of them. The young man who did women's work sat quietly by the window, listening, but never rose to add his opinion to the discussion.

Juanita smiled at some of the young girls who sat with their families: Ada Sandoval, Marian Shorte, Ruby Chavez, Ida Platero, girls who helped her at the day school. It was evident that they had dressed carefully for the Chapter meeting. Clean top skirts, the glitter of a ten-cent brooch among the silver buttons on their velvet blouses, and hair combed neatly and ornamented with small colored combs or a carefully arranged row of hair pins.

Among their California friends, Luciano had at first been eager and proud to talk about Cañoncito, and their jobs at the day school. It was enjoyable seeing their old friends, hearing them remark about how well they were looking, how well they must be doing, hearing them exclaim over the girls. But after two weeks, Juanita and Lu seldom spoke of Cañoncito when they visited friends, except to answer questions. Instead, they talked of home when they were alone, wondering if the men had started planting corn, if the white-faced mare had dropped her foal, if the affair between Seraphina's daughter and a returned schoolboy had been settled.

Before, Juanita had known homesickness through Luciano. Now she knew it for herself. When her husband sat on the edge of their bed early one morning, staring past her out the window, and said, "If we packed today, could we take a train home tonight?" their vacation was little more than half over.

"I think we could," she answered evenly, knowing it was also what she wanted to do.

The Chapter meeting was over. The families wandered toward the door. Little "Washeengtone" held fast to his mother's skirt, ducking his head shyly and grinning when Juanita spoke to him. Old Seraphina stopped to pet Rosita and Toni, making clucking noises through her stubby teeth. George Abeyta called across the room to Luciano, "How are things out West?"

They moved along slowly with the people toward the door and touched hands with them. Decidero Platero spoke, his eyes smiling. Alice Watson and her husband, Pah-des-bah Earl Begay greeted them also.

Looking from one to another of the familiar faces, Juanita felt gladness and contentment spread over her like a warm blanket. It was good to be home.

Juanita and Luciano were just leaving the school grounds on Lady and Raven when Charlie Sandoval, Earl Begay, Arturo Chavez, and Manuel Secatero came riding through the cut in the mesas.

"We're going on a rabbit chase. Want to come along?" Manuel called to Luciano. The young men rode up beside them. Charlie carried a short, knobbed-at-one-end rabbit stick.

Juanita sat quietly on her horse, debating whether to ride off by herself toward Arrowhead Mesa, the way she and Lu had planned to go, or to ask to go along on the chase. She'd always wanted to go on a rabbit chase since it promised to be a hard and exciting ride, but she'd hesitated to ask because she knew it wasn't customary for women to go.

Raven was restless. He began to stamp his feet and toss his head. Juanita stroked his neck and tried to quiet him. George Abeyta was riding toward them, crossing the arroyo bridge. Allen rode up from his mother's hoghan on Pete. Luciano reined Lady close to Pete and began to talk with Allen in a low voice. Allen's white teeth flashed in a grin. Manuel smiled as he overheard the conversation.

Luciano turned to his wife and said rather sternly, "You'd better trade horses with Allen. Pete's a seasoned rabbit chaser. If you're going along we can't be bothered with you getting pitched off." The laughter in his eyes softened his words.

As Juanita got on Pete, George Abeyta called, "Are you going with us?"

She nodded.

"Well, wait a minute." He rode along the base of the low mesas and then rode toward them with a very long, very large stick. "Here, Juanita, you'll need this to club the rabbit."

The young men lounging in their saddles looked at Juanita slyly and began to laugh.

"No, you keep it for yourself, George," Juanita told him. "I'll do well if I stay in the saddle this time."

As they rode east past various hoghans, men on horseback joined them: Richard Platero, Tony Chavez, Frank Woods. There were perhaps twenty-five riders when the men began to spread out in a long line across the open country.

It would be hard riding all right, Juanita thought as she surveyed the country ahead, cut with small arroyos and outcroppings of rock, dotted with cholla cactus and chamise. The line was moving forward, each rider's eyes intent upon the bushes ahead for the first rabbit to be scared up.

"Aiiiiiyeeee," a high long cry sounded from the center of the line as a frightened jack rabbit darted from beneath a chamise bush and scurried ahead of the horses. Immediately, the furthermost riders began closing in toward the center.

The rabbit dodged one way and men and horses on that side of the ragged pack formation followed. The rabbit dodged to the other side and short yells preceded the charge of a few riders in that direction. The rabbit was rapidly losing ground and one of the men ahead was able to ride it down, bending from the saddle to club it sharply behind the ears.

There was a quick pulling up on the lead horses. The riders farthest out rode in toward the knot of men and horses. "Who got it?" someone asked.

"Frank got the first one."

Frank Woods was off his horse, picking up the limp rabbit. In one quick movement he broke the hind legs at the joint, then hooked them over one of the leather thongs behind his saddle, knotting the leather securely above the broken bones.

The line began to spread out again to beat up another rabbit from the bushes. They rode forward, converging as another rabbit streaked across the ground ahead. Juanita had found that trying to control Pete made not the slightest difference. He wheeled sharply when the other horses wheeled, and plunged ahead into the converging pack when the rabbit was just ahead. Dust smarted in Juanita's eyes and in her nostrils, and as she rode, head down, her only thought was to stay in the saddle.

Allen got the second rabbit. The men rested their horses for a moment and settled back in their saddles, a few of them lighting cigarettes. Pete stood trembling a little, anxious to go again.

"How are you doing?" Lu asked casually as he rode up beside her.

"I haven't been pitched off yet."

The chase lasted until the sun was hot: several minutes of hard riding, then a pause while a rabbit was tied behind a saddle, some talk and laughter, and the line slowly spread out again. It was fun, and a little dangerous. The rough country made it almost as hard on the horse and rider as on the rabbit, except that the rabbit almost always lost.

Riding home, men turned off at well-worn trails or rode off across country. When they reached the cut in the mesas, Juanita, Lu and Allen rode on through.

"We're all going again next Sunday," George Abeyta called after them. "I'll save that rabbit stick for you, Juanita."

At the day school, Allen put lead ropes on their horses and started off toward the hoghan, three limp jack rabbits dangling from his saddle. "Better luck next time, brother."

Luciano smiled but did not answer, and Juanita didn't tell her husband that in spite of the wind and dust in her eyes and the confusion of men and horses about her, she had seen him riding not far behind her, instead of up in the lead after a rabbit.

School would soon be starting. Everything was ready for the fall term except the building, which needed one last thorough cleaning before opening day. New dresses were made, two for each girl, bright prints and ginghams cut from a magazine pattern rather than in the full-skirted Navajo style. Juanita spent most of the summer days sewing these dresses and hemming additional bath towels and tea towels to stock the linen closet.

Luciano repaired and painted the playground equipment, hauled and cut wood for the depleted wood pile, washed the windows, washed the walls of the kitchen and wash rooms, and spent some of his evenings at the forge on silver work for the new trading store.

"Shall we ride over to our land today?" Luciano asked as they were saddling Lady and Raven.

Lu and Allen had worked almost all day on a new hoghan for Shimah, while Juanita and Lupe and the two girls stayed in the brush shelter with the family. Shimah had a rug up and Lupe worked awhile on it, taking her sister's teasing good-naturedly when Yee-ke-nes-bah said that going to school had dulled her fingers.

The almost completed hoghan looked raw and new against the background of the two old rock houses. The clean yellow and white rock of the walls had not yet been streaked and worn by wind and rain; the newly cut post supports of the doorway were raw and yellow where the axe had stripped the bark, as were the heavy logs which began the curve inward for the dome. Even the packed earth of the dome appeared new and raw, with no scattering of grass and weeds growing from it as from the earth on the poled roofs of the old rock houses.

"We'll put the door up tomorrow," Luciano told her as they rode away. Shimah was proud of the new door and cupboards Lu had built, wide-shelved with doors.

They followed the day school road across the arroyo bridge and raced Raven and Lady along the smooth surface of the dirt road until they reached the top of the steep hill. Pulling their horses in, they descended the hill at an easy lope. Lu's allotment was just over the next hill. To one side of the road were the tumbled rocks of an abandoned sheep corral. To the other side was the narrow wagon trail which led toward Cottonwood Spring behind the far red mesa.

"Next time we go to Albuquerque we'll bring back an empty fifty-gallon oil drum. I've got an idea about making a stove from one of those for the hoghan." Luciano expanded his idea, telling how he intended to set the open end up on rocks, and have the fire built underneath. The flat round top of the drum would have a hole made in it to attach a stove pipe that would go on up to the smoke hole in the ceiling. "Should take less wood and give more heat."

They were on top of the second rise. Marhilde Chavez's corn field in the spread of low ground where the arroyo widened was lush and tall. The heavy tassels were like creamy white foam on a sea of green. Their own land stretched before them, one hundred and sixty acres girded by two strands of barbed wire. Chamise bushes and a few stunted junipers dotted the rolling pasture land, and cholla cactus raised spiked arms from the sloping hill.

"When we build a house, we'll build a fireplace in it. I like an open fire," Lu said as he dismounted to unhook the strands of wire stretched across the gateway.

They rode around their land, Lu pointing out a thick patch of thistles. "The Medicine Men come here for these." A circle of rocks at one far corner was the remains of Shimah's hoghan when the family had lived on Lu's land for a short time while he was away at school. There was a battered kettle and a soleless moccasin among the gray chips where wood had once been piled.

"Here's a good place for peach trees or a cornfield." Lu indicated a low spot, the earth dried and cracked where water stood after rain.

They dismounted on the top of the sloping hill. Lu nudged broken bits of pottery with the toe of his boot. "We used to find arrowheads up here when we were kids; I guess some of the ancients once lived on top of this hill." He walked along leading Lady, trampling a few late yellow wildflowers underfoot. "But down there on the slope is where we want to build."

Juanita could see the house in her mind, low, thick-walled against the wind and the rain, nestled at the base of the hill. She saw the long line of mesas on the horizon to the west, Des Jin and the chain of low hills to the north, a view of the Sandia Mountains far off beyond Albuquerque to the east. She could picture the afterglow of sunset on deep-silled, square-paned windows.

A small wind rustled across the top of the hill. She could hear its voice in the yellow grass, see its path down the hillslope.

Luciano was at the new hoghan putting up the stove. The girls had walked over with him, and Rosita promised Toni a ride alone on her mare.

Lupe and Juanita finished the housework and changed into shirts and Levis, "just in case someone's rounded up the horses," Juanita said, winding a red band around her head to hold the heavy coil of hair in place. Walking across the pasture land, they could see a column of thin gray smoke coming from the dome of the new hoghan. "There's no smoke coming out the door," Lupe observed, "I guess the new stove works."

Khee was leading Rosita's mare around and around the hoghan, Toni holding gravely to the mane, her little legs scarcely long enough to clamp against the horse's middle. Luciano stood in the doorway of the new hoghan. "Now give her the reins."

The mare stood still while the reins were looped over her head and handed to Toni. She continued to stand when Toni jiggled the reins and urged her ahead.

"Kick her, Toni," Luciano instructed.

Toni kicked, almost upsetting herself. Wide-eyed, she clutched the reins as the mare resumed her leisurely pace. "Pull her head this way." Lu came from the doorway of the hoghan to follow on one side of the mare. The mare turned and began a circle around the hoghan. "Loosen up your reins a little."

Juanita watched, smiling. Toni was little to begin riding, but no smaller than Rosita had been. Shimah sat under the shelter carding wool, stopping occasionally to shoo flies from Yee-ke-nes-bah's baby sleeping beside her. She nodded approvingly as she watched her granddaughter managing the horse alone. She pursed her lips for a moment and then said, "All the women of this family are good riders." Her hand flicked out against the flies. "When I was a young girl, I rode my horse in races." Lu's mother smiled, remembering. "I won, too."

Juanita sat down, leaning against the corner post of the shelter. Luciano was so proud of the girls' love for horses and the way they spoke Navajo around the hoghan. He often spoke to them in Navajo at home, just to hear the shy, soft answers. He had begun running toward the east with them early each morning, pretending to race with Rosita while Toni shouted gleefully from his shoulders. He'd begun to talk about their education, wondering if an Indian school would be advisable since the girls would not have to make the adjustment in thought and language that most Indian children had to make.

Allen and Lorencito were driving the horses toward the corral. Juanita went into the hoghan for her saddle. "Ask my brother if I may use his," Lupe called after her.

"Lupe wants to ride over and see Ada before going back to school," Juanita explained to her husband. "We won't be gone long."

As they rode north toward the canyon where the Sandovals lived, they passed an old man on horseback who stared at them. He was a stranger to Juanita. His long hair was looped into a club knot, small strings of turquoise hung from his ears, and a bright-colored Pendleton was tied behind his saddle.

"I think I remember that man," Lupe said when they were some distance past him. "He looks like a Medicine Man from Torreon who used to visit my father."

They were within sight of the Sandovals' hoghan when Lupe stopped Pete. "I heard something nice about you this summer," she said shyly to her sister-in-law.

Juanita pulled up on Raven, smiling. "Tell me. I love to hear nice things about myself."

"While I was staying at the hoghan and you were in California, some men from Crown Point visited Lorencito. They were talking one night about their sister marrying a white man. They don't like their sister's husband; he and the family don't get along. They said a lot of things about how it isn't good for Navajos to marry with white people and that they're trying to get the sister to separate from her husband. Lorencito listened and when they were through talking he said, 'My younger brother is married to a white girl, and she gets along well with our family. We would not complain about her.'"

Juanita thought a moment. "That's rather nice coming from my brother-in-law. Thank you, Lupe."

When they returned to Shimah's, the stranger they had met on the trail was sitting in the brush shelter. Lorencito, Lu, Yee-ke-nes-bah—the whole family—were there with him. Shimah had begun to cook something for the visitor. The stranger stared at Juanita and Lupe as they dismounted, pulled the saddles and blankets off at the hoghan door, and led the horses to the corral. He was still staring as the girls walked to the shelter. An angry frown began to pucker his forehead.

"What is he saying?" Juanita asked Lupe as the man began to talk and gesture first to Luciano and then to Shimah.

Lupe knelt and then sat down on the sheep pelts. Juanita sat beside her and slightly behind Luciano. "He's telling my brother he shouldn't allow his wife to wear men's pants."

"Oh," Juanita turned to watch her mother-in-law's face.

"He's telling my mother that it's disgraceful for her daughter-in-law to wear such clothes. And that you're a bad influence on me. Remember, he's a long hair from Torreon."

Shimah sat quietly for a long time, her hands folded neatly in her lap. Juanita couldn't help remembering a night when Shimah herself had been just as upset about a pair of Levis. She waited.

Her mother-in-law began to speak softly, quieting the stranger. "I'm an old woman as you are an old man. A long time ago I thought as you, that such a thing was bad. But now I have seen them so much, and they do no harm; I think those pants are all right."

The long hair from Torreon made a noise through his nose. It sounded like a snort.

Juanita thought she saw the beginning of a smile at the corners of her mother-in-law's mouth.

TWENTY-TWO
Unmasking the Yei

It was after the beginning of the fall term that news spread of a Yei-be-tchai to be given in Cañoncito. Such a ceremony had not been held in the community in Lu's lifetime. Only a wealthy family could afford to give the nine-day-and-night ceremony of the Yei-be-tchai. The payment to the Medicine Man and the cost of feeding his assistants and the other people connected with the rites was too expensive.

Antonio Shorte was not a wealthy man but his wife had been afflicted with constant headaches and occasional spells of blindness. The ceremony was to be held over her. Other Cañoncito families had agreed to share in the expense, among them Shimah's family, and the contributing families in turn would share in the blessings of the Yei—the Gods—invoked during the nine days and nights of song, prayer, sand painting, and dancing. Juanita and Luciano gave money to Shimah to be added to the family's share of the expense.

Katharine Teller, the new school teacher, sent money as she too wished to contribute to this Yei-be-tchai. Katharine was the tall, handsome Navajo girl added to the school personnel at the beginning of the fall term when the forty-four or forty-five pupils were divided into two classes; the White Haired Woman took the older students, while Katharine took the younger ones.

When the messenger returned from Crown Point with word that the Medicine Man would conduct the Yei-be-tchai, a large new hoghan for the ceremony was built in a shallow, treeless valley, several miles from the day school. But it was a few days after the beginning of the Yei-be-tchai before Juanita and Lu were able to leave their work at the school.

That there was a nine-day-and-night chant being held in the community was soon evident. Many families moved temporarily to the valley where the Medicine hoghan had been erected. School attendance dropped. The children were too interested in the activities of the large camp to come to school. Those who did attend had their minds on other things or were too sleepy to cope with studies.

On the afternoon of the sixth day of the chant, two masked Yei came to the day school begging for gifts. Juanita was busy in the kitchen, as it was bread-baking day, when Luciano called her to the door. They walked to the edge of the playground to watch the two figures that had appeared in the cut between the mesas—two figures stripped to breech clout and moccasins, ruffs of spruce about their necks, and buckskin masks completely covering their heads. The taller figure gave a peculiar call which sounded like "wuu hu wuu hu" and then they ran with short, halting steps to the day school. Following them at a distance were four men on horseback, half-full flour sacks tied behind their saddles. They had come to carry the gifts collected. Juanita recognized Richard Platero, Frank Woods, and her brother-in-law Khee.

The Yei were continuing the short, running steps in front of the school building, the taller figure giving the cry "wuu hu wuu hu."

"That's Ha-ste-yalti, the Talking God," Lu told her. Juanita looked long at the white buckskin mask topped with eagle feathers like an open fan. "He's sometimes called Yei-be-tchai, Grandfather of the Gods."

Children were coming from the school building to watch the Yei. Some of the older boys laughed, others stood in awed silence. Most of the little ones were frightened. They clustered about Katharine Teller, trying to hide their faces in her skirt. Toni and Rosita stood at the apartment door with Alice Watson.

"The one in the blue-decorated mask is To-ne-nili, the Water Sprinkler. He's the clown at the dances."

"That funny running step they're doing, is it part of a dance?"

Luciano grinned. "These October days are chilly to be without clothes. Maybe they have to do that to keep warm."

The riders with the flour sacks had stopped before the school. Luciano started across the playground. "I'll take Rosita and Toni to the trader's. They'll want to give something to the Yei."

Ha-ste-yalti and To-ne-nili continued to run up and down in front of the school, Ha-ste-yalti uttering his weird cries.

Juanita returned to the school kitchen to wrap some of the fresh-baked bread in a tea towel for the Yei. She saw the White Haired Woman coming across the school grounds with an armful of canned goods.

The Talking God paused in the completion of a circle as the women approached him with their gifts. He accepted the food silently and passed it to one of the men on horseback. Bending over he took the box of cookies from Rosita's outstretched hand. She stared at the square painted mouth and eyes, the corn stalk painted where the nose would be, the spread of down-tipped eagle feathers. Her solemn brown eyes were round with wonder.

Luciano lifted Toni from beside him. She buried her face against his shoulder, only peeking at the masked figure, and put her hand out shyly with her gift to the Yei.

After the Yei had left the school grounds and started across the arroyo to beg gifts at the scattered hoghans, the children stood outside watching, talking excitedly to each other. The White Haired Woman turned to Luciano, spreading her upturned hands in a helpless gesture. "The only sensible thing for me to do is to dismiss the school until the Yei-be-tchai is over."

Luciano took Juanita, Katharine, and the girls to the Yei-be-tchai for the last three days and nights of the ceremony. Cutting across the shallow valley in the school truck, they passed open campfires with blackened cook-pots set up on rocks, brush shelters of fresh green juniper boughs, temporary sheep corrals, and tents stretched from the sides of wagons and from the backs of trucks. Some of the camps seemed deserted, the families visiting other families. Other camps were full of activity, food being prepared, children sprawling about their mothers' knees as the women sat talking and attending bubbling pots. While older children played games about the camp, dogs were being continually shooed away from the cook-fire. The older boys had organized a ball game. At the far end of the shallow valley some of the men were racing their horses.

"Not many strangers," Juanita observed.

"Khee said there were a few Navajos from Puertocito and some teachers from the art department of one of the schools. Oh, yes, and some policemen from Crown Point to see that no liquor is brought in."

The Medicine hoghan was yellowish and new. Not too far distant was the oval brush shelter where the women of some of the families who were helping with the chant cooked for the Medicine Man and his assistants.

They found Shimah's substantial brush shelter, recognizing the old spring-wagon parked tongue down and empty beside it. One of Lorencito's horses grazed nearby.

Katharine, Juanita, and the girls got down from the truck, taking their bundles of food into the shelter. Luciano drove on in search of some of the boys whom he would join in the last night's dancing.

On the afternoon of the eighth day, Juanita went into the Medicine hoghan with Lu to see the large sand painting which almost covered the whole floor. Men and women were crowded into the small space left between the walls and the sand painting. A small fire burned beside the Medicine Man—a faint incense filled the hoghan.

Antonio Shorte's wife sat in the center of the sand painting, the folds of a new bright blue skirt smoothed about her legs, her feet outstretched before her. From the bright blue skirt her upper body rose brown, bare, and beautiful. Her hair was smoothly combed into two shining dark fanshapes, and her face and eyes were calm and utterly still.

"The figures in the sand painting are Water Gods," Luciano told Juanita when they were outside again. "That's all I know. Lorencito would be able to tell us more about it."

He left her at the brush shelter. "I'm going down here," he jerked his head toward another brush shelter where several horses were tied. "Some of the men are having a game."

"Gambling?" Juanita looked over her shoulder. "Well, if you feel lucky, maybe you'll get into the game and put up something to back up the way you feel."

Shimah was helping at the large oval cook-shelter near the hoghan. Juanita asked Katharine if she'd like to walk over. "Maybe we'll get something special to eat." Rosita and Toni were busy playing with their cousins; they would eat later with Yee-ke-nes-bah and the family.

Women nodded to Juanita and Katharine from their places beside the evening cook-fires, and some of the children ran out to walk beside the new teacher. Juanita and Lu had often spoken of the way Katharine fit into the community, visiting the mothers of her pupils at the hoghans, to attending one-night Sings. Lu said the children seemed to be learning fast under her instruction because she could explain things in both English and Navajo.

Juanita had wrapped her Pendleton about her shoulders, the chill of the October evening seeming to pierce her blue gingham dress. She and Katharine sat down against the wall of brush shelter, laughing a little as she resorted to her best Navajo to tell Shimah they were hungry.

They were eating blue cornmeal cakes and a bowl of stew liberally sprinkled with chili when the Medicine Man and his assistants came from the hoghan for their evening meal. The Medicine Man might have been forty and he might have been sixty. He was square-faced, medium tall, and solidly built. His black hair hung long about his shoulders and was tied with a silk kerchief; his Pendleton was unfringed and broadly striped in purple, gray, and green.

He spoke a moment with the older women about the cook-fire and then sat down cross-legged, the silver buttons on his high reddish-brown moccasins gleaming in the firelight. As he reached to take a bowl of stew, Juanita noticed the heavy strands of drilled shell and deep blue turquoise about his neck.

While they ate, the Medicine Man and the men around him talked occasionally in low tones. Finally he looked across the fire at Katharine, asking her where she was from.

"Ganado," she answered. "I am one of the school teachers here."

"Do you know the Yei?"

"I was sent to a mission school before I was old enough."

The Medicine Man looked at Juanita, asking Katharine who she was. Katharine started to explain that she was the wife of the Navajo assistant at the day school.

Shimah interrupted. "She is my daughter-in-law."

Making a gesture with his hand which included Juanita and Katharine, the Medicine Man said, "Both of you come to the hoghan tonight for the Unmasking of the Yei."

Shimah seemed pleased with this.

When the Medicine Man had gone, Katharine explained to Juanita that every Navajo was supposed to attend one unmasking of the Gods, usually after he was eight or nine years old. It was then said that he knew the Yei, that he had been initiated. But with being away at school in the wintertime when the Yei-be-tchais were given, few school children became initiated until they were grown.

"What is the unmasking ceremony?" Juanita asked.

"I don't know except what I've heard. The Yei are supposed to remove their masks and reveal their faces. It's supposed to explain to children who have believed that the masked figures were really the Gods themselves, that they are only men impersonating the Gods. The real Gods cannot be seen."

When it came time for the unmasking, Juanita was standing outside the Medicine hoghan with others of the uninitiated. Katharine and Frank Woods were beside her. Juanita noticed that Frank still wore his cowboy boots and looked rather funny stripped down to a breech clout, his long, thin legs rising from the ornate leather. Several of the school children were waiting in a group.

Someone in the doorway of the hoghan gestured that everything was ready. He gave them final instructions. They were to keep their heads down and their eyes downcast at all times until they were told to look up. He asked Juanita to remove all of the hairpins from her hair. Juanita drew the pins out and let her hair fall about her shoulders. She could scarcely see where she was walking as she followed

Katharine to the back of the hoghan and sat down. A small fire was the only light. With her head inclined she could just see the moccasined feet and the bright skirt edges of the people who crowded the hoghan to watch the initiation.

When the Medicine Man began to chant there was no drum, only the rhythm of his voice. Although the words had no meaning for her, Juanita could sense the dignity and solemnity of the ritual. The rhythm seemed to invade her body, to soothe her senses, and make her newly aware of oneness with everything about her. Moccasined feet were moving sideways toward her. Brown hands holding something wrapped in spruce twigs—ears of corn—pressed the bottoms of her feet, ankles, legs, chest, arms, shoulders, the back of her neck and her forehead. The moccasined feet moved on.

The Medicine Man spoke instructions. Katharine whispered to Juanita to look up.

Standing in the firelight were two men, dark bodies bare except for moccasins and breech clout; one held the elaborate eagle-feathered mask of the Talking God, the other held the square blue-painted mask of one of the female Gods. The figure with the blue-painted mask moved from one initiate to another and held the mask for a moment before each face, then returned to stand beside the impersonator of the Talking God.

The Medicine Man again addressed them.

"He says to look well at the faces of these men and always remember them. They will always remember you," Katharine told her.

Juanita looked at the two strange faces dim in the firelight. She looked beyond them to all the solemn faces of the figures against the wall. The rhythm of the chant still possessed her body and her mind. With ceremonies like this one and the reverence and solemnity with which it was regarded, the Navajos had kept their tribal entity. It seemed to her that this moment revealed more than the faces of the Gods—it revealed the strength of a people.

On the ninth and last day of the chant, a large brush shelter was built east of the Medicine hoghan for the use of the

dance teams who would take part in the all-night masked
dancing. Toward night, wagons and the few cars and trucks
were lined up on either side of the dance ground, forming a
wide lane from the hoghan to the north. Wood was brought
and stacked in piles along the edge of the dance ground.

The trader had put up a temporary stand of canvas and
brush, decorated with crepe paper streamers, at the far end of
the lane. Other members of the trader's family were there
helping him. Already some of the Navajos were drifting to the
stand to buy hamburgers and hot coffee.

Luciano drove the truck up beside the dance ground, lifted
out the leather seat, and carried it to the front of the truck
where the women could sit to watch the dancing. Shimah
threw a few sheep pelts on the ground, while Juanita spread
blankets in preparation for the long night ahead. When
Juanita looked up, Luciano was walking away in the
darkness toward the dancers' brush shelter.

The ceremonies of the last night began as the Talking God
cleared the wide lane for the dancers, walking among the
people muttering only his "*Hash shal tigi.*" The fires along the
edge of the lane were lighted. The Talking God seemed even
taller in the shadows cast by the fires. He looked like a
supernatural personage in the white, eagle-plumed mask and
the large soft buckskin thrown over his shoulders.

When the Medicine Man summoned the four masked figures
of the male Gods from the shelter, they lined up silently
before the hoghan while Antonio Shorte's wife sprinkled them
with cornmeal. The four male Dancing Gods, in oval-shaped
blue masks, had whitened bodies. A fox skin hung from the
back of each one's silver concho belt. Each dancer held a
gourd rattle in one hand and a branch of sacred spruce in the
other. They stood swaying, lifting one foot in rhythm while
the Medicine Man chanted and the patient chanted each
phrase after him.

A long whoop. Then an answering whoop from the four
dancers as they turned and scooped their rattles toward the
ground. In procession, they stamped and lifted their feet
rhythmically, singing: "Oh ho ho ho, Yee yee yee."

Rosita and Toni watched fascinated as the four masked
figures moved in rhythm, singing words, repeating them,

facing one direction and then another as their voices lifted into "Oh ho ho, Ee hee hee."

On both sides of the lane people were watching, dark eyes, dark faces intent upon the dancers. Women and children sat on high wagon seats or wrapped in blankets on the edge of the dance ground. Men leaned against wagon wheels or rested against saddles thrown upon the ground.

After the Starting Dance a larger group of masked dancers came forward. Six male Gods in oval-shaped blue masks and six female Gods in square blue masks began the dancing and singing which would continue until dawn. They performed sedately, dancing in double lines and simple formations, lifting and stamping their feet, shaking their gourd rattles and singing a song not unlike the Starting Song. The "Oh ho ho ho, Ee hee hee hee" sounded far away and unlike earthly voices as it came through the mouth slits of the masks.

Juanita remembered what Lu had told her about the difficulty of singing behind the buckskin mask, how forced and loud the voices had to be to carry through the small mouth openings. Once a dancer put the mask over his head he must not talk or laugh or cough—he must make no noise but singing.

When the formations had been repeated and all the words repeated the proper number of times, the masked dancers formed a single line and danced back to the brush shelter to remove their masks and pass them to the next group of dancers.

First one group and then another of these dancers appeared at intervals. Their appearance was always announced from the darkness by the call of the Talking God, and their voices answered from the shelter. The same songs and the same dance steps were repeated over and over. To-ne-nili, the Water Sprinkler, clowned about the dance ground, imitating the Talking God and the dancers. The people didn't seem to tire of watching.

As the fires died down more wood was added. The flames leapt high, sparks showering. People gathered around the large fires to warm themselves. In the intervals between dances, men and women walked down to the trader's stand for hot coffee.

Juanita touched Shimah's arm when she saw the tall slender figure of Wounded Head's son approach the large fire nearest them.

"Ee-yah," Shimah exclaimed softly. "It's the first time this winter I've seen anyone of that family."

The son looked much like his father in the firelight. His thin face was devoid of expression, his long hair gathered into a club knot. He warmed himself for a moment and then disappeared into the darkness.

The "wuu hu wuu hu" of the Talking God announced the return of the masked dancers. Juanita was trying hard to stay awake. Both Rosita and Toni were asleep beside her. She spread another blanket over them and wondered sleepily which one of the dancers might be Lu. Did he dance with this group or another one? The dark masked figures looked very much alike in the firelight.

As the dancers returned to the shelter this time, To-ne-nili, who had been vigorously dancing beside the last masked figure, continued to dance, unaware that he was now all alone. Smiles and soft laughter greeted his predicament. He looked to one side and then the other, dashed frantically along the dance ground in the wrong direction looking for the rest of the dancers, dashed back the other way, dropping parts of his costume and stooping to retrieve them, and ran along after the last dancer who was just disappearing into the shelter. As he reached the corner of the shelter he tripped and fell sprawling. Laughter rewarded this vigorous exhibition of clowning. Juanita and Katharine started toward the trader's stand for a cup of hot coffee.

As the sky turned lighter and the stars dimmed, the singing grew louder and the dancers' stamps became softer and softer against the ground. Families began to gather up the pelts and blankets on the ground and put them into the wagons; women carried sleeping children to the wagon beds and covered them for the ride home.

With the first gray light in the east the people gathered once more about the dance ground. The dancers assembled facing east. With the dawn the Medicine Man and his assistants began the Bluebird Song in the hoghan. It was at dawn that the Yei gathered for their ascent to their sky homes; they were looking down upon the people and listening to their prayers.

The dancers, led by the Talking God, sang the Bluebird Song, their voices rising in the prayer for good corn, rain, and the blessing of the Gods. As the song ended people approached the Talking God for a pinch of yellow pollen from the buckskin bag he held out to them. Pollen to the tongue, pollen touched to the forehead, pollen sprinkled upon the impersonators of the Yei standing with masked faces to the east.

What had been a large busy camp was now deserted. Juanita sat on the running board of the truck waiting for Lu.

"I think I'll get back here with the girls," Katharine said as she climbed into the truck bed. "I'm too sleepy to sit up any longer."

The shallow valley was dotted with empty brush shelters and the scattered gray ashes of dead campfires. Over everything was a thin white covering of frost. Two men on horseback disappeared over the rim of the valley.

Luciano came from the dancers' shelter, walking briskly toward the truck, his breath white before him.

"I left Haswood in the shelter. He's going to wait a while longer until he's sure the policemen have had time to get out of Cañoncito," Lu told her as he turned on the ignition and pulled out the choke.

"What has Haswood done?"

"Oh, nothing much. He had some wine last night. The policemen found out about it and started looking for him." Lu pushed the starter button. The starter ground for a long time before the motor finally started. He sat working the hand throttle while the motor warmed. "The only way he could get them off his trail was to crawl under their pick-up truck. They didn't think of looking there. He spent a long cold night under there—no blanket. Just before daylight he came to the shelter. He doesn't want them to catch him now after being safe but almost frozen all night." Luciano drove slowly along the valley, past deserted brush shelters, and followed the wagon trail up over the rim.

The eastern sky was pale yellow and misty. The ground and the mesas were awakening to color.

"I had a little trouble getting dressed," Luciano said casually. "I couldn't find all my clothes. Haswood helped me look for them. I'm minus an undershirt and one sock." He laughed a little but his eyes were serious as he pulled up the leg of his Levis and displayed one bare ankle.

"Well, I wouldn't worry about it," Juanita pulled her Pendleton about her sleepily. "It's a cold morning. One of the boys probably needed some extra clothes."

As they drove along the road toward the day school, Juanita could see the faint wagon trails branching off across the pasture land—wagon trails that led to the scattered distant hoghans. Frost lay in the narrow ruts. Far across the pasture land were the figures of men and horses faced homeward, and the dull white top of a covered wagon swaying along a trail. The air smelled clean and sweet, and felt cold against her cheek. "I love early mornings," she said drowsily.

Luciano smiled, not looking at her, searched on the seat beside him until his long strong fingers closed over her hand.

TWENTY-THREE
Luciano Is Nothing

Rosita and Toni were disappointed because their mother was going to Albuquerque, and they couldn't go. They followed her around as she dressed.

"But, Mama, when will we see the toys in the stores, and when will we see Santa Claus?"

Juanita slipped the brown silk dress over her head. "There are two whole weeks yet," she reminded her older daughter. Opening the dresser drawer, she unfolded a fresh white collar.

Tonita continued the argument. "But how will Santa Claus have time to get what we want if we wait so late to tell him?"

"Next week will still be plenty of time; we'll all go in next Saturday."

When Luciano found that the basketball schedule had not been canceled, and that he would either have to drive the schoolboys to Pinedale or else be deliberately insubordinate to the White Haired Woman and to government orders, he finally agreed to make the one trip upon the teacher's promise to do all in her power to get the rest of the schedule canceled. Juanita and Lu decided that while he was making the trip to Pinedale, she would ride to Albuquerque with the trader to keep a final dentist appointment and do her last minute Christmas shopping. Then the following Saturday they would take the girls to town and make a day of it.

Juanita put a towel over her shoulders and began to unbraid her hair. "You two girls go watch for Alice." She shooed them toward the window.

It was always so hard for Lu to carry out orders that he knew were foolish and wasteful. The basketball schedule was another impracticality of a system in an experimental stage.

295

Some sports-minded official had probably planned it, thinking of the exercise and development of sportsmanship among the boys of the day schools, and not thinking or knowing that most of the day schools were a hundred or so miles apart. It was a long way over reservation roads, and most of the boys were not old enough to have acquired the skills needed for the competitive games. Luciano had every right to complain to the teacher as he had. Driving small boys a hundred miles away to play a game they knew little about was a foolish thing.

Juanita brushed her hair until it was smooth and glossy and wound it back from her forehead into two heavy coils on the back of her neck; she leaned toward the mirror to apply powder and lipstick. She hated for Lu to have to do anything he so thoroughly didn't want to do. But he seemed resigned to it, and even teased her as he left by tucking his Levis with studied carelessness into the intricately stitched tops of his new cowboy boots.

He and the boys didn't leave as early as they intended; they waited for an hour for little Miguelito Secatero. Juanita could still see Miguelito running along the road to the day school, crying because he was late, crying because his mother was at first going to keep him home after the dream he'd had—a dream about a train.

"Here comes Alice," Rosita said as she ran to the door to let her in.

Alice was puffing from her walk to the day school. She settled her ample body in a kitchen chair.

"I left coffee for you on the stove," Juanita told her, "and fix whatever you and the girls want for lunch."

A horn sounded outside. "That must be the trader." Juanita slipped into her brown plaid coat and picked up her gloves and purse from the dresser. "Now you be good girls." She bent to kiss them. There were traces of pouting still on her daughters' lips.

Albuquerque was festively decorated for the Christmas season. There was greenery about the lamp posts and strings of colored lights. Banners fluttered reading "Merry

Christmas—Happy New Year." Small stalls along the street displayed evergreen and holly wreaths. Bits of mistletoe and holly berries were intended for coat lapels. No snow, but the cold wind and overcast sky held a promise.

Juanita walked along Central catching glimpses of miniature snow scenes and impressive tableaus of the first Christmas. The crowd parted for a moment and she could see the store windows. She wanted to buy small gifts for the girls, inexpensive ones that would give them more packages to open on Christmas morning. She and Lu had already ordered the big gift, a play table and chairs from Montgomery Ward. Nadine and Michel had written that they were sending dishes.

The ten-cent store was crowded. It was an effort for Juanita to make her way down the aisles. Various odors assailed her: cheap perfume from the cosmetics counter, chocolate and spicy peppermint from uncovered heaps of Christmas candy; and the steamy odors of sandwich meats, coffee, and minced pie from the lunch counter.

Juanita bought hair ribbons, jumping ropes, large red rubber balls, and two books of paper dolls for the girls. There were a few Christmas cards she'd forgotten, and she edged her way toward the stationery counter. Her shopping would be completed—except for Lu's gloves. She knew exactly what she wanted: lined driving gloves, dark-gray gauntlets which would be warm and at the same time dressy-looking.

The men's store where Juanita went to buy the gloves was not especially crowded, but all the clerks were busy. The glove counter was directly beneath a large red tissue-paper bell. Juanita looked through the stacks of gloves on the top of the counter and found a dark gray pair, exactly what she wanted, but the size was too large for Lu. As she waited for a clerk, she saw a pair of soft brown calfskin gauntlets. By the time a clerk came to the counter she couldn't decide which pair she wanted. Glancing at the clock, she noticed it was almost time for her appointment with the dentist.

"I'm sorry," she told the clerk, "but I can't seem to decide what I want. I'll come in again next week."

As she turned to leave the store she was conscious of the big red bell swinging overhead. How stupid of me. I knew exactly what I wanted when I went there.

Leaving the dentist's office, she had just enough time to walk to the parking lot where she was to meet the trader. News boys were calling an extra on the street; something about a train wreck. The words were unintelligible, and she caught only a glimpse of the black headlines as the crowd jostled her along.

The trader was waiting for her. Some Navajos stood by the truck—Lena, and two male relatives of Juan Chavez. The men climbed into the back of the truck. Lena got in front with Juanita and the trader.

"We'll stop at Juan Chavez's on the way to the day school and let these people off," the trader told Juanita.

In the late afternoon sunlight, the compound around the Chavez hoghan was still and peaceful. A bay horse stood in the large corral, leaning its head over the sturdy cedar-post fence. Someone had driven the sheep and goats into their low brush enclosure where they huddled together *baaing* plaintively. There was no wind; the row of bare-branched peach trees stood motionless.

The men got down from the back of the truck, stamping their feet and stretching their legs. Lena got out and started toward the hoghan. The tall, dignified figure of Mrs. Juan Chavez came from the doorway. Lena stopped to greet her relative, but Mrs. Chavez didn't seem to see or hear her as she walked past her toward Juanita.

Juanita knew that something terrible was wrong the instant she saw Mrs. Chavez's face. All signs of serenity, poise and composure that held her strong, handsome features together were gone. Her face was completely broken up. Mrs. Chavez began to cry.

"What is it?" Juanita asked in Navajo, putting her hand on the older woman's arm to comfort her.

Mrs. Chavez laid her hand over Juanita's and tried to speak through the sobs that wracked her body. Juanita could not quite understand her. The older woman spoke Luciano's name and then repeated over and over something about her sons.

"What is it about Luciano?" Juanita asked. A numbness was creeping into her chest and throat. Juanita couldn't understand. "Luciano is nothing." That phrase was only used in Navajo when someone was gone—dead.

The trader was speaking to Mrs. Chavez rapidly in Spanish. Her answers were blurred and broken as the tears coursed over her cheeks. The trader started the truck with a jerk. "There's been an accident with the school truck."

As the trader's truck lurched over the narrow wagon trail toward the day school road, the trader told Juanita that a train had hit the school truck. "Mrs. Chavez's two sons were killed. The others—I don't know about."

Mrs. Chavez' words kept repeating themselves in Juanita's mind. "Luciano is nothing. Luciano is nothing." She stared ahead through the windshield, numbness tightening her chest until she felt that she could not take another breath. I won't think now. I can't think now. Surely someone will be at the day school who knows what has happened.

A government car was in front of the apartment. Two strange women met Juanita in the hallway. She could see Alice's sober face and troubled eyes behind them.

"Tell me what has happened."

"Your husband has been badly injured, Mrs. Platero," the heavy, gray-haired woman began. "He's at Wingate. We drove here to get you."

Juanita turned to the door. She must get to Luciano. Then she remembered. "The boys?"

"Some of them were killed—the others injured. They're at Wingate too."

How could she get word to those families? Most of them were off piñon picking on Walking Around Mountain; the trader had taken them there at the beginning of the season. "Could you go tonight after the boys' families?" she asked the trader. "Do you know where to find them?"

The trader nodded.

Juanita began to name the families—there were six in all. "Lu's mother; she's with the pickers."

Juanita followed the government women as they started out the door. Rosita and Toni clung to her coat. "Alice, will you stay?" Juanita said. She turned to the girls, "You aren't to worry," she kissed their upturned faces. "Daddy's been hurt, but he'll be all right."

These government women have no reason to tell me anything but the truth, Juanita thought as she got into the car with them. Lu is only injured. I didn't understand all that Mrs. Chavez was saying.

It was a long ride to Wingate. The two government women immediately began a light but steady conversation. Juanita sat between them, at times watching the needle climb around the circle of the speedometer, occasionally having to shield her eyes from the glare of approaching headlights.

As she drove, the younger woman was talking about a dress she was making, dark blue silk with a peplum. "I haven't the figure for a peplum, but they're becoming quite fashionable." She made a small shrugging gesture with her hand and shoulder.

"We women shouldn't be like so many sheep and allow our dress styles to be dictated, should we?" the gray-haired woman asked Juanita.

"No, I guess we shouldn't," Juanita agreed. She was wondering just what the earlier statement, "badly injured," might imply."

"Navajo women may be backward in some ways, but they keep their fashion problems simplified." The gray-haired woman paused. "Come what will, they wear the same style skirt and the same style blouse. On special occasions, just a little more jewelry."

The younger woman smiled. "We might try that sometime and see how long we get away with it."

Juanita stared ahead into the darkness beyond the car lights. I hope it doesn't mean the loss of an arm or leg. Lu could never stand being anything but whole. There were so many questions she wanted to ask these women about the boys and Lu, and yet she knew that whatever they told her about her husband, her mind would not accept until she had actually seen him.

The needle dropped rapidly on the speedometer. "We'd better gas-up here," the younger woman said as she turned onto the graveled path between the pumps of a filling station. "We may not find another station open along the road."

They were on their way again; the two government women continued chatting steadily. Juanita waited for a long enough pause.

"Could you tell me how it happened?"

There was an awkward silence. The two government women seemed to be looking at each other in the semi-darkness of the car.

The older one finally spoke. "It happened before noon. The mail train from Chicago to California was an hour late, trying to make up time. That's what the crew told Mr. Bogard. The train hit the truck on a crossing."

"But Lu is a careful driver. He wouldn't drive on a crossing when a train was coming," Juanita said.

"I've seen the crossing," the gray-haired women continued. "The railroad track rounds a low mesa. A train would not be fully visible until within a few hundred yards of that crossing, and there's no wig-wag." [4]

"A fast train could travel that distance in a few seconds," the younger woman added.

Juanita waited. The picture of a train and the school truck was painfully clear in her mind. Little Miguelito had dreamed of a train. "Did you see any of the boys? Do you know how badly they are hurt?"

Both women shook their heads. The boys had already been removed to the hospital at Wingate when Mr. Bogard had asked them to drive to Cañoncito.

Juanita leaned back against the seat. Questions only seemed to deepen the uncertainty. There was nothing to do but wait.

---

4 In the 1930s, some railroad crossings had a simple signaling device that moved back and forth that signaled if a train was coming. This was called a wig-wag.

And waiting would not be easy. Many miles stretched ahead in the darkness. The needle climbed farther around the dimly lit circle of the speedometer. Conversation was spasmodic. It lagged, and then finally there was silence. The three women sat side-by-side as the car sped along the almost deserted highway.

When they arrived at Wingate, the government women drove directly to Mr. Bogard's house. The downstairs was brightly lit. Soft light came from one of the upstairs windows.

Mr. Bogard met them at the door. Juanita had seen him many times at the day school, and he always looked and acted the same. His rather heavy body was always erect and immaculately dressed, giving him the appearance of even greater height. His dark hair was smooth and in place, and his manner was always efficient but friendly.

"Come in, Mrs. Platero," he said. His tone was friendly and the words were short as he directed her to the divan. The two women followed her.

Juanita stood hesitantly in the middle of the living room floor. "If you don't mind, may I go to the hospital to see my husband first?"

Mr. Bogard shook his head, neither his face or his voice altering. "We thought it best to wait until you were here in Wingate to tell you. Your husband is dead. He was dead when the men removed him from the wreck."

Juanita stood very still in the center of the room. "Luciano is nothing," Mrs. Chavez had said. The room closed about her; everything seemed very close and very clear: the overstuffed furniture, the plain rug, the gray-haired woman, the younger one who had driven the car, Mr. Bogard standing beside her looking at her with concern. The people, the furniture, and the walls of the room began to recede. Nothing was clear after that. Everything was dim and unreal.

"You must sit down, Mrs. Platero, and try to adjust yourself to this," Mr. Bogard was saying. "Naturally, it has come as a great shock to all of us."

Juanita remained standing. "Will you take me to my husband?" How could she make them understand that she must see Lu—she must see him no longer alive before she could ever believe him dead.

"I'm sorry," Mr. Bogard answered. "This accident is a terrible thing, and you must understand that we're only trying to make things easier for you. It will be tomorrow evening or possibly the day after before you can see Mr. Platero."

TWENTY-FOUR
The Winds Erase Your Footsteps

She was not the one who stood in Mr. Bogard's living room watching these families come quietly in and sit upon the edges of the chairs, and upon the floor. She was not the one who touched hands with them and saw the deep sadness in their eyes before they turned their faces into their blankets. This was someone else, and she, Juanita, was watching from a great distance.

There were no words to speak when Shimah came in with Lorencito. To hold the frail hands, to watch the tears through her own tears, that was all she could do.

Lupe sat close to Juanita, as if her nearness might bring comfort. When Mr. Bogard came in, the strain of the day before was on his face, but it had not broken through his usual efficient manner. As he spoke to the people, Lupe interpreted for her brother and Lorencito repeated the words quietly. Words were so inadequate and yet certain things must be said—certain decisions must be made while the families were together.

Unreality cloaked Juanita's thoughts. How could Lupe be here when she was at school in Santa Fe . . . Miguelito Secatero's father . . . Willie Platero. . .quiet, slender-faced Juan Chavez, Frank Woods, John Apachito's father . . . and the blanket-shrouded figures of women who helped her at the day school . . . and Shimah—what were they all doing in Wingate? This must be part of a terrible dream from which she would awaken.

She was numbly aware that Mr. Bogard had spoken to her. What was her preference in regard to her husband? If the families agreed, the government would conduct services over all of the boys together and bury them here in Wingate.

Juanita turned instinctively to Shimah. Lupe spoke for her.

Luciano's mother sat quietly for a moment and then raised her face from the shielding Pendleton. "If my daughter-in-law thinks that Wingate is all right . . . that is all right."

It was the third day—a soundless, windless day. The girls had gone with Lupe for a walk along the mesas to hunt for bits of pottery. Juanita sat before the fireplace; she needed to be alone for this. The fire blazed up as she fed things into it. Juanita knew that these unreal feelings must eventually give way to reality and the full impact of her loss. She would have to meet these feelings alone—no one could help her. Everyone had been kind. Mrs. Skinner had come to Wingate to stay with her. Nadine had called long-distance to ask if she needed any money. There had been other phone calls and telegrams. But they had only served to make more solid the fact that there was nothing anyone could do. Some things must be faced alone, and from this would come the strength for going on.

Fragments of conversation and half-clear pictures filled her mind. The old grandfather leaned forward to the sound of her voice, telling her that now when Luciano's body was safely laid away his spirit must be thought of. All of his clothing and personal belongings should be burned. And after tomorrow she must not grieve. He held up four trembling fingers. After four days the spirit was ready to begin its journey. To grieve after that would hold the spirit here, and that was not good.

Juanita placed a stack of papers in the fire. She could still see Allen's face as she told him that he was to have Lu's silver tools and that Lu's horses were to be divided among the other brothers—all the horses except Lady. It had been difficult to keep her voice steady as she told Allen how Lu had felt about Lady.

She replaced the empty dresser drawer and brought another to the hearth. One by one she added the garments to the fire. When she came to the purple velveteen shirt, she ran her hands over the material. Clearly into her mind came the picture of Luciano as she had first seen him . . . silver conches against bright purple, silver bracelets against dark wrists, red silk against black, black hair . . . cheek bones sharply cut, mouth stern and proud, eyes large and dark and unfathomable. Surely it would not be wrong to save something. She refolded the purple shirt and placed it back in the drawer.

Everything was consumed in the fire, Luciano's clothing, letters, all of his personal possessions. Juanita sat staring into the dying flames. "Everything is done now, and after tomorrow I must not grieve," she repeated softly. Shimah had told her this too as they rode home from Wingate—a composed Shimah, fingering the remaining two strands of her shell necklace. She would never forget Shimah as she stood by Luciano; the bright Pendleton drooping from her shoulders no longer seemed colorful and gay. She was separating one strand of shell beads and lifting them over her head—placing them upon her son.

Lupe explained afterward, "My mother did that so when my brother gets to the end of his journey he will think of her."

Juanita sat beside the smoldering embers a long time and then she heard the footsteps she was waiting for. Allen came in quietly and walked down the long hall to the living room. His eyes were dark with shadows, his face taut, his lips set into a firm line. He stood Luciano's shotgun in the corner by the fireplace, and when he spoke, his voice was so low that she could barely hear the words.

"That part is taken care of."

Lupe and the girls were back from their walk. Rosita and Tonita both tried to climb into Juanita's lap at once and show her the pieces of pottery they'd found. Searching for pottery shards had been one of their chief pleasures since Lu had told them about the "ancients."

Tonita succeeded in gaining Juanita's lap first, and Rosita stood leaning against her. When all of the pieces of pottery had been displayed and duly praised, Rosita touched her mother's face.

"Mama, you've been crying again."

"I know, dear."

"Why do you cry? You told us not to."

"I didn't mean to cry, dear, but I was burning Daddy's things. It made me sad."

"Lupe told us that was what you were doing. Does everyone burn the things when people die?"

"I don't know, but the Navajos do."

She knew this was the hard part, answering the questions that the girls would ask. She had to answer them truthfully, yet leave nothing sordid, nothing fearful to mark their young minds. It had been difficult to explain to them that they would not see Lu again for a long time. She knew that every time the door opened she would expect to see him. Every time a car came down the road she would look up expectantly.

She stood up, sliding Tonita to the floor gently. "Come on in the kitchen, girls, it's warmer there. It will soon be supper time."

Lupe had built up the fire and put water on to boil. Juanita got out the potatoes and a tin of corned beef. Lupe began to clean and peel the potatoes, while Juanita put the plates and silverware on the table.

There was a soft knocking at the door, and then it was opened. Alice Watson and one of the Chavez women came into the kitchen.

"Sit down, Alice," Juanita told her and then slid another chair across the floor for Mrs. Chavez.

The talk was about the weather and when the day school would open again. Finally Alice spoke of the reason for their visit.

"Juan Chavez's wife—her sister-in-law," she tilted her head toward the other woman—"is very sick, grieving over her two sons. They're going to have a Sing over her. They want to borrow your two baskets."

Juanita nodded and started toward the living room for the wedding baskets.

Alice Watson continued, "and they'll need a piece of new cloth."

Juanita gave the baskets to Mrs. Chavez, who slipped them under her Pendleton. The three women walked over to the day school.

It was cold inside the building and there was the odor of soap, furniture, and disinfectant in the stale air. Juanita unlocked the supply closet and pulled the bolts of material forward on the shelf. Mrs. Chavez indicated the bolt of white. Juanita turned the bolt twice, slit the salvage and tore off the material.

"Count this against my work," Alice told Juanita as they left the school building.

Juanita stood for a moment watching the two Pendleton-wrapped figures cross the school grounds. Then she returned to the warmth of the kitchen to help Lupe with dinner. Corned beef fried with potatoes should be enough—a can of tomatoes, perhaps. It was difficult to plan a meal; she wondered if she would ever be hungry again.

Lupe opened the bread drawer. "The bread is used up, Juanita."

"Then I'll make biscuits."

The dough was rolled out and ready to cut when there was another knock at the door. Frank Woods came in, holding his wide-brimmed hat awkwardly.

"You're in time to eat with us, Frank. Sit down, and I'll go on with these biscuits."

Juanita was buttering a biscuit for Tonita when Frank asked if the day school would reopen.

"Why, yes, after the Christmas holidays. I haven't heard anything otherwise."

"Some of the families are talking. They say they won't send their kids to school no more."

"Because of the accident?"

Frank nodded. "They say it's the teacher's fault. She shouldn't send little kids so far away to play games."

Juanita thought this over. A few families could do a lot of talking and influence other families. "Frank, how do you feel about it?"

"Well, I lost a boy in that wreck, but if the school opens, I'll send the others."

"When people talk to you like these families are talking, will you tell them the truth? The teacher doesn't make the rules here. She didn't send the boys on that trip. The orders came from someone above her, and it is her job to carry them out. When she received the schedule for those ball games she showed it to Luciano. I was there. Lu said that all of those places were too far away. The teacher said that she would try to get the schedule canceled. But she didn't get an answer in time to stop that trip."

"I'll tell them that," Frank promised, "and I'll tell them they should send their kids to school just the same."

Lupe looked up from her plate. "I've heard some of the people talking like Frank says, but I thought maybe it was just talk."

"Lorencito should be able to stop talk like that. Lupe, will you ask him about it? And tell him that it isn't fair for the people to blame the teacher. This accident wasn't anyone's fault. It just happened."

When Frank rose to leave he asked, "Do you have the pictures that Luciano took of Tom on the horse?"

"I think so."

"Tom's mother lives a long way from here. I have to send her word of this and I'd like to send her one of those pictures."

The wind began to blow early that morning—not a gentle wind but a strong, steady, howling wind. It swooped down the chimney and scattered ashes out upon the hearth. It plucked at the windows with ceaseless, prying fingers. When Juanita went outside for wood, the wind was a force that she had to match her strength against. It resisted every step she took, tugging at her skirt, swirling sand into her eyes. The mesas were hazy and indistinct through the clouds of sand and dust that hung over Cañoncito. The sun shone as through a heavy veil.

Lupe and the girls were busy in the kitchen measuring flour, sugar, milk, and butter into a bowl. Tonita and Rosita stood upon chairs watching impatiently, while Lupe measured the small quantities of salt, baking powder, and vanilla. "Let me break the egg, let me break the egg," Tonita begged, jumping up and down.

"Careful," Lupe said as she steadied the chair with one hand. "Then Rosita gets to beat it."

They each had a turn at rolling the dough, and after Lupe had cut the large cookies, they used a thimble to cut the uneven leftovers of dough into doll cookies.

Juanita wandered about the house, sweeping rugs that had been swept, dusting where there was no dust. If the wind would stop blowing for only a few minutes.

Katharine brought in freshly made tortillas for their lunch. Juanita opened some cans of soup. They all had to eat some of the crispy doll cookies and compliment Rosita and Tonita on their baking.

"I'll be glad when school starts again," Juanita told Katharine. "I believe I'll feel better with things to do that have to be done."

"I'd think it would be better if you took the girls and went to California for a while—if you got away from here," Katharine suggested.

Juanita shook her head.

In the late afternoon the wind still blew. If there was a moment's quiet, it was a moment in which the wind renewed itself and returned in full force, to sweep more sand into the air, to call out wildly as it battered against the walls of the house, against the windows.

Juanita saw Shimah as she passed the kitchen window. Her slender figure, shielded by the Pendleton, seemed to be propelled along. Juanita held the door with both hands as she let her mother-in-law in. "Shimah, you shouldn't be out on a day like this. You'll blow away."

Shimah settled herself on the rug by the fireplace. She held out her hands to her granddaughters, talking softly to them until they came to sit beside her. Tonita edged into her grandmother's lap, touched the silver buttons on her blouse with curious fingers, and reached up for one of the silver earrings.

"Isn't this wind terrible, Shimah?"

"It always comes like this," her mother-in-law told her, "the fourth day after there has been a death."

Juanita waited.

Shimah took her arm from around Rosita and made motions of the wind scooping up sand and then smoothing it out again. "Nothing left—no footprints left."

"She means that the wind comes on the fourth day and erases the footprints of the ones no longer here," Lupe explained.

"My daddy's footprints, too?" Rosita asked.

Shimah's eyes misted.

Juanita rose quickly and went to the kitchen. I'm going to cry, she thought, and that will upset the girls. She fumbled for the leather jacket in the corner of the hall, and opened the door just wide enough to slip out quietly.

It all went together: destroying or giving away everything that had been Lu's, and not grieving after the fourth day, and now the sand swirling into great clouds and dashing to earth again until no trace remained.

Juanita walked on blindly until she gained the road that cut between the mesas. The wind had become a purposeful thing. It tore at her jacket and loosened her hair, but she struggled against it. Fighting the wind seemed to unleash pent-up emotions. The tears came fast, and sobs broke through, sobs that were soundless against the voice of the wind. Juanita stopped in the shelter of a rock ledge. She watched the gnarled cedars bend and twist and listened to the wild voice of the wind moaning in the trees, shrieking across the rocks. The question rose to her lips that had lain four days in her mind.

"Why did it have to happen? Why?" She cried aloud into the wind—"why?"

But the wind moaned on in the trees, and shrieked on across the rocks. It was for calling. . .never for answering.

TWENTY-FIVE
Leaving Cañoncito

The thought of leaving Cañoncito had not occurred to Juanita. Cañoncito was home. Her parents wrote from Texas; there was a place for her and the children with them. Nadine wrote that certainly if Juanita wanted to return to California, she should think of staying no place but with her and Michel. But not once did Juanita herself think of leaving Cañoncito.

The day school was reopened. Katharine was sent to another school, leaving the White Haired Woman again the only teacher. Frank Woods came to help with the heavy work, getting wood, coal, water and cleaning the building. The trader went after the children in his truck and took them home. The government would send a new school truck as soon as possible. Lupe stayed with Juanita at the apartment to take care of the children. Some things were different, but they were not unbearable—Juanita had no desire to run away.

The same tasks awaited her at school. It was comforting to have these things to do: hot lunch at noon, bread to be baked each week, shirts and dresses to wash and iron. The women came as always to help in the kitchen: Alice Watson and Lena, Pah-des-bah, Gladys Del Garito. The day school schedule was not different, but no longer did a clear high voice ring through the empty building, punctuated by the swabbing of the mop. When Juanita was tired, no longer did the "funny old man with the squeaky wooden leg" hobble through the kitchen, or the "Pueblo lady attempting to balance a jar on her head" walk past the dining room windows.

Seeing Lu's family every day, being able to look out the kitchen window at Blue Clay Gap, standing in the door and seeing Waling Around Mountain cloaked in snow, Des Jin, the mysterious blue canyons and mesas beyond—all these things made Lu seem less far away. They made it more believable that her family had lived here together in happiness.

But Juanita couldn't put these things into words the day that the White Haired Woman came into the kitchen to talk to her.

"I wanted to wait until you were more yourself before talking about this," the White Haired Woman began in her timid voice. "I know you're anxious to take your girls and go back among your own people."

Juanita turned from the pan of white beans she was soaking for the next morning. Her face was marked with bewilderment.

"This has all been so hard on you. Please don't feel that it's your duty to stay on here until the end of the term. It will be no trouble to ask the Agency for another housekeeper. I think Alice Watson could manage here for awhile if you want to leave right away." The teacher's eyes were damp behind her glasses. "I know how much easier it will be for you when you get away."

"But I've no intention of going away," Juanita told her. "I intend to stay here. I want to stay here." There was no such thing as going back among her own people. Lu's people were her people too, and they were especially her children's people.

Frank came in with a scuttle of coal. He looked at the water buckets. One was almost empty. He poured the remaining water into the other bucket and started outside again.

The teacher still stood in the doorway. "Perhaps you haven't been in this country long enough to know of the custom. I've been among Navajos a good many years." She lowered her voice. "When a man dies, his family always expects the widow to marry the older brother."

Juanita smiled. "That may have been true a long time ago."

"It's still true," the White Haired Woman said meaningfully.

Frank brought in the water. "I think everything's done, Juanita. I'll go now."

"Don't forget tomorrow's wash day; we'll fire up early." When Juanita turned to the doorway, the teacher was gone.

Juanita closed the cupboard doors, locked the kitchen door, and went out through the front of the building. She had never heard of the custom of which the teacher spoke. Not that it couldn't exist. Anyhow, Lu's family would never attempt to force her to do anything like that. Rosita and Toni were waiting at the door of the apartment; they ran to meet her. Still, it might be well to find out about it. And, too, there was the beginning of a feeling that the White Haired Woman, although concerned about her, had something else on her mind.

"Lupe," Juanita said as she removed her leather jacket and hung it behind the door. "While I set the table, will you run over to the hoghan and tell Lorencito I'd like to see him?"

Lorencito came back with Lupe. He stood in the kitchen doorway for a moment.

"Will you eat with us?" Juanita asked as she reached up to the cupboard for another plate.

Lorencito nodded, smiling. He put his weather-beaten, broad-brimmed hat on the window sill and went to the sink to wash his hands. Juanita noticed the two new, heavy bracelets when her brother-in-law passed his cup for coffee. "*Nah-zhun.* Where did you get them?"

"I did some Medicine work in Torreon," he answered in Navajo.

Juanita wanted to be certain that her brother-in-law understood what she had to say. She buttered bread for Toni and Rosita, waiting until everyone was served before asking Lupe to interpret for her.

She told Lupe what the teacher had said about the Navajo custom of a widow marrying the elder brother. Lorencito began to smile before Lupe had finished repeating the words.

"Is there such a custom?"

Her brother-in-law nodded slowly, the pendants in his ears swinging.

"Is it still practiced?"

He nodded again and then began to talk to Lupe. His face was growing more serious.

Lupe laid down her knife and fork thinking over what her brother had told her and how to express herself. "He says that's a very old custom. A custom of the clans to keep their members. It prevents the widow from going somewhere else and taking the children." Lupe paused. "This is hard to say in English as he means it. He wants you to know that our family would not expect you to do anything you didn't want to. You are one of us—but different."

"I understand." Juanita reached to the stove for the coffee pot. "I wasn't really worried about it, but I wanted to get it straightened out." Then Juanita asked Lupe to tell Lorencito about the teacher urging her to go away and about her strange feeling that perhaps the teacher really didn't want her to continue to work at the day school alone. "I want to stay here. There's no reason for me to go anywhere else."

Lorencito listened quietly, and sipped his coffee.

"Some of the men are going to the big Agency at Window Rock. I'm going with them. One of the things we will ask is that they appoint a man here to take Luciano's job, but that they leave you, Juanita, at the school. We have already had a meeting over that."

A Chapter meeting was held on the day the men returned from Window Rock. The people began to arrive in the early afternoon. Juanita could see the bright-blanketed figures through the kitchen window as they walked across the snow-covered school grounds to the Chapter House. Snow had been falling since daylight. Large soft flakes were drifting down from the low gray sky. The mesas were obscured; the fringe of chamise bushes along the arroyo extended as far as she could see.

Some of the women came into the kitchen to warm themselves at the big woodstove before going on to the meeting. They pulled one of the wooden benches close to the stove and held their wet moccasins and trading store shoes out to the warmth. The heat against the wet leather, the snow-wetted ruffles of heavy skirts, and the damp Pendletons filled the kitchen with the strong odor of mutton grease, stale wood smoke, and wet wool.

Lupe came into the kitchen with Juanita's Pendleton over her head; the girls were bundled into their dark blue coats. "Lorencito said that you must come to the meeting as you always have."

Juanita smiled a little. "Will you go along to interpret all the things I won't understand?"

One of the women by the stove held out her hand to Rosita and Toni; they walked shyly to her and listened. They sometimes answered softly as she spoke to them in Navajo.

Juanita hurried with her work in the kitchen—setting the bench back against the wall when the women left, mopping up the marks of their wet footprints. Then she took her jacket from the pantry door.

It seemed that everyone had gathered inside the Chapter House. Most of the benches were full, and a few old men sat on the bench behind the barrel-shaped woodstove. The old grandfather was there, leaning against his crude walking stick; little Joe Chavez sat on the floor at his feet. Juanita went first to the grandfather, clasping the hand he held out, as she spoke to him. The other old men nodded, while murmuring "yah et eh" over and over and touching hands with her. There were the older women to speak to—Seraphina, Frank Woods' mother, George Abeyta's mother—and then Juanita sat down on the bench between Lupe and Shimah. Toni slid down from her place beside Lupe and came to lean against her mother.

Once, all of these faces had been those of strangers, but it had been a long time ago. She recalled how she had worn the blue and gray suit that Luciano liked and most of his jewelry. He had been proud and a little self-conscious coming back home and bringing a new wife. She remembered the look on the old grandfather's face when he saw Luciano—the way he said, "my son." She remembered so many things. Seeing George Abeyta she thought of a red velvet shirt. Seeing Frank Woods she heard again his and Luciano's wild high voices echoing through the school building. Seeing little Washeengtone, she saw him young, with Luciano squatting on his heels beside him, calling him "Little Brother." And seeing Mrs. Juan Chavez huddled in the corner, her saddened face nearly hidden by the folds of her Pendleton, Juanita heard her voice again: "Luciano is nothing." She knew that Luciano was nothing now except all the things she could remember. Seeing these faces of relatives and friends brought Luciano back in memory, and comfort with the pain.

Lorencito was talking and the room was quiet. The only sound was the opening and closing of the door as some of the young men entered and took their places, unobtrusively, among the other men along the wall by the doorway. One of the men who had gone with the group to the Agency got up to tell what he had said, and what the answer had been. George Abeyta, who had interpreted for the group, stood up to tell the people the messages which the Agency had sent back.

"They're only discussing when the new school truck will arrive, and who will drive it, and what they said at the Agency about sending a teacher to replace Katharine as soon as the school attendance is at forty-five," Lupe told Juanita.

One of the old men by the stove took a few sticks from the wood box and added them to the fire.

"Decidero is asking if they know yet at the Agency how that accident happened. Did something go wrong with the truck?" Lupe interpreted.

The old men behind the stove began to talk together. The grandfather nodding his head and doing much of the talking. Lowered voices came from other parts of the room. Mrs. Willie Platero began to cry, covered her head with her Pendleton, and slipped out the doorway.

Juanita knew that few of the people in the community had been able to understand about the wreck. Why did it happen? What was the cause? No one could say. It just happened. To these people that answer wasn't enough. These people, like all people who live simply and close to the earth, needed an answer—a reason for why this had happened. When they couldn't find a reason, their imaginations supplied one.

The explanation Mr. Stacher had given her on the evening she saw him in Albuquerque was not an explanation which could be adequately put into Navajo. Since the consolidation of the Agencies into one large Agency at Window Rock, Mr. Stacher was no longer at Crown Point, but in the Navajo Land Offices in Albuquerque. After the accident he sent word to Juanita to stop and see him the first time she was in town. He and Mrs. Stacher had a box of Christmas things for the girls. It was that evening when Mr. Stacher told her that the magnetism of the mail train's huge diesel motor might have stalled the motor of the school truck as soon as the truck was on the rails. But how could she explain it in Navajo?

"My mother says that many of the people here are saying *ma-itso* caused the wreck."

"How could *ma-itso* have caused it?"

"Haswood told about my brother not finding his undershirt and a sock at the Yei-be-tchai. The old men say that with something like that to work over the *ma-itso* could have caused it."

Juanita shook her head.

The old grandfather stood slowly.

"He's saying that the members of the *ma-itso* which caused the wreck will die within a year. The *ma-itso* wasted many lives to bring about the death of his son." Lupe paused. "I've heard about that old belief: a curse falling on the *ma-itso* when too many are killed in order to kill one person."

The older people were nodding as the grandfather sat down. Lorencito tried to get the meeting back to order. George Abeyta stood up to speak again.

The Agency would send someone out to the next Chapter meeting, and the people were to select a man from the community to do the work of the Indian assistant at the day school until the Agency could appoint a new assistant. The men at the Agency had listened when Lorencito told them about the people wanting Luciano's wife to remain as housekeeper. They had said they would think about the matter carefully. The Agency liked to have a man and his wife in those jobs; it worked out better, and the living quarters were planned that way, but the Agency would think about what the people said.

When the people were leaving, pulling their blankets about them before going out into the steadily falling snow, Lorencito walked over to where Juanita stood with Lupe and Shimah. "I talked for you. We all talked for you at the Agency. Maybe they'll listen to what we say."

"Thank you, Lorencito."

"One of the things they told us there," he turned to Lupe to be sure Juanita would understand what he was saying, "was that the government will send you money every month—fifty-five dollars because my brother had civil service papers."

"I know about that, Lorencito. The government money will help us but I'll have to have a job, too. We want to build a house, and someday the girls will need to go away for school."

When the notice came from the Agency of her transfer to a larger day school over one hundred and fifty miles away, Juanita was not too surprised. The transfer would be effective at the end of the term.

"I guess far back in my mind I've been expecting this," Juanita told Lupe. "The Agency can't change its policy for one isolated case. And yet I really hadn't thought out what I'd do if this happened."

Lupe ran her fingers through her thick dark hair; her eyes were troubled. "You won't go back to California?"

"No, but there's no point in accepting the transfer. In some ways it would be as far away from Cañoncito as California is." Juanita sat down on the studio couch, still holding the letter in her hand. "The Albuquerque Indian Service has offices in Albuquerque. Perhaps I could get a transfer there. Albuquerque isn't too far from Cañoncito."

The next few days Juanita planned what she would do. Saturday morning she would ride into town with the trader. She'd go to see Mr. Stacher. He might be able to advise her where to go and who to see at the Indian offices.

But Saturday morning did not go the way she had planned it. Mr. Stacher was no longer in Albuquerque. The secretary at the Land Office told her he had been sent to the Ute Agency. Juanita walked to the tall new building beside the post office that housed the Indian offices. She knew of one person to ask for: Dr. Aberlee, head of the United Pueblo Agency.

"Do you have an appointment with Dr. Aberlee?" one of the secretaries in the large outer office asked.

"No," Juanita began to draw the brown kid gloves from her hands, "but I'll wait. Would it be possible to see her sometime today?"

The secretary smiled. "About what did you wish to see Dr. Aberlee?"

"About work."

"In that case you can just fill out one of these applications."

The secretary returned with a large printed form and a pen.

Juanita felt trapped. "Wouldn't it be better if I saw Dr. Aberlee personally?"

The secretary returned to her desk.

The trapped, helpless feeling persisted as Juanita filled out the application form. There were the usual questions about age, education, and previous experience. So much couldn't be stated in "Yes" or "No," or in dates, in the small space left for remarks. Juanita signed her name, laid the pen down and began to draw on her gloves. She watched as the secretary opened a steel cabinet, took out a bulging file, and wedged her application in with similar forms.

"Thank you for coming in."

There was a sinking feeling in Juanita's stomach long before she reached the elevator. She was certain that by the time she heard from her application, if ever, it would be too late to be of any help. She needed a job soon. The school term would be over in another month. If she were to get anything in Albuquerque before that, it would be a job which she would find herself outside of the Indian Service.

From habit, Juanita stopped at the White Eagle Trading Post. She and Lu had always stopped to see Mr. Palm when they came to Albuquerque. She needed a little cheering up right now.

Mr. Palm greeted her as he came from the back of the store. "How are the wild Indians out your way?"

"Wild as ever." She tried to keep her feeling of dejection from her voice.

"And the little girls? You surely didn't come in without them."

"This isn't exactly a holiday," Juanita began. And then as Mr. Palm leaned against the counter and nodded understandingly, she told him of the transfer and her decision to look for work in Albuquerque.

"Didn't you mention a long time ago that you'd worked in a bank?"

"Yes."

"Well, there are two banks here: Albuquerque National and the First National." Mr. Palm looked at his watch. "Say, why don't you try the First National this morning. I know one of the officers, Mr. Rogers. Tell him I sent you over."

Mr. Rogers was cordial; he gave her an application blank to fill out, but he was not encouraging. "We have only one woman bookkeeper, and she's been with us a long time; the rest are men. We prefer to hire men because we can work them into other departments." He assured her that her application would still be considered.

I've accomplished nothing, absolutely nothing, Juanita told herself as she walked to the parking lot. Unless reaching a decision might be counted as something. When the school term was over, and she still had no definite prospects of work, she'd move into Albuquerque anyway and continue the business of looking for a job systematically until she'd found one. She'd have to find a house in Albuquerque between now and the end of the month, and she'd have to write a letter to Window Rock advising the Agency of her intention to resign from the Service.

Shimah sat very quietly, looking at the hard-packed earth floor of the hoghan, while Lupe talked for Juanita and explained about leaving the day school.

"You'll be taking the girls away?" Shimah asked without raising her eyes.

"No farther than Albuquerque, and as soon as we can afford an old car we'll come out weekends. Albuquerque isn't so far, Shimah," Juanita added gently.

"She'll be lonesome with Bijo and Keetso in Crown Point and you and the girls in Albuquerque," Lupe observed. "I haven't told her yet that I'm going with you."

Juanita knew that leaving Shimah would be one of the hard things about leaving Cañoncito. She dreaded beginning to pack, and she dreaded the actual driving away; but she must not look too closely at what lay immediately ahead. She must look farther to the things that working in Albuquerque would make possible.

Shimah rubbed her hands along her skirt. "We'll be moving too. Leaving this place." She gestured to the walls and ceiling of the hoghan. She hadn't been sleeping well in this hoghan which Luciano had helped build. Allen and Lorencito were going to tear it down. An owl had been coming here.

"An owl?" Juanita questioned Lupe.

"Sometimes when spirits visit places they know, they come in the form of an owl."

"Where will you live, Shimah?"

Luciano's mother pointed with her lips to the mesas beyond the day school. A new hoghan would be built on top of those mesas. Her sons would begin to haul rock, and logs as soon as the corn was planted. "I can see all around from that mesa. I can see Luciano's land." Shimah smiled a small, wise smile. "Someday if there's a house there, I will be able to see the smoke."

TWENTY-SIX
Dreams Fulfilled

It was a small house, and there was no beauty in it, the yard, or the neighborhood. One narrow frame house followed another, crowded side by side, with small patches of trampled-over grass separating front porches from sidewalks, and sidewalks from streets. Overhead was only a narrow view of smoke-streaked sky.

This small house had been better than many. It was clean, and there was a fenced backyard where the girls could play; it was near a school and within walking distance of the business district, and the rent fitted the budget.

The budget was important. Until Juanita found a job, fifty-five dollars would have to be stretched to cover all the expenses for herself, Lupe and the two girls. It could be done by careful managing, but there would be nothing left over.

Their own furniture made the house seem less strange, but there had been a loneliness about hanging pictures, spreading rugs, and arranging books and pottery by herself . . . no one to pretend that the pictures weren't straight, the rugs at a right angle. . .no one to frown and rearrange the books, to make an elaborate gesture of straightening the edge of a scarf.

There was also loneliness for Cañoncito. Sometimes relatives rode into town with the trader, and dark, friendly faces and soft-spoken Navajo words made Juanita realize that Cañoncito was not so far way. But it seemed very far away when she walked downtown into the confusion of automobiles and milling crowds. Gasoline fumes, dirt and grime, jostling elbows and loud voice assailed her senses.

"Looking for work makes you half a person," she thought. Going hopefully to a place, returning discouraged, answering question after question and then getting the doubtful assurance, "We'll call you if we need you." Giving references to someone's secretary whose look quite plainly says, "We have a long list of people waiting who've had more experience at this work." It does something to you; it takes something away that you can't regain until you have a job. Juanita thought of Lu and the days he'd spent in Albuquerque looking for work. This same feeling must have haunted him.

After weeks of watching ads, revisiting firms where she'd filled out work applications, following other people's suggestions (like going to the Liberty Cafe when Mr. Palm heard that the cashier was leaving and investigating the Fred Harvey Courier Service that the Skinners had written about), there came the telephone call asking her to appear at the First National Bank for an interview.

This was the job she most wanted. It meant regular hours and that she would have evenings and holidays with the girls. The salary would allow for the eventual fulfillment of her plans, and Lu's. But, it was this job that she was least hopeful of getting; Mr. Rogers had not been encouraging.

Juanita dressed carefully in the tailored white linen from last summer, coiled her dark hair close to her head for coolness, and gave her white pumps an extra buffing to remove excess polish. She started downtown early. Third and Central was several blocks away.

The interview was with Mr. Carson, a tall, dignified man whose desk was labeled "President." Everything about this man—the slender, erect figure, his manner of speech, the close-clipped gray hair—suggested a military background. Juanita found it odd that the manner of a bank president left her personality intact, whereas an assistant secretary seemed to strip it from her. Mr. Carson told Juanita that the bank's need for a bookkeeper was immediate. He asked how long it had been since she'd been employed in the Huntington Park Bank?

"Seven years."

"Isn't that too long to be away from work requiring a high degree of efficiency? Can you pick it up again? Especially when it will be necessary to keep up with men bookkeepers here."

Juanita did not hesitate to speak as she thought. Mr. Carson would never mistake frankness for impertinence. "I've always worked with men bookkeepers and kept up with them. As for the seven years that have passed since I did that work, bookkeeping is something not easily forgotten, and I worked at it for more years than I've been away from it. I don't believe the time I've been away will make any difference."

Mr. Carson glanced up at Mr. Rogers and then back down at the papers in front of him. "Is there anyone that you can give as reference that we can get in touch with easily?"

"Mr. Bogard at Wingate. I worked directly under him for two years. He might be easier to reach than Mr. Crosby at the Huntington Park Bank.

Mr. Carson made a note of both names and handed them to Mr. Rogers.

"Now don't plan too much on this job, Mrs. Platero. The unforeseen can happen in any business firm. But discounting that, you should receive a call as soon as we've had time to check these references."

The call came that same afternoon at four o'clock. "Would Mrs. Platero report for work at eight o'clock the next morning?"

The bookkeeping room was familiar, a little larger than the one in Huntington Park, and not quite as large as others in Los Angeles. But there was a sameness about bookkeeping rooms: barred windows, the peculiar light created by powerful electric globes burning in daylight, adding machines, posting machines, typewriters, and people working over bundles of checks. The noise of the machines combined with the almost continual jangling of a telephone. An overall atmosphere prevailed that could only be described as "well-ordered hurry."

It was all familiar; only the people in the room were strange. But they were friendly through their preoccupation when she was introduced to them. A young man named Dade Rogers came to help her with her set of books. (The minor details of handling accounts were different in each bank.) He asked if she was accustomed to an all-electric posting machine. She was not, and she found the intricacies of the new-style machine at first bewildering.

I'm here on trial as it is, she thought. There are people to be convinced that a woman bookkeeper is as satisfactory as a man. I mustn't be slow about any of this. She devoted every thought, every energy, to mastering the new machine. She worked all day, every day, at high tension.

After the third day on her set of books, Dade Rogers came only occasionally to see how she was getting along. "You don't need me any longer," he told her. After a week, it seemed that she had never been away from a bookkeeping room.

It was time to enroll Rosita in school. Juanita realized that summer was over. Rosita needed school dresses and shoes, and what Juanita bought for Rosita, she had to buy for Tonita. The fact that Rosita was going to school and Tonita wasn't was hard enough to explain; Rosita getting new clothes and getting to go to school also would have seemed unjust discrimination to her smaller daughter. So Juanita outfitted them both, and the amount that went into her savings account that month was much less than she had planned.

She had started the savings account on her first pay day. Aside from their increased living expenses for winter time, the wages that she could now pay Lupe for staying with the girls, and the few more suitable clothes that she would need for work, the rest of her salary was earmarked for one purpose.

The home that she and Lu had planned on his land in Cañoncito would not remain a dream. As soon as she had saved enough that home would be built. Somehow her life would seem less incomplete with that much of their plans realized. Cañoncito would always be home for her and for her children. The rest of the plans would follow. The girls would learn in Cañoncito what Lu had wanted them to learn, and the love of all the things that he had loved would be their heritage. And here in Albuquerque their education would be assured, and their lives would be equally balanced. Perhaps for the girls, the middle path might be gained more easily.

Juanita thought that after a few months in Albuquerque, she would become accustomed to the confusion of automobiles, the people, and the new job. But that was not true. Each month seemed to add its weight to the other months before it, and the pressure was becoming unbearable.

I mustn't let this get me down, she told herself. I must think of the ways in which I'm lucky. I have a job—a salary that pays expenses and leaves something to be saved. I have the girls and someone whom I trust to take care of them. I have so much. But always the thoughts of Cañoncito broke through. Cañoncito, where the land was rolling pasture and rock-ledged mesas, where little canyons wandered and ended between high walls of red rock—little canyons like the one where Lu was born, and the one where the old grandfather planted his peach trees. Cañoncito, where the sky was limitless. Juanita would turn from her machines to face the barred window that looked out upon the brick wall of another building. Above the wall was a narrow strip of sky. In the afternoons, a shaft of sunlight brightened the rows of red brick along the top of the wall. As the light fades, Juanita would fumble for a handkerchief to hide the tears that blinded her.

Buying the second-hand roadster was a necessity. At least she and the girls could drive to Cañoncito when they wanted to, and that was often: every weekend, every holiday. A day spent at Shimah's hoghan did much to make the other days in town more bearable. And it was easier with a car to stop and get figures at the different lumber companies for the cost of the two-room house for which she'd drawn rough plans. She realized following visits to three companies that even the simplest two room house would cost twice what she had figured. It would be less without a fireplace, but she wouldn't strike that from the plans.

She and the girls stopped at the allotment in Cañoncito almost every Sunday and paced off the smallest kitchen into which a woodstove, a cabinet, and a breakfast table and chairs could be fitted. Juanita thought to herself, the door would be here, shielded from the wind, and there could be a rough porch of flat rock added later, and the kitchen windows would be here and here—one with a view of the sloping hill, two with a view of the Sandias and Manzanos. The living room would do with windows at each end, which would leave a long wall with the fireplace in the center. On the other wall would be space enough for the tall bookcases on either side of the cedar chest.

"And under these windows will be a couch for Toni and me." Rosita made marks with her shoe in the place that her mother had often indicated. "And under those windows will be a couch for you."

The house was almost as real to the girls as it was to Juanita. She had talked over most of the plans with them. They knew that the pile of rocks from their grandmother's old hoghan would be built into the foundation. They knew that hollow tile would be used for the walls and plastered over later. The ceiling would be left unfinished, rafters showing, because it would be cheaper.

But how much longer would they plan? They needed this house to come to, and they needed this house to think of when they were in Albuquerque. It would take too long to save the money. It was too much time to wait.

Had it been any other man but Mr. Carson, Juanita would never have had the courage to ask about a loan. Five hundred dollars was a lot of money, and she'd worked at the bank only a few months. But a home on Lu's land meant so much. After all, Mr. Carson could do no more than refuse, and his refusal would at least be kind.

So she stood at the marble-topped counter in front of his desk.

"We like to help our employees when we can," he told her, "but you must admit that you have no security to offer except your job here. What do you need the money for?"

"A house. I want to build on my husband's land in Cañoncito."

"Cañoncito, that's Indian land. Indian land cannot be used as security. Isn't that true?"

Juanita nodded. It seemed a long time before the bank president spoke again.

"How long before you'd be ready to start work out there?"

"Three or four months, as soon as the winter weather is over for sure."

"What arrangements could you make to repay the loan?"

"I could pay thirty-five, perhaps forty dollars a month. I'm not making payments on anything else."

"This is most irregular." Mr. Carson smiled and tiny wrinkles appeared at the corners of his eyes. "But you save as much as you can in the next three months and then I'll take your loan up with the Board of Directors."

It was the beginning of summer. White clouds floated lazily across the sky. Juanita steadied Raven; there would be no racing with Tonita riding behind the saddle. Rosita trotted along beside them on her mare. They rode to the spring below Des Jin; pools of yesterday's rain were still in the worn depressions of the rocks, and sunlight flashed against the water. Small white and yellow flowers, like daisies, carpeted the grass-grown slopes; brilliant red trumpet-shaped blossoms grew among the rocks, along with bell-like flowers of palest apricot.

Guiding the horses down the bank, they followed the stream as it flowed from the spring and formed its own small canyon, cutting through the rocky, juniper-dotted pasture land. The canyon bed was smooth and sandy.

"Let's gallop, Mother, just a little ways," Rosita begged. "I'll hold fast to the reins."

Juanita looked back at her youngest daughter. "All right? Then hang on tight."

They galloped easily along the streambed. When they pulled up on the horses, Rosita was laughing with excitement. "I'll be glad when I'm old enough to go really fast."

"I'd be glad if I had a horse that was my very own," Tonita sighed from her place behind the saddle.

"When my mare has a colt, you can have it," Rosita promised her.

Shimah was waiting for them when they returned. She had already begun to slap dough for bread. A pot of stew simmered over the fire outside the brush shelter. Juanita unsaddled Raven, took the small blanket off Rosita's mare, and Allen led them to the corral.

It was cool and peaceful in the brush shelter. Juanita watched the girls playing tag with Wudy around the hoghan. "What can I do, Shimah, set out the plates?"

Her mother-in-law nodded and then paused in her bread-making.

"You know Wounded Head's son?" She turned her face toward the mesa where the family lived. "He died this winter. No one knows when. We didn't see him for a long time. Then his mother told someone that he was dead." Shimah continued to nod her head slightly, as if she'd known all along that it would happen that way.

"Within a year," Juanita recalled the words. Who could say whether this death proved the prophecy, or was just coincidence? She looked far out to where Shimah's flock of sheep was moving homeward. Khee drove them slowly; there were many lambs running beside the ewes this year.

The stew was good, mutton with potatoes and chili. The slapped bread was thick and hot. Juanita sat quietly, eating, listening to news of the family as Shimah told it. Lorencito had gone back to Torreon; his new wife's people lived there. Allen and Khee had planted the cornfield. Next year they would plant a field on her land.

Then everyone finished eating, and the boys got up and wandered outside into the twilight. Juanita began to gather up the dishes. Shimah brought two small red apples from a paper sack and gave them to her granddaughters.

It was much later, and the moon was bright when Juanita drove the roadster down the wagon trail from the mesa. The girls were tired, and she had hardly reached the day school road before they were both asleep beside her.

Driving at night like this brought thoughts that seldom came to her in the day time. There was no sound except the motor of the car against the stillness. When she reached the little side road that led to their land, she turned the car into it and slowed to a stop beside the fence. Rosita roused from her sleep for a moment and then settled back against the seat. Juanita sat there a long time, looking at the half-finished walls rising dark in the moonlight. This was the beginning. Sometime afterward there'd be money to drill a well so that they could plant shade trees, even an orchard. And when the girls finished school perhaps . . .

It would take longer this way—without Lu—much longer. And yet there was her whole life before her. She leaned her head against the frame of the roadster top and her thoughts found voice softly, earnestly.

The earth has swallowed you . . . the winds have erased your footprints . . . your possessions are divided among your relatives . . . or are ashes in the fire. But all the years ahead cannot erase one smallest memory from my heart. The life we planned together, I'll live that with our children, and I'll never be afraid. But I'll always be lonely . . . Luciano.